"James Dolezal offers an exceptionally rich, lucid, and creative insight into the meaning and significance of the doctrine of God's simplicity. Engaging in a lively, sincere discussion with the major contemporary opponents and with representatives of the broad theological tradition, he gives not only a thorough introduction, but also advances the debate: Dolezal translates the discussion about ontotheology into an analytical framework and suggests a new solution for the compatibility of God's simplicity and freedom."

—Harm Goris
Tilburg University

"At a time when the simplicity of God has fallen on hard times, James Dolezal does a fine job of navigating current objections to this central aspect of theology proper. In particular, Dolezal shows the intimate relationship between those who would affirm God's absolute character, and an affirmation of divine simplicity. He brings Aquinas' affirmation of simplicity into the contemporary debate in a way that Thomas himself might have done."

—K. Scott Oliphint
Westminster Theological Seminary

God without Parts

God without Parts

Divine Simplicity and the Metaphysics of God's Absoluteness

JAMES E. DOLEZAL

PICKWICK *Publications* · Eugene, Oregon

GOD WITHOUT PARTS
Divine Simplicity and the Metaphysics of God's Absoluteness

Pickwick Publications
An Imprint of Wipf and Stock Publishers
199 W. 8th Ave., Suite 3
Eugene, OR 97401

www.wipfandstock.com

ISBN 13: 978-1-61097-658-9

Cataloguing-in-Publication data:

Dolezal, James E.

   God without parts : divine simplicity and the metaphysics of God's absoluteness / James E. Dolezal.

   xxii + 240 pp. ; 23 cm. Includes bibliographical references and index.

   ISBN 13: 978-1-61097-658-9

   1. God—Simplicity. 2. God—Attributes. 3. God (Christianity)—History of doctrines. 4. Thomas, Aquinas, Saint, 1225?–1274. 5. Protestant Scholasticism. I. Title.

BT148 D56 2011

Manufactured in the U.S.A.

For Courtney

"Though we cannot comprehend him as he is,
we must be careful not to fancy him to be what he is not."

—Stephen Charnock, *The Existence and Attributes of God*

Contents

Foreword

Dr. James Dolezal's treatment of divine simplicity, which provides a defense of this doctrine in perhaps its strongest form, is a first-rate piece of work. He shows himself to have a grasp not only of the primary and secondary intellectual sources but also of the arguments of contemporary critics as well as of defenders of the doctrine, especially those in analytic-style philosophical theology, "analytic theology" as it is coming to be called. He does not simply dust off the cobwebs of old ideas and rehearse antiquated positions. Not content with mere exposition, able as this is, the author likes to argue, presenting robust defenses of divine simplicity against some of its eminent detractors and modifiers—for example, Alvin Plantinga, Thomas Morris, and Eleonore Stump. He takes these on, utilizing some current arguments of Brian Leftow, William Mann, and others, but also offering arguments of his own. The result is the best full-length philosophical treatment of divine simplicity that I know.

God's simplicity is a central element in the "grammar" of classical Christian theism. The data regarding the essence and nature of God, as revealed in Scripture, have by and large an occasional and unsystematic character to them. But because Scripture, as God's word, is self-consistent, the varied data must be self-consistent, and when properly appreciated must also be *seen* to be. Or, at the very least, it may be recognized that alleged inconsistency cannot be proven. The classical conceptual shape of Christian theism offers a template in terms of which that consistency may be appreciated. For it provides rules, drawn from the varied data of Scripture, in terms of which the varied language of Scripture about God, not only in his unity but also in his trinitarian glory and in his actions in the economy of redemption, can be learned and used without falling into inconsistency or serious error. It is not so much an explanatory as a *grammatical template*.

So in thinking about divine simplicity as an account of divine unity we are not to think of it primarily as a *description* of that unity, much less as an *explanation* of it, but as offering rules for appreciating and employing the character of divine unity. This is a central part of the fuller grammar of Christian trinitarianism. It aims to bring together a way of thinking and speaking about divine unity—that God is one and that the Lord our God is one Lord—that does justice to the manifold witness of Scripture to that unity and to ways of handling its apparent references to divine complexity and disunity in a way that considering each isolated datum in turn could never do. Fundamental to that grammar is a conviction about God, made evident throughout the Scriptures, that he is the creator of space and time and all that it contains, existing at a point beyond space and time and not therefore subject to it. God is not spread out in space or in time, a creature among fellow-creatures. How then are we to think and speak of him?

Part of the answer to that question is that we are to think of God partly in negative terms, as we have just been doing: *not* in space, *not* in time. An account of divine unity must be consistent with such timelessness and spacelessness. But there is more. For in being the Creator, and not a creature, or creaturely, God does not depend for his existence on operations or forces working upon him. He is not fashioned or the product of parts forming themselves into a unity in an arbitrary fashion. He is necessary, self-existing. This means, for example, that God is not composed of elements that are more ultimate, in a logical or metaphysical sense, than he himself is. It is by attention to such considerations that the doctrine of simplicity has been developed, in order to safeguard that divine sovereignty and transcendence to which Scripture richly testifies. Divine simplicity is not the doctrine that God has no features, an infinite *tabula rasa*. Nevertheless he has no parts and so is not divisible.

But what of the Trinity? Christian theologians have routinely stated that the threefoldness of the Trinity—that God is Father, Son, and Holy Spirit, each person being wholly divine—refers to *distinctions* in the Godhead, not to *divisions* in it. All divisions involve distinctions, but not vice versa. This distinction between distinctions and divisions has been in service in trinitarian thinking a long time; it can be found, for example, in Tertullian.

To suppose that the distinction between the Father and the Son, for example, is a *division* between them is to suppose that the terms "Father" and "Son" denote different *parts* in God, each of which is separable from the other. A triune Godhead that consists of a divisible threeness would thus be made up of three parts—Father, Son, and Spirit—who together comprise it. The obvious problem with such a proposal is that it violates the biblical affirmation that God is one, which the doctrine of divine simplicity articulates. Another consequence of supposing a division between the persons is that Father, Son, and Spirit would each be part of God, and so not the whole God, and so not wholly divine.

God the Creator is one God, and not creaturely. Because God is timeless he is changeless, immutable. Not simply in the sense that he has chosen to be so, or covenanted this, proposals which offer a rather unstable account of God's changelessness and are probably incoherent. He is *metaphysically* changeless. Such changelessness in turn entails divine impassibility, an idea frequently misunderstood and derided. But impassibility is not to be confused, as it often is, with impassivity or with dispassion. Although it may seem paradoxical, the stress on impassibility is meant to safeguard the fullness of God's character. He is eternally impassioned, unwaveringly good, not moody or fitful as he is buffeted by the changes of his life, some of them, perhaps, unexpected changes.

Another way of entering this territory, a way which is quite consistent with what we have been thinking about, is via the idea of God as the most perfect being. God is a being than which no greater can be conceived. This is not a piece of metaphysical speculation, but is clearly stated or implied in Scripture, as in Hebrews 6:13–14, which refers to God as one besides which there is none greater. For had there been a greater than God then in establishing his covenant God would have sworn by that greater. But he swears by himself and so establishes a covenant that is immutable and which for that reason is utterly trustworthy.

Of course, there are other biblical data to support the wonderful verses of Hebrews in their assertion about God's unsurpassable greatness. David refers to the greatness of God and the fact that there is no God besides him (2 Sam 7:22); Nehemiah refers to the great, the mighty God (Neh 9:32; also Jer 32:18; Titus 2:13). Besides, the Lord is a great God and a great King above all gods (Ps 95:3); he is to be feared above all gods (Ps 96:4; 77:13); he is greater than all gods (Exod 18:11); his greatness is unsearchable (Ps 145:3). It is hardly plausible to suppose that God's kingship over other gods is a mere contingent matter of fact. Paul's "golden chain" (Rom 8:31–39) is mere rhetoric if is not supported by a view of God who necessarily transcends his creation. And so on.

It is not that these biblical writers suppose that there could be a greater than the God of Israel, and that one day there might be. The God who is the creator of the heavens and the earth is one than which no greater can be conceived. How could God be worshipful if he could have been greater than in fact he is? If there is a being greater than God then why is that being not God instead? So, all the grammatical features of the doctrine of God that we have mentioned express metaphysically necessary truths.

James Dolezal's favored way of approaching divine simplicity is through the distinction between act and potency. He offers a close and careful reading of Thomas Aquinas. A subject's potency or potentiality expresses its liability to change and develop, or to be changed. So it is a sign of compositeness. Every creature in space and time has such potency. By contrast, a simple God does not develop by acting, much less by being acted upon. He does not develop at all. His actions express his perfection; they do not contribute to its attainment. I think it is fair to say it is in this area, of God's freely expressing his perfection in creation and in human redemption, that the sense of ineffability and incomprehension of the doctrine of God's absoluteness is at its highest.

Noting the author's close adherence to Thomas's approach to divine simplicity, some may think that this book is a work of "Catholic" theology, meaning by this an exclusively Roman Catholic theology. But this judgment would be seriously mistaken. Dr. Dolezal is at pains to show that adherence to the doctrine, and an appreciation of both its strengths and of its profundities, is the property of the entire "catholic" church. He draws the reader's attention to Stephen Charnock, John Owen, and other Reformed and Puritan theologians, to Reformed confessional statements, as well as to their present-day expositors, notably Richard Muller. He flags up the thought of a notable Dutch Reformed theologian who straddled the nineteenth and twentieth centuries, Herman Bavinck. The work deliberately reinforces the view that divine simplicity is the property of truly "catholic" Christian theology.

It might be objected that if an argument for some fundamental feature of God's existence, such as divine simplicity, concludes in emphasizing the ineffability and incomprehensibility of the life of the Creator, we ought to suspect its premises. Dr. Dolezal touches on such matters in his fascinating dialogue with a contemporary evangelical philosophical theologian, Jay Richards, over the conflict, or apparent conflict, between divine simplicity and divine freedom to create worlds other than our world, or to refrain from creating any world at all. This is, in effect, a debate about a concept of God who is first and foremost anthropomorphic and anthropopathic, and, on the other hand, of a God who creates and upholds everything that exists in space and time, as their transcendent Creator and Lord, while working immanently within the creation.

It is God's transcendent will, the expression of his simple nature, that generates in the most acute way in the creatures' apprehension the sense of incomprehensibility and ineffability. This is hardly surprising. Indeed, it would be surprising if such bafflement were not felt. Yet its presence hardly amounts to a reason for denying or attenuating God's absoluteness, central to which is his simplicity.

Such debates will be taken further, and without doubt Dr. Dolezal's work deserves to be an impressive and powerful stimulus to them.

Paul Helm
Teaching Fellow, Regent College, Vancouver

Preface

ORTHODOX CHRISTIANS ARE UNIVERSALLY committed to the confession that God is absolute but they are not always agreed on how to characterize this absoluteness. Historically the doctrine of divine simplicity (DDS) has been regarded as indispensable for establishing the sufficient ontological condition for divine absoluteness. Accordingly, the Westminster Confession of Faith 2.1 confesses both that God is "without parts" and is "most absolute." But there no longer seems to be a broad consensus on the truth or usefulness of the doctrine of God's simplicity. Indeed, the doctrine has been criticized and dismissed by many recent Christian philosophers and theologians alike on the grounds that its supposed theological benefits can be preserved by less recondite doctrines. Moreover, many are convinced that the classical form of the doctrine is simply incoherent. It is the contention of this study that to forfeit the doctrine of divine simplicity is to jettison the requisite ontological framework for divine absoluteness.

The classical doctrine of simplicity, as espoused by both traditional Thomists and the Reformed scholastics, famously holds forth the maxim that there is nothing in God that is not God. If there were, that is, if God were not ontologically identical with all that is in him, then something other than God himself would be needed to account for his existence, essence, and attributes. But nothing that is not God can sufficiently account for God. He exists in all his perfection entirely in and through himself. At the heart of the classical DDS is the concern to uphold God's absolute self-sufficiency as well as his ultimate sufficiency for the existence of the created universe.

The pages that follow set forth both metaphysical and theological arguments in favor of divine simplicity. Along the way I seek to answer some of the leading recent critics of the doctrine—most notably those objecting from within the modern school of analytic philosophy. The assumption that God and creatures are correlatives within a univocal order of being dominates this school of philosophy and is arguably the chief reason why their criticisms of the DDS fail to hit the mark. By appealing to God's simplicity I aim to show that God and the world are related analogically and that the world in no sense explains or accounts for God's existence and essence. If God were yet another being in the world, even if the highest and most excellent, then the world itself would be the framework within which he must be ontologically explained. But as Creator, God is the sufficient reason for the world's existence and thus cannot be evaluated as if he stood together with it in the same order of being. It follows from this that God can neither be measured, nor his simplicity refuted, according to the modalities unique to created beings.

Throughout the volume I make extensive use of both classic Thomist and Reformed sources. It should not be thought that this study offers a proper historical or philosophical analysis of the critical texts of Thomas Aquinas or his Protestant successors. I deploy these older writers simply in order to rehabilitate the power and subtlety of their insights for our modern philosophical-theological milieu. In addition to the older sources I also utilize the recent expositions of Aquinas and the Reformed scholastics by scholars such as John Wippel and Richard Muller. Undoubtedly, some will think that this harkening back to the metaphysics and theology of pre-Enlightenment Christians betrays nothing more than nostalgia for a golden age that has been forever de-stroyed by Kantian philosophy and the rise of modern science. But this is not the case. The return to Thomistic metaphysics, and to the classical orthodox understanding of God's simplicity, is taking place today not only among historical scholars and theologians, but also among philoso-phers such as David Oderberg and Jeffrey Brower. Just as older Reformed accounts of God's simplicity benefited from many of the insights of the medieval scholastic philosophers, it my persuasion that the modern Reformed account of the DDS can be similarly bolstered by some of the newer contributions of certain analytic Thomists. I trust that this study will show how even recent philosophical contributions can still be put into the service of classical theology.

The chapters of this volume are logically arranged so as to make the claims and conclusions of the classical DDS clear. Chapter 1 introduces the basic argument of the volume and seeks to orient the reader to both the traditional Christian witness to divine simplicity as well as the main lines of argumentation currently leveled against the doctrine. Chapter

2 sets forth an extended consideration of precisely what is meant by denying composition in God. In this connection I offer a brief survey of act-potency metaphysics and then proceed to examine six different variations of act-potency composition and the reason why each is denied of God. One needs a fixed idea of what is meant by "simple," "composite," and "parts" before considering the theological motivations for the doctrine or precisely how it enables one to account for God's absoluteness. Chapter 3 lays out the dogmatic motivations for the traditional DDS. Many have criticized the doctrine as being overly speculative and insufficiently biblical. Thus, I intend to show how various other doctrines require adherence to the classical DDS as a good and necessary consequence, including: divine aseity, unity, infinity, immutability, and eternity. The claims of the DDS are indispensible to the classical formulation of each of these doctrines.

In chapters 4 and 5 I aim to apply the conclusions of the previous two chapters to the questions of God's existence and essence respectively. Chapter 4 examines the significance of the claim that God is subsistent existence itself (*ipsum esse subsistens*). In particular, the importance of Thomas Aquinas's insistence upon the real distinction between existence and essence in all creatures is explained as well as his understanding of God's relation to "being in general." Divine simplicity is necessary for a proper understanding of the distinction between the being of God and the being of creatures and for understanding the absolute self-sufficiency of God's existence. Chapter 5 is concerned to explain how it is that God has his attributes such that he depends upon nothing in order to be what he is. The central claim is that God is what he is in virtue of his Godhead and not by virtue of properties inhering in him. This stands in contrast to the contingency that marks all creaturely property bearers. I conclude the chapter by arguing that the "truthmaker" theory of divine predication is one way in which the classical claims of divine simplicity can overcome many of the popular "property" criticisms propounded by certain analytic philosophers.

In chapters 6 and 7 I turn my attention to the implications of the DDS for our understanding of God's knowledge, will, and freedom. Chapter 6 considers how it is that God can be simple given the fact that he both knows and wills many *different* things. Would not the knowledge of multiple things entail that God have multiple ideas and that he is therefore intellectually composite? I first endeavor to show that God's knowledge is simple because, though he knows many things, he does not know them through multiple intelligible species, but rather through his own nature as imitable. Next, I argue that God is really identical with his will and its primary object. Inasmuch as God's has only one ultimate end, namely, himself, he has only a single act of will. What's more, his act of will is not in him as an accident, determining him to be in some volitional sense. Rather, the very act by which he wills himself and all things is identical with the act by which he exists. Finally, chapter 7 explores the knotty question of how a simple God can be free with respect to creation. Many regard this difficulty as the Achilles heel of divine simplicity. Does simplicity leave God sufficiently free in his creation of the world? I consider various recent attempts to rescue divine simplicity and freedom. In the end I propose that God's freedom cannot be modally characterized as passive counterfactual openness; in fact, the *modality* of divine freedom is entirely beyond our grasp. It is concluded that while simplicity roots the absoluteness of God's freedom, neither of these divine characteristics is comprehensible to us though both are indispensible to the confession that God is most absolute.

It is my hope that this volume will revitalize the confession and defense of divine simplicity among orthodox Christians and will be a serviceable introduction to the doctrine for those who have hitherto found it elusive or impenetrable.

James E. Dolezal
Philadelphia, Pennsylvania
July 14, 2011

Acknowledgments

M ANY PEOPLE HAVE CONTRIBUTED both directly and indirectly to the completion of this volume. Dr. K. Scott Oliphint of Westminster Theological Seminary proved to be a thoughtful and challenging advisor throughout my preparation of this work. Dr. Gregory T. Doolan of The Catholic University of America offered many useful insights and correctives to an earlier version of this material. Any errors that remain are, of course, solely my responsibility. Others who have aided me in thinking through the questions of metaphysics and divine simplicity include: Dr. Lane Tipton, Dr. Yannick Imbert, Jeffrey Waddington, Jim Cassidy, Jonathan Beeke, Camden Bucey, and Robert LaRocca. Also, I am grateful to Paul Helm for his encouragement toward the publication of this book and his gracious willingness to supply the foreword.

The greatest encouragement in the production of this volume has come from my family. My parents, Richard and Leta Dolezal, have provided unflagging support. My children, Judah and Havah, have been a great source of joy and happy diversion to me throughout my research and writing. Most of all, I owe more than I can say to my wife Courtney, whose tireless sacrifice, encouragement, and love have made this study possible. It is to her that this work is dedicated.

1

Friends and Foes of the Classical Doctrine of Divine Simplicity

> There is but one only, living, and true God, who is infinite in being and perfection, a most pure spirit, invisible, without body, parts, or passions; immutable, immense, eternal, incomprehensible, almighty, most wise, most holy, most free, most absolute.

WITH THESE WORDS THE Westminster Confession of Faith begins its chapter, "Of God, and of the Holy Trinity" (WCF 2.1). The plain intention of the authors is to express those ways in which God is distinct from and superior to all creatures. This distinction is most broadly summarized in the affirmation that God is "most absolute." This means that no principle or power stands back of or alongside God by which he instantiates or understands his existence and essence. He alone is the sufficient reason for his own existence, essence, and attributes. He does not possess his perfections by relation to anything or anyone other than himself.

But the question is asked: What is the ontological condition by which such absoluteness is ascribed to God? Or, put differently, what is it about God's existence and essence that permits one to say that he is the entirely sufficient explanation for himself? The same article of the Westminster Confession supplies the answer to these questions when it states that God is "without parts." This curious verbiage signifies the Westminster divines' commitment to the classical doctrine of divine simplicity (DDS). It is divine simplicity that enables the Christian to meaningfully confess that God is most absolute in his existence and attributes. Adherents to this doctrine reason that if God were composed of parts in any sense he would be dependent upon those parts for his very being and thus the parts would be ontologically prior to him. If this were the case he would not be *most* absolute, that is, wholly self-sufficient and the first principle of all other things. Thus, only if God is "without parts" can he be "most absolute." It is this argument that forms the central thesis of this volume: *Simplicity is the ontologically sufficient condition for God's absoluteness.*

The doctrine of divine simplicity teaches that (1) God is identical with his existence and his essence and (2) that each of his attributes is ontologically identical with his existence and with every other one of his attributes. There is nothing in God that is not God. The Reformed theologian Stephen Charnock explains simplicity in terms of God's supreme existence: "God is the most simple being; for that which is first in nature, having nothing beyond it, cannot by any means be thought to be compounded; for whatsoever is so, depends upon the parts whereof it is compounded, and so is not the first being: now God being infinitely simple, hath nothing in himself which is not himself, and therefore cannot will any change in himself, he being his own essence and existence."[1]

In similar fashion, the medieval theologian and philosopher Thomas Aquinas contends that, "every composite is posterior to its components: since the simpler exists in itself before anything is added to it for the composition of a third. But nothing is prior to the first. Therefore, since God is the first principle, He is not composite."[2] Again, the argument of both Charnock and Aquinas is that God cannot be the ultimate ontological explanation for himself or for anything else if he is composed of parts.

The theological value and implications of the doctrine of divine simplicity have been variously explained and applied throughout the history of the church, though in recent decades the classical version of the doctrine has fallen into disrepute. Many seek to banish it from Christian theology altogether while others aim to preserve it by softening its philosophical or theological austerity. It is my contention that God's absoluteness is diminished to just the extent that one denies or softens the DDS. This argument is developed in various ways throughout the chapters of this book.

---

1. Charnock, *Existence and Attributes of God*, I: 333.

2. Aquinas, *Scriptum super libros Sententiarum*, I.8.4.1.

Before delving into the particular elements of my thesis, it is first crucial that we should have some sense both of the historical and present status of the doctrine of divine simplicity. My aim, then, in the remainder of this chapter is to briefly sketch the historical Christian witness to the DDS and after that to survey some of the recent criticisms of the doctrine. Following these two sections I will conclude with an initial response to the doctrine's critics.

THE HISTORICAL WITNESS TO DIVINE SIMPLICITY

Historian Richard Muller informs us, "The doctrine of divine simplicity is among the normative assumptions of theology from the time of the church fathers, to the age of the great medieval scholastic systems, to the era of Reformation and post-Reformation theology, and indeed, on into the succeeding era of late orthodoxy and rationalism."[3] The following is a brief sketch of what some of the church's leading theologians have said about the DDS in the last two millennia.

Patristic Witness

The early church fathers first gave expression to the DDS in response to the classical Greeks' philosophical quest for a single ultimate principle by which to account for the universe, that is, to discover the unity that lies back of all multiplicity. Wolfhart Pannenberg distills the basic logic of the Platonic and Aristotelian notion of simplicity that came to be appropriated by the early church fathers: "Everything composite can be divided again, and consequently is mutable . . . Everything composite necessarily has a ground of its composition outside itself, and therefore cannot be the ultimate origin. This origin must therefore be simple."[4] In his *Against Heresies*, Irenaeus appeals to divine simplicity in order to

---

3. Muller, *Post-Reformation Reformed Dogmatics*, III: 39. This is cited hereafter as *PRRD*.

4. Pannenberg, *Basic Questions in Theology: Collected Essays*, II: 131. See Plato, *Republic* B. 382e; *Timaeus* 41a, b; Aristotle, *Metaphysics* 1074a33–38; 1071b20f.; 1072a32f.; 1072b5–13; and 1015b11f. All citations from Aristotle are taken from *The Complete Works of Aristotle*. The Greeks never truly arrived at the notion of a simple God because they were committed to a dualistic conception of reality. The early Christians recognized that if one posited two first principles, such as God and matter, then neither principle could be *absolutely* simple or suffice as the absolute explanation of the universe. For a helpful summary of the views of Plato and Aristotle relevant to divine simplicity see Immink, *Divine Simplicity*, 51–73.

prove to certain Greek emanationists that God neither exhibited passions nor underwent a mental alteration in the production of the world: "He is a simple, uncompounded Being, without diverse members, and altogether like, and equal to himself, since He is wholly understanding, and wholly spirit, and wholly thought, and wholly intelligence, and wholly reason, and wholly hearing, and wholly seeing, and wholly light, and the whole source of all that is good—even as the religious and pious are wont to speak concerning God."[5]

The DDS was quickly established as a central ingredient to the orthodox Christian understanding of the divine nature.[6] Though it was initially expressed in the apologetical conflict with the Greeks, it soon came to be used to establish the full deity of the Son and the Holy Spirit and to defend the monotheistic credentials of orthodox trinitarianism. Gregory of Nyssa argues that the Son and the Holy Spirit could not be semi-divine, as some heretics insisted, because the DDS proves the indivisibility of the divine essence. Thus, wherever the divine essence is present it must be *wholly* present.[7] As for the Trinity, the DDS was used to prove the indivisible singularity of the divine essence and thus refute the accusations of tri-theism. Lewis Ayres remarks, "[T]he deepest concern of pro-Nicene Trinitarian theology is shaping our attention to the union of the irreducible persons in the simple and unitary Godhead."[8] It is the DDS that ensures this is not a union of three gods.

Following the Cappadocian fathers, Augustine appeals to divine simplicity in his *De civitate Dei* to argue for the unchangeableness of each person of the Godhead: "It is for this reason, then, that the nature of the Trinity is called simple, because it has not anything which it can lose, and because it is not one thing and its contents another, as a cup and the liquor, or a body and its colour, or the air and the light or heat of it, or a mind and its wisdom. For none of these is what it has."[9] In *De*

5. Irenaeus, *Against Heresies*, II.13.3.

6. See the discussion on "Unity and Generality in God" in Stead, *Divine Substance*, 103–9.

7. See Gregory of Nyssa, *Against Eunomius*, bk. 10, sec. 4, and *On the Holy Spirit*. For a penetrating study of the two Cappadocian brothers on this topic, see Radde-Gallwitz, *Basil of Caesarea, Gregory of Nyssa, and the Transformation of Divine Simplicity*.

8. Ayres, *Nicaea and its Legacy*, 301. See also, Pelikan, *Christianity and Classical Culture*, 246–47; Kelly, *Early Christian Doctrines*, 268–69; Barth, *Church Dogmatics*, II/1: 446–47 [§31.1].

9. Augustine, *The City of God*, XI: 10.

trinitate he further elaborates on the DDS in his attempt to establish the uniqueness, independence, and singularity of the divine nature:

> But it is impious to say that God subsists to and underlies his goodness, and that goodness is not his substance, or rather his being, nor is God his goodness, but it is in him as an underlying subject. So it is clear that God is improperly called substance, in order to signify being by a more usual word. He is called being truly and properly in such a way that perhaps only God ought to be called being . . . But in any case, whether he is called being, which he is called properly, or substance, which he is called improperly, either word is predicated with reference to self, not by way of relationship with reference to something else. So for God to be is the same as to subsist, and therefore if the Trinity is one being, it is also one substance.[10]

This passage affirms the identity of God's existence and essence and denies that God's attributes are in any way separable from his essence. God simply is whatever is predicated of him and none of his essential attributes is really or conceptually separable from him. The denial that God is identified "with reference to something else" is surely calculated to express God's absoluteness in contrast to those beings that have their existence and substance with reference to him. God is not correlative to any non-divine thing.

Medieval Witness

This doctrine of the fathers and Augustine was later endorsed by Boethius and then by Anselm. Boethius uses the DDS to prove God's immutability and independence:

> But the Divine Substance is form without matter, and is therefore one, and is its own essence. But other things are not their own essences, for each thing has its being from the things of which it is composed, that is, from its parts. It is This *and* That, *i.e.,* it is its parts in conjunction; it is not This *or* That taken apart. Earthly man, for instance, since he consists of soul and body, is body *and* soul, not body *or* soul, separately; therefore he is not

---

10. Augustine, *The Trinity*, VII: 10. Augustine further affirms the identity of God's existence and essence when he writes, "What is God's knowledge is also his wisdom, and what is his wisdom is also his being or substance, because in the wonderful simplicity of that nature it is not one thing to be wise, another to be, but being wise is the same as being" (ibid., XV: 22). See also, Ayres, *Augustine and the Trinity*, 208–11.

his own essence. That, on the other hand, which does not consist in This and That, but is only This, is really its own essence, and is altogether beautiful and stable because it does not depend upon anything.[11]

Likewise, Anselm also employs the DDS to explain God's self-sufficient independency. In the *Proslogium* he writes, "But undoubtedly, whatever thou [God] art, thou art through nothing else than thyself. Therefore, thou art the very life whereby thou livest; and the wisdom wherewith thou art wise; and the very goodness whereby thou art good to the righteous and the wicked; and so of other like attributes."[12] Also, he understands the DDS to ensure God's absolute immutability and unity:

> For whatever is composed of parts is not altogether one, but is in some sort plural, and diverse from itself; and either in fact or in concept is capable of dissolution. But these things are alien to thee, than whom nothing better can be conceived of. Hence, there are no parts in thee, Lord, nor art thou more than one. But thou art so truly a unitary being, and so identical with thyself, that in so respect art thou unlike thyself; rather thou art unity itself, indivisible by any conception. Therefore, life and wisdom and the rest are not parts of thee, but all are one; and each of these is the whole, which thou art, and which all the rest are.[13]

The doctrine of God's simplicity reaches the zenith of expression and sophistication in the thought of Thomas Aquinas. He regards the DDS as the centerpiece of the Creator-creature distinction and he makes recourse to the doctrine both explicitly and implicitly throughout the vast corpus of his theological and philosophical writings. Several factors enabled Thomas to nuance the doctrine in ways that his Christian predecessors had not. The most important of these was reappearance in the Latin West of the writings of Aristotle. The Stagirite supplied an extensive conceptual framework by which Thomas was enabled to articulate a more detailed account of just how it is that God is not a composite being. In his *Summa contra gentiles* he writes,

> Every composite . . . is subsequent to its components. The first being, therefore, which is God, has no components. Every com-

11. Boethius, *De Trinitate*, II, 30–40. See also, Nash-Marshall, "God, Simplicity, and the *Consolatio Philosophiae*," 225–46.

12. Anselm, *Proslogium*, 12.

13. Ibid., 18. See also, Anselm, *Proslogium*, 22, and *Monologium*, 16–18.

posite, furthermore, is potentially dissoluble. This arises from the nature of composition . . . Now, what is dissoluble can not-be. This does not befit God, since He is through Himself the necessary being. There is, therefore, not composition in God. Every composition, likewise, needs some composer. For, if there is composition, it is made up of a plurality, and a plurality cannot be fitted into a unity except by some composer. If, then, God were composite, He would have a composer. He could not compose Himself, since nothing is its own cause, because it would be prior to itself, which is impossible.[14]

Thomas's greatest contribution to the advancement of the DDS is found in his teaching that every created thing, even relatively simple things such as human souls and angelic spirits, are at the very least composed of existence and essence. No created essence is identical with its act of existence and is therefore relative and dependent in some sense. But God's essence is identical with his existence and therefore God is absolutely necessary and self-sufficient. Thomas explains:

> [I]f the existence of a thing differs from its essence, this existence must be caused either by some exterior agent or by its essential principles. Now it is impossible for a thing's existence to be caused by its essential constituent principles, for nothing can be the sufficient cause of its own existence, if its existence is caused. Therefore that thing, whose existence differs from its essence, must have its existence caused by another. But this cannot be true of God; because we call God the first efficient cause. Therefore it is impossible that in God His existence should differ from His essence.[15]

There is very little development in the DDS after the time of Thomas, though John Duns Scotus differs somewhat from Thomas by arguing for the doctrine primarily based upon the conception of God's infinity. With his characteristic subtlety, Scotus maintains, "From infinity every type of simplicity is inferred . . . If the essence were composed its components would be in themselves either finite or infinite. In the first case, the composite would be finite, in the second a part would not be less than the whole."[16] The point is that if God's perfections are infinite

14. Aquinas, *Summa contra gentiles*, I.18 [3]–[5]. This is cited hereafter as *SCG*.

15. Aquinas, *Summa theologiae* I.3.4. This is cited hereafter as *ST*. For a thorough treatment of Aquinas's doctrine of simplicity, see Weigel, *Aquinas on Simplicity*.

16. Duns Scotus, *A Treatise on God as First Principle*, 4.75–76.

then no one of them can be less than the whole, that is, other than the divine essence itself. From this Scotus concludes that each attribute is identical with God himself and so with all the other attributes. He offers the following prayer to God: "You are the ultimate in simplicity, having no really distinct parts, or no realities in your essence which are not really the same."[17]

Reformed and Modern Witness

The Protestant Reformers and their scholastic heirs did not alter Thomas's account of the DDS in any significant way except to make the biblical motivations for the doctrine more explicit. The words of William Perkins, an early English Puritan, are strikingly similar to those of Aquinas and Duns Scotus: "The simpleness of his nature, is that by which he is void of all logical relation in arguments. He hath not in him subject or adjunct . . . Neither is God subject to generality, or specialty: whole, or parts: matter or that which is made of matter: for so there should be in God divers things, and one more perfect than another. Therefore, whatsoever is in God, is his essence, and all that he is, he is by essence."[18] Richard Muller rightly notes, "the underlying assumptions governing the doctrine of God during the eras of the Reformation and Protestant orthodoxy are very little different from those governing the discussion during the Middle Ages."[19]

John Owen, another Puritan, employs the DDS in his arguments against the Socinians. By it he proves that God is the absolute first and independent being: "Now, if God were of any causes, internal or external, any principles antecedent or superior to him, he could not be so absolutely first and independent. Were he composed of parts, accidents, manner of being, he could not be first; all of these are before that which is of them, and therefore his essence is absolutely simple."[20] With reference to Exodus 3:14–15, Owen also explains God's unity via the DDS: "[W]here there is an absolute oneness and sameness in the whole, there

17. Ibid., 4.84. On Scotus's DDS see Cross, *Duns Scotus on God*, 99–114.

18. Perkins, *Workes*, I: 11. The spelling has been updated in the citation.

19. Muller, *PRRD*, III: 97. It should be noted that in Reformed hands the DDS did not remain the special preserve of academicians, but was passed on to common churchmen in the form of ecclesiastical confessions. See for example: Thirty-Nine Articles (art. 1); Belgic Confession (art. 1); Westminster Confession of Faith (2.1); Savoy Declaration (2.1); and Second London Confession of Faith (2.1).

20. Owen, *Vindiciae Evangelicae*, XII: 72.

is no composition by an union of extremes . . . He, then, who is what he is, and whose all that is in him is, himself, hath neither parts, accidents, principles, nor anything else, whereof his essence should be compounded."[21] Owen's treatment of God's simplicity is representative of Reformed Orthodoxy as a whole. His continental counterpart, Francis Turretin, declares, "[T]he orthodox have constantly taught that the essence of God is perfectly simple and free from all composition."[22]

The Christian witness to the DDS was strongly maintained by the Reformed and Thomist traditions well into the nineteenth and twentieth centuries. The Dutch Reformed theologian Herman Bavinck stresses the significance of the DDS to Christian orthodoxy in a passage worthy of lengthy citation:

> This simplicity is of great importance . . . for our understanding of God. It is not only taught in Scripture (where God is called "light," "life," and "love") but also automatically follows from the idea of God and is necessarily implied in the other attributes. Simplicity here is the antonym of "compounded." If God is composed of parts, like a body, or composed of *genus* (class) and *differentiae* (attributes of differing species belonging to the same *genus*), substance and accidents, matter and form, potentiality and actuality, essence and existence, then his perfection, oneness, independence, and immutability, cannot be maintained. On that basis he is not the highest love, for then there is in him a subject who loves—which is one thing—as well as a love by which he loves—which is another. The same dualism would apply to all the other attributes. In that case God is not the One "than whom nothing better can be thought." Instead, God is uniquely his own, having nothing above him. Accordingly, he is completely identical with the attributes of wisdom, grace, and love, and so on. He is absolutely perfect, the One "than whom nothing higher can be thought."[23]

In these words one discovers the teaching of Augustine, Anselm, and Aquinas reasserted for the modern age. Again, Bavinck's point seems to be that if God were not simple he could not be absolute.

Among twentieth-century theologians one finds the DDS affirmed by figures diverse as the Reformed theologian Louis Berkhof and the

---

21. Ibid.

22. Turretin, *Institutes of Elenctic Theology*, 3.7.1. This is cited hereafter as *IET*.

23. Bavinck, *Reformed Dogmatics*, II: 176. This is cited hereafter as *RD*.

Roman Catholic theologian Réginald Garrigou-Lagrange. Berkhof
stands squarely with the church fathers, medieval schoolmen, and
Reformed scholastics in remarking that the DDS "implies among other
things that the three Persons of the Godhead are not so many parts of
which the Divine essence is composed, that God's essence and perfections are not distinct, and that the attributes are not superadded to His
essence." He also observes, though, that Christian support for the DDS
had waned in the late nineteenth and twentieth centuries: "In recent
works on theology the simplicity of God is seldom mentioned. Many
theologians positively deny it, either because it is regarded as a purely
metaphysical abstraction, or because, in their estimation, it conflicts
with the doctrine of the Trinity."[24]

Garrigou-Lagrange is representative of the enduring commitment
to the DDS among twentieth-century Roman Catholics when he writes,
"Now there can be no kind of composition in the self-subsisting Being
. . . [E]verything in the self-subsisting Being is identified with this very
Being, and there is no imperfection in Him. We may consider all the
modes of composition, and not one of them can be applied to Him."[25]
Although the DDS finds wide-ranging support in the modern Reformed
and Thomist traditions, its positive development seems to have peaked
in the high medieval period.

From this brief survey of the church's historical witness to the
DDS we find that numerous aspects of the Christian doctrine of God
are thought to depend upon the truth of God's simplicity, including: his
unity, necessity, immutability, self-sufficiency, independence, perfection,
and infinity. In spite of this broad historical affirmation of the doctrine,
though, it has been criticized in recent decades by a host of detractors
ranging from atheistic philosophers to evangelical theologians. In order
to better understand the challenges facing modern adherents to the DDS
we turn now to consider some of the leading contemporary opponents
of the doctrine.

---

24. Berkhof, *Systematic Theology*, 62. One still finds an affinity for the DDS in some
modern evangelical theologians. See for example, Erickson, *God the Father Almighty*,
210–32; Grudem, *Systematic Theology*, 177–80; Holmes, "Something Much Too Plain
to Say," 137–54.

25. Garrigou-Lagrange, *God*, II: 43.

RECENT PHILOSOPHICAL AND THEOLOGICAL CRITICISM OF DIVINE SIMPLICITY

Numerous modern philosophers oppose the DDS on the grounds that it is philosophically incoherent, while theologians tend to oppose the doctrine on the charge that it undermines some of the most basic features of the Christian understanding of God. Many of the current objections to the DDS, especially those issued by the analytic philosophers, are highly nuanced and demand close attention. They represent a formidable opposition to any who would appeal to simplicity as indispensible to an orthodox doctrine of God in the twenty-first century. I will have occasion to refer back to the following criticisms as I seek to articulate the function and importance of the DDS in subsequent chapters.

Richard Gale

In his book *On the Nature and Existence of God*, atheistic philosopher Richard Gale discusses the perceived inadequacies of some of the recent Christian philosophical accounts of God's simplicity, especially those propounded by Eleonore Stump, Norman Kretzmann, and William Mann.[26] Gale identifies two versions of the DDS, "the property and instance identity versions," which he explains as follows: "When it is said that God is identical with his properties, say omnipotence, it could mean that he is identical either with the property of omnipotence itself or with his instancing of omnipotence."[27]

Against the version of the DDS that claims God is identical with each of his properties and that each divine property is identical with all the others, Gale raises three objections.[28] First, properties, rightly understood, are abstract entities and so could not possibly be identical with the God of Christianity since he is understood as a concrete, personal creator. How could a personal God be identical with anything abstract? What's more, it is a sound argument lodged by Aristotle against the Platonic doctrine of forms that abstract forms or properties cannot be causal factors; only concrete entities that instantiate the requisite

---

26. See Gale, *Nature and Existence of God*, 23–29. For recent defenses of the DDS to which Gale objects see Stump and Kretzmann, "Absolute Simplicity," 353–82; Mann, "Divine Simplicity," 451–71; Mann, "Simplicity and Immutability in God." 267–76; Mann, "Simplicity and Properties: A Reply to Morris," 343–53.

27. Gale, *Nature and Existence of God*, 24.

28. Ibid.

properties can function as causal principles. Second, if God were identical with each of his properties then none of those properties could be shared by creatures since in the case of a creaturely instantiation the creature would be an instance of God himself. But creatures do have certain properties in common with God, even some of his intrinsic properties such as being a person, being an entity, being self-identical, and so forth. If the property identity version is true of God then no individual other than God could possibly have any one of his properties. Third, the property identity version seems to make all of God's properties to be one and the same and this simply is not true. Omnipotence, for instance, is not omnibenevolence. Inasmuch as these two differ in sense they must also differ in ontological reality since, as Gale insists, "the sense of each is the property it expresses." Also, it will not help to argue that power and benevolence may be different in their limited creaturely expressions but not in their unlimited divine instantiations as *omni*potence and *omni*benevolence. Gale explains why: "Since ordinary power and benevolence obviously differ, there is all the more reason to hold that increasing degrees thereof differ."[29] An unlimited mode of instantiation, as Christians claim for God, does not alter the fundamental ontological difference between his properties. But the property identity account is not the only version of the DDS currently on offer.

The property instance account, contra the property identity account, holds that God is identical with the *instantiation* of each of his properties but not with the properties as such. This has the supposed advantage of side-stepping the abstraction argument that seems to plague the property identity account. Gale acknowledges that the property instance version of the DDS seems at first more plausible since, as he notes, "it is now a familiar story that two referring expressions can be coreferential though differing in sense."[30] In other words, the instance of a property may be identical with the instance of another property even if the properties themselves are not identical and even if they still differ in sense. He considers two analogies put forward by Stump and Kretzmann. First, just as the "morning star" and "evening star" are two distinct ways of referring to the same thing, the planet Venus, so "perfect power" and "perfect knowledge" are two ways of referring to the same thing, God. Moreover, just as the morning star is ontologically identical

29. Ibid. We shall have occasion to answer these arguments in chapter 5.
30. Ibid., 25.

with the evening star, so it is not inappropriate to hold that perfect power is ontologically identical with perfect knowledge.[31] Second, "'Perfect power is identical with perfect knowledge' does not entail that power is identical with knowledge any more than the fact that the summit of a mountain's east slope is identical with the summit of its west slope entails the identity of the slopes."[32]

Gale is not convinced that these property instance explanations actually exonerate the DDS from the difficulties that attend the property identity version. First, calling the properties of power and knowledge "perfect" does not thereby enable them to transcend the real difference that exists between ordinary power and knowledge. There is no degree of perfection or even perfect instantiation at which the difference disappears. Second, the slope analogy is inadequate since the summit of the slope represents the limit or termination of the slopes and this is obviously contrary to the unlimited perfection that Christians claim for all God's "omniproperties."[33] Third, and possibly most devastating to the property instance argument of Stump and Kretzmann, is that it "violates God's absolute aseity or independence, since it conceives of God as instancing properties and thus as dependent upon them."[34]

Finally, Gale rejects William Mann's solution in which he attempts "to grab this dilemma by both horns by identifying God's properties with his instancing of them."[35] Mann denies that properties are abstract entities and is thereby able to propose that all God's properties possess some causal capacity.[36] Gale responds, "Even if we were to grant that properties are certain sorts of causal powers, it is unclear both how this escapes the aseity objection and how it establishes that God's different properties bestow one and the same causal power(s) upon him."[37] Mann's notion that each divine property is a causal power is problematic for the DDS, as Gale deftly observes: "Omnipotence is having the causal power to bring about anything . . . while benevolence is having the causal dispositions to perform or bring about good actions. A person's instanc-

---

31. Stump and Kretzmann, "Absolute Simplicity," 356–57.

32. Ibid., 357.

33. Gale, *Nature and Existence of God*, 26.

34. Ibid., 25.

35. Ibid., 27.

36. Mann, "Simplicity and Properties," 352–53.

37. Gale, *Nature and Existence of God*, 28.

ing of one of these properties seems to bestow on him a different set of causal powers than does its instancing of the other."[38] In Gale's final analysis both the property identity and property instance versions of the DDS fail. Indeed, in seeking to avoid the philosophical unpleasantries of the property identity account the advocates of the property instance account seem to abandon altogether one of the classical motivations for the DDS, the aseity of God.

Christopher Hughes

Christopher Hughes, a Christian philosophical theologian, offers a lengthy critique of Thomas Aquinas's version of the DDS from a distinctly analytical perspective. In his volume *On a Complex Theory of a Simple God* he is particularly opposed to Thomas's identity of God with being itself (*ipsum esse*). He confesses, "I don't know how to construe Aquinas's claim that God is *ipsum esse* in such a way that it fails to come out necessarily false."[39] Hughes explains just why he finds it so troubling to claim that God is identical with existence itself:

> [I]f God were pure subsistent existence, then He would be identical with His existence. In that case—since God is not the existence of anything distinct from Himself—God would be an existence, which was not the existence of anything but that existence. But supposing that something could be an existence, without being the existence of anything but that existence, is like supposing that something could be a shape, without being the shape of anything but that shape, or be a shadow, without being the shadow of anything but that shadow. It is like supposing that something could be the whiteness of itself, and nothing but itself . . . Surely, though, existence is no different from whiteness on this score, in which case neither God nor anything else could be just its own existence.[40]

This is an enlightening passage for understanding just what Hughes thinks existence is. He likens it to accidental forms, shadows, and colors. In other words, existence stands in the order of accidents that of themselves cannot subsist. Existence, like shapes, shadows, and colors must find expression *in* something other than itself. Identifying God with

---

38. Ibid.

39. Hughes, *On a Complex Theory*, 5.

40. Ibid., 21.

his own existence, as Thomas's classical version of simplicity does, is, in Hughes's estimation, to strip God of the richness of his being so that nothing can be said of him except that he just is:

> Although there is something more to Socrates than Socrates' existence, there is nothing more to God than His existence. In that case, it looks as though God will just exist, because there will be nothing else in Him over and above His existence. Since there will not be anything in God but existence, and the existence of a thing does not make it anything but existent, God will be nothing more than existent. But it seems clear that nothing subsistent could be just existent: a merely existent substance is too thin to be possible.[41]

Hughes finds the identity of God with his act of existence non-compelling because he conceives existence to be "thin," functioning as nothing more than an on-off toggle switch, as it were. How can God possess all of those other properties that Christians ascribe to him if he is nothing but existence itself?

Hughes also disputes Thomas's claim that every composite is potentially dissoluble. Indeed, Hughes discovers composite creatures in Thomas's own theology that are not dissoluble, namely, angelic spirits. Hughes reasons, "If dissolution is understood in the most natural way, there are in fact good Thomistic reasons to deny that every composite is potentially dissoluble."[42] Thomas believes that angelic spirits can be annihilated, but they cannot be dissolved by reduction to their elements since they are not composed of parts such as matter and form or genus and species. But they are composed of existence, essence, subject and accidents. This being so, it must follow that not *every* composite can undergo dissolution since angels can only undergo annihilation. Their parts can be destroyed but not removed. Thus, Hughes deduces, if angels are neither prior nor posterior to their parts and yet are still composites God may very well be a similar sort of composite, only more durable.

There is also a problem with Thomas's insistence that all of God's properties are identical in him. Specifically, Hughes contends that if God has some shared properties, such as wisdom, and some "insular properties," such as omnipotence, then these properties cannot be identical in God because one would be "conspecific" with the creature (e.g., his

41. Ibid.
42. Ibid., 37.

wisdom with Socrates' wisdom) and one would be insular (e.g., neither
Socrates nor any other creature exemplifies omnipotence).[43] To borrow
the language of some Reformed theologians, if one of God's attributes is
communicable to creatures and another is incommunicable then it must
follow that these properties cannot be identical. Instead of indentifying
each of God's attributes with the others, Hughes proposes the possibility
of constructing an "intimate relation" account in order to explain the
harmony between God's attributes.[44]

Possibly the most formidable argument Hughes wields against the
DDS is that respecting God's freedom. He reasons as follows:

> God could not be the same as all His intrinsic attributes unless
> God has all the same intrinsic attributes in every world He in-
> habits . . . There presumably are beings whose intrinsic attributes
> do not vary from world to world: sets, numbers, and (I think)
> regions of space. But . . . there are worries about whether *God's*
> intrinsic properties could be constant from world to world, given
> that He is omniscient. If these worries are well founded, we shall
> have to give up not just the identity of God with His intrinsic at-
> tributes, but also the identity of God with His essence: if God has
> properties that are neither included nor follow upon that essence,
> He cannot very well be the same as His essence.[45]

In short, how can a God who is omniscient and free to create if and what
he pleases possibly be simple? If an intrinsic property, such as God's
specific knowledge, could change from world to world then God cannot
be identical with his intrinsic properties. Consequently we must either
posit a real distinction between God's essential nature and his intrinsic
properties or sacrifice the doctrine of immutability and conclude that
God's essence changes from world to world. Either way the identity
account of the DDS is bound to fail. Furthermore, if God could have
known the world other than it is (thus a different actual world) then is
this possibility not an instance of passive potency in him? Hughes summarizes: "If some intrinsic attributes of God are had by God in every
world in which He exists, and others are had by God in only some of the
worlds in which He exists, then those attributes cannot be the same as

43. See Ibid., 69.
44. Ibid., 71.
45. Ibid., 106.

one another, and cannot both be the same as God; so it must be false that whatever is an intrinsic attribute of God, just is God."[46]

Thomas Morris

Christian philosopher Thomas Morris identifies three distinct commitments of divine simplicity: God lacks spatial parts, temporal parts, and metaphysical parts.[47] Morris affirms divine spatial simplicity, that is, that God lack physical parts. He is skeptical of temporal simplicity as it seems to entail the unacceptable conclusion that God is atemporal. But Morris's strongest criticism is reserved for metaphysical simplicity, which he understands as the denial that God exemplifies numerous different properties ontologically distinct from himself. He accurately summarizes the chief concern of "property simplicity": "[I]f God were like us in exemplifying properties distinct from himself, then he would depend on those properties for what he is, in violation of divine aseity."[48]

Morris issues a host of criticisms against the DDS. First, he takes the line popularized by Alvin Plantinga (see below) that if God is identical with his properties then either his properties are concrete or God is abstract. "Either view," he remarks, "seems startlingly counterintuitive, in violation of any standard concrete-abstract distinction."[49] Second, if God does not possess a real multiplicity of properties then many of the standard distinctions we make when predicating attributes of God just don't make sense. For instance, Christians believe that some things are necessarily true of God, such as his omnipotence, while other things are contingently true of him, such as his use of that power to create the world. But the real distinction between necessary and contingent properties seems to be entirely inaccessible to us if we insist, per the DDS, that each of God's attributes are identical with him and with each other. Morris applies this challenge to the issue of God's knowledge. God is necessarily a knower but only contingently a knower of specific contingencies, such as knowing the color of the shirt one wears on a particular day. One's choice of a specific shirt to wear surely cannot belong to God's necessary knowledge even if it is necessary that he know the contingent

---

46. Ibid., 114.

47. Morris, *Our Idea of God*, 114.

48. Ibid.

49. Ibid., 117.

choice once it is made. "Thus, there is both necessity and contingency with respect to God. And there seems to be no other good way to capture this truth than to say that God has both necessary (essential) and contingent properties."[50]

Much of Morris's criticism of the DDS is leveled against William Mann's "rich property" account in which Mann fashions a unique property instance argument that conceives God as an instance of a single property, namely, divinity.[51] Morris contends that this version of the DDS still fails to make the modal distinctions between necessary and contingent properties in God: "God's properties obviously cannot differ among themselves in modal status if he is in reality only one property. But theists traditionally hold that God is essentially omnipotent, omniscient, and good, yet only contingently or accidentally such that he created this world, called Abram out of Ur, spoke through Moses, and so forth. It follows from Mann's [property instance] account of divine simplicity, as well as from the property view, that no such modal discriminations can be made with respect to God. And surely this is unacceptable."[52]

Additionally, the DDS, whether conceived according to the property identity account or Mann's property instance account, suffers from a "supervenience problem" in which certain properties entail the presence of other distinct properties. Morris distills the essence of this argument:

50. Ibid. Elsewhere Morris explains this problem as one of "modal uniformity": "For consider any exemplification of an apparently accidental or contingent property. God will have the property of knowing this property to be exemplified. And this piece of knowledge will be identical to his omniscience. Thus, it will be essential to him. But if this is so, and God is a necessarily existing being, it will be a necessary truth that the original, apparently contingent property is exemplified, and that it is exemplified by the particular object which otherwise appeared accidentally to have it. It then follows of course that the actual world is the only possible world, that all our properties are essential, and so on. This is the extreme of modal uniformity" ("On God and Mann," 311).

51. Mann explains, "There is a rich property of which God is an instance. Unlike the case of created persons, whose rich properties are complex and chock-a-block with accidental properties, the rich property appropriate to God has none of these features. The instance-instance identities [i.e., each property instance in God is identical with every other], along with the thesis that God has no accidental properties, gives us the result that the rich property associated with God has but one element—*being a Godhead*, which is the same property as *being omniscient, being omnipotent*, and all the rest. So the DDS . . . does have the upshot that God is a property instance, but . . . I see nothing untoward or embarrassing about that" ("Divine Simplicity," 467).

52. Morris, "God and Mann," 307. For more on Morris's conception of necessary and contingent divine attributes see his, *Anselmian Explorations*, 76–97.

"Standard conceptions of some divine attributes seem to be conceptions of essentially supervenient properties—properties which can be exemplified only in virtue of other distinct properties being exemplified." Supervenience can be explained as follows: "If a property F supervenes a property G, then an instance of F essentially depends on there being some instance of G in association with which it exists, in the sense that no instance of F could exist unless some underlying instance of G existed simultaneously."[53] For God to be omnipotent, for example, he would have to have the ability to perform a set of various tasks and that ability to perform each task is not itself identical with omnipotence. The same can be argued for omniscience. God must have the capacity to know many distinct things and this capacity for knowing is not itself identical with omniscience.[54] So the property of omnipotence supervenes the property of capacity-to-perform-tasks and the property of omniscience supervenes the property of capacity-to-know. Morris is of the school of thought that anything that can be truly said of a subject counts as a numerically distinct property. Thus, any truths that must supervene or be entailed in any other truths automatically indicate the presence of multiple distinct properties.

Finally, Morris offers a version of the shared property critique based upon "Leibniz's Law," which he formulates as follows: "(x) (y) $(x = y \equiv (F)$ $(Fx \equiv Fy))$, according to which, roughly, an object x is identical with an object y if and only if x has every property y has, and vice versa."[55] In particular, Leibniz's Law of identity poses a problem for divine uniqueness. God seemingly cannot have both a property unique to him and a property shared by another individual since the DDS argues that all of God's properties are identical. It follows from Leibniz's Law that if *any* of his properties are unique to him, such as aseity, then *all* of his properties are unique to him. If he has any shared properties, ones instantiated both by God and some non-divine thing, then those properties "could not be identical with an instance of a unique divine property."[56] The only options seem to be "that either (1) All of God's properties are shared, or (2) None of God's properties is shared." Morris highlights the problem: "If God has an individual essence, or any properties distinctive of deity,

53. Ibid.
54. Ibid., 308.
55. Ibid., 313.
56. Ibid.

(1) cannot be true. And if we can make any justified assertions about God at all, (2) cannot be true. Indeed, (2) is not even coherent except on a non-standard and extremely restricted view of what counts as a property."[57] The reason Morris thinks (2) is obviously absurd is because if we can truly predicate that God has no shared properties then he obviously has the shared property of being predicated of truly. Morris concludes against both the property identity and property instance versions of the DDS, writing, "It is hard for me to see how an acceptance of either (1) or (2) could amount to anything other than a relinquishing of the substance of traditional theism."[58]

Alvin Plantinga

The single most influential polemic against the DDS in the past fifty years is arguably Alvin Plantinga's 1980 Aquinas Lecture, *Does God Have a Nature?* In this work he seeks to demonstrate that Aquinas's doctrine of divine simplicity is philosophically incoherent and theologically problematic. Plantinga is fully aware of the historical pedigree of the DDS: "The idea that God is simple has been embraced by thinkers as diverse as Duns Scotus and Louis Berkhof; it is to be found both in the ancient creeds of the church and in such relatively recent declarations as the Belgic Confession."[59] But the "dark saying" of simplicity faces two great difficulties: first, it is hard to grasp or construe; second, it is difficult to see why anyone would be inclined to accept it as it is traditionally explained.

Plantinga begins his critique by identifying Thomas Aquinas's motivation for holding the doctrine: "the fundamental reason is to accommodate God's aseity and sovereignty."[60] The DDS preserves God's aseity by ensuring that God is not dependent upon his properties. Identifying God with each of his properties seems to be the only way to guarantee that he is not subsequent to them in some sense. Also, according to Plantinga's reading of Thomas, the DDS makes certain God's sovereignty over all things inasmuch as he would not be sovereign over any properties he possessed by participation. If God participated in any property

---

57. Ibid., 314.

58. Ibid.

59. Plantinga, *Does God Have a Nature?* 27.

60. Ibid., 28.

that property would have to precede him and exist independent of him in some sense. But then God would have no control, no sovereignty, over that property. By identifying God with each of his properties and with his existence the DDS effectually precludes God's participation in any property. Plantinga explains the concerns of aseity and sovereignty:

> If God were distinct from such properties as wisdom, goodness and power but nonetheless *had* these properties, then he would be *dependent* on them . . . in a dual way. First, if, as Aquinas thinks, these properties are essential to him, then it is not possible that he should have existed and they not be "in" him. But if they had not existed, they could not have been in him. Therefore he would not have existed if they had not. This connection between his existence and theirs, furthermore, is necessary; it is not due to his will and it is not within his power to abrogate it. That it holds is not up to him or within his control. He is obliged to put up with it. No doubt he wouldn't *mind* being thus constrained, but that is not the point. The point is that he would be dependent upon something else for his existence, and dependent in a way outside his control and beyond his power to alter; this runs counter to his aseity.[61]

Furthermore, if God participates in properties with which he is not identical then he also depends upon those non-divine entities for his character. "He is, for example, *wise*. But then if there had been no such thing as wisdom, he would not have been wise."[62] What's more, God did not cause this dependence situation: "[H]e didn't bring it about that he is thus dependent; this dependence is not a result of his creative activity; and there is nothing he can do to change or overcome it. If he had properties and a nature distinct from him, then he would exist and display the character he does because of a relation in which he stands to something other than himself. And this doesn't fit with his existence *a se*."[63] But Plantinga is not convinced that God is *a se* in the strong traditional sense. After all, beside the divine properties we also have to account for "the rest of the Platonic menagerie—the propositions, properties, numbers, sets, possible worlds and all the rest."[64] These things do not depend upon God in any way. "That there are natural numbers, for example, is

61. Ibid., 32–33.
62. Ibid., 33.
63. Ibid.
64. Ibid., 35.

not up to God; he didn't create them and couldn't destroy them. They do not owe their character to him."[65] In keeping with this Platonic vision, Plantinga concludes, "there are innumerable beings whose existence and character are independent of God."[66]

Beside his skepticism of God's aseity and absolute sovereignty, Plantinga is also critical of Thomas's denial that God possesses any accidental properties. Thomas issues this famous denial in response to the challenge of contingency: How can a simple God have accidental or contingent properties? Most adherents to the DDS deny that he does. Plantinga summarizes: "All of God's properties are essential to him; each property he has is one he couldn't possibly have lacked."[67] In contrast, though, Plantinga points out that the Scriptures are replete with examples of contingency in God, such as his creating Adam and knowing that Adam sinned. Moreover, Thomas's reply that "having created Adam" and "knowing that Adam sinned" are not real properties in God is objectionable: "even if *having created Adam* isn't a *property* it is at any rate something that *characterizes* God, and it is something such that its characterizing him makes him different from what he would have been had it not characterized him."[68] Plantinga extends his argument against Thomas's denial of divine accidents to his denial of passive potency in God as well. If all of God's attributes are essential then there is no way God could have been other than the way he is and there is no way that God could yet be in the future that he is not already. But this seems patently wrong. Consider Plantinga's argument: "No doubt he [God] hasn't yet created all the persons he will create; he will create persons distinct from all those that have so far existed. If so, there is at least one individual essence E such that God does not now but will have the characteristic of causing E to be instantiated. If so, he is in potentiality with respect to that characteristic."[69] So, upon an ordinary understanding of time and the biblical narrative it seems the DDS is flawed in its denial of accidents and potency in God.

The most important and perplexing denial of composition is, in Plantinga's view, the claim that in God there is no complexity of proper-

65. Ibid.
66. Ibid.
67. Ibid., 39.
68. Ibid., 42–43.
69. Ibid., 44.

ties and that God is identical with his nature and each of his properties: "God isn't merely good, on this view; he is goodness, or his goodness, or goodness itself. He isn't merely alive; He is identical with his life. He doesn't merely have a nature or essence; he just *is* that nature, is the very same thing as it is. And this is a hard saying."[70] Two difficulties stand out. First, this seems to make each of God's properties identical with all the others and thereby suggests that God has only one property. But clearly he has several properties that are by no means identical, such as power and mercifulness. Second, if God is identical with his properties then he must be a self-exemplifying property. But this conclusion is fraught with theological drawbacks. Plantinga notes, "No property could have created the world; no property could be omniscient, or, indeed, know anything at all. If God is a property, then he isn't a person but a mere abstract object; he has no knowledge, awareness, power, love or life. So taken, the simplicity doctrine seems to be an utter mistake."[71] Also, it will not help the DDS to modify the claim to say that God is identical with his *having* power or his *having* wisdom so that the identity is not between properties as such but between God's *having* of these properties. The reason this maneuver is not available to the DDS adherent is that it simply shifts the property identity problem over to the category of states of affairs. To deny that God is identical with his properties seems to rescue one from the charge that the simple God is an impersonal abstract. But to say instead that God is identical with his *having* this and that property and that his *having* this property is identical to the state of affairs of his *having* that property still leaves one with an abstract God because states of affairs are just as impersonal and abstract as properties. Plantinga concludes, "If God is a state of affairs, then he is a mere abstract object and not a person at all; he is then without knowledge or love or the power to act. But this is clearly inconsistent with the claims of Christian theism at the most basic level."[72]

---

70. Ibid., 46–47.

71. Ibid., 47. The argument that the DDS makes out God to be an abstract and depersonalized object is not original with Plantinga. Daniel Bennett, for one, suggested this difficulty some years before Plantinga's lecture was published, writing, "The assumption that the states (or activities or episodes) of a thing are properties, and the view that God is simple, lead to the consequence that God is a property! This is devastating to commonly held views about God" ("The Divine Simplicity," 100).

72. Ibid., 52–53.

Plantinga lays many and serious charges against Thomas's DDS but he also leaves open the possibility that he has not rightly understood the Angelic Doctor's claims: "Perhaps when he argues that God is identical with his essence, with his goodness, with goodness itself, and the like, he doesn't mean to identify God with a property or state of affairs at all, but with something quite different. If so, it isn't easy to see what sort of thing it might be."[73] But if Plantinga's understanding of Thomas is correct, "the Thomistic doctrine of divine simplicity seems entirely unacceptable. Like the views that our concepts do not apply to God [analogy?], it begins in a pious and proper concern for God's sovereignty; it ends by flouting the most fundamental claims of theism."[74]

In a final salvo against the DDS Plantinga challenges any who might appeal to the notion of analogical predication in an attempt to excuse the infelicity of claiming that God is both a person and a property: "If we can't rely on our usual modes of inference in reasoning about God, by what right do we argue . . . to the conclusion that God is not distinct from his properties? Suppose it is a fact that our language about God is analogical: if that fact vitiates the argument *against* divine simplicity, it pays the same complement to the arguments *for* this doctrine."[75] Finally, the DDS cannot be the way to account for God's relation to the "Platonic horde" inasmuch as "it scouts intuitions much firmer than those that support it."[76]

Evangelical Critics

Evangelical theologian Ronald Nash's assessment of the DDS basically follows the arguments put forth by Plantinga. Nash wryly declares, "The doctrine of divine simplicity has a public relations problem."[77] In particular, the problem with denying that God has any parts is that "[h]uman

73. Ibid., 53.

74. Ibid., 53–54.

75. Ibid., 58–59.

76. Ibid., 61. This is a crucial statement for understanding how Plantinga weighs the arguments for and against the DDS. What he means is that the intuition about the absolute non-identity of persons with properties is much firmer than the intuition about the nature of God's sovereignty-aseity relative to Platonica. In the end it seems better to Plantinga to modify the traditional understanding of God's sovereignty and aseity than to challenge modern semi-Platonic notions about properties and persons.

77. Nash, *Concept of God*, 85.

beings could never have knowledge of any absolutely simple essence."[78] Absolute simplicity of the sort traditionally ascribed to God renders him incomprehensible to finite knowers. Suggesting that humans know God by way of analogy does not ease Nash's concerns. He asks, "If human beings necessarily conceive God differently than He really is, is their conception of God not therefore false?"[79]

Nash considers the medieval motivations for the DDS with special attention given to the challenges of extreme realism, on the one hand, and nominalism, on the other. The extreme realist threat is summarized as follows:

> The threat that extreme realism posed to the Christian doctrine of God resulted from its tendency to take properties like wisdom and goodness and hypostatize them into existing entities. With respect to the properties of God, the problem was obvious. If the properties or attributes of God are hypostatized existents, then God is a composite being. In other words, the extreme realists took properties such as being wise, being powerful, and being good and turned them into substances like wisdom, power, and goodness. This effectively made God's nature a construct of more basic building blocks, namely, the hypostatized attributes.[80]

Nash is sympathetic to the Christian resistance to such strong realism, observing: "Theological claims that God is not composed of parts are attempts to avoid the absurd or heretical implications of a hyper-realist interpretation of the divine attributes."[81]

The nominalist threat took the far opposite position in contending that there aren't any differences at all between the divine attributes. In effect, nominalism denied that such things as properties exist; only particulars exist. It follows that God cannot have properties and therefore has no nature. All distinctions between the divine attributes are made subjectively in the human mind and do not correspond to any external reality. Nash correctly observes that nominalism was rejected by most medieval adherents to the DDS, but he suspects that many of them came close to it in their denial of any real distinction between God's attributes. Although Nash acknowledges that the Scylla of extreme realism and

78. Ibid.
79. Ibid., 86.
80. Ibid., 87–88.
81. Ibid., 88.

Charybdis of nominalism are both perilous to an orthodox Christian doctrine of God, he is unconvinced that the DDS, with its concomitant emphasis upon the analogy of being, is an adequate way to navigate between them.

His skepticism of the DDS is fueled in part by his acceptance of Plantinga's basic theses. The challenge of how God can have a nature and still be sovereign and *a se* is especially vexing for Nash:

> [E]ither God's properties have always existed or God created them. But if God created His properties, there was a time when He did not possess those properties. And if this were so, then properties like goodness, justice, and wisdom could not be essential properties of God. But if, on the other hand, God has always been good, then there seems to be a sense in which God depends on His properties; His existence seems conditioned or limited in some sense by His properties. God could not be good unless goodness existed. That God has essentially a property like goodness is something that is beyond His control. Moreover, the belief that God has a nature (properties) seems to limit God in other ways. Each of God's essential properties has characteristics that are beyond God's control.[82]

Even if one rejects extreme realism, the divine attributes themselves seem to place traditional Christian theism, and especially its commitment to God's aseity, in a logical and theological quandary.

The DDS demands acceptance of several counterintuitive notions. First, in equating God with each of his properties one is also forced to identify each property with all the others and consequently God has only one property. "But this is mystifying, to say the least." While Nash is willing to acknowledge that many things about God are incomprehensible to us, the notion of property identity cannot be one of them: "one of the things we do seem to know very clearly is that power and love and knowledge and mercy are not identical properties."[83] Second, the DDS conflicts with the Christian belief that God is a person and even "leads to the odd suggestion that the biblical teaching that God is characterized by a variety of distinct properties is wrong."[84] Third, Nash contends that the DDS does not do enough to make God unique since it appears that there is a sense "in which every human essence is also simple."[85] Admittedly, this criticism is difficult to square with Nash's other claim that divine simplicity makes God out to be a depersonalized single property. What he appears to be saying is that insofar as the DDS teaches that God's essence is an indivisible unity it does not claim anything different from what is claimed for any individual human essence. If human essences are indivisible wholes, wherein if one part were removed the essence would cease to be, then human essences are just as simple as God; ergo the DDS is unnecessary.

Nash concludes that the liabilities of the DDS are too much to bear since they demand conclusions "that conflict with other important tenets of Christian theism." He adds, "It would appear that Christian theologians have no good reason to affirm the doctrine of divine simplicity. It seems doubtful that the doctrine adds anything significant to our understanding of God."[86]

John Feinberg, another evangelical theologian, agrees. The first problem he discovers with the DDS is its apparent lack of biblical support. Appeals by Reformed theologians, such as Herman Bavinck and Louis Berkhof, to texts that seem to identify God with his attributes (e.g., Jer 23:6 with righteousness; John 1:4, 5, 9 with life and light; 14:6 with truth and life; 1 Cor 1:30 with wisdom; 1 John 1:5 with light; 4:8 with love) seem to "beg the question and wrongly use surface grammar as indicating that these verses teach the doctrine."[87] Are the biblical writers really making a metaphysical point in these passages? Furthermore, would not any passage that speaks of God as *possessing* attributes argue equally well for the position that God is *not* identical with his attributes? Feinberg concludes that the biblical data "underdetermine the issue." Indeed, this lack of explicit biblical data for the DDS "should be disconcerting at the least, and a good argument against it at most."[88]

Feinberg affirms many of the leading criticisms of the DDS proffered by Morris and Plantinga, including: (1) that God has only one property; (2) that God is a property or state of affairs and thus not a person; (3) that God has only essential properties (which seems obviously false) or that he is identical with his accidental properties and thus

---

85. Ibid.
86. Ibid.
87. Feinberg, *No One Like Him*, 328.
88. Ibid., 329.

is himself contingent (which also seems obviously false); and (4) that
Mann's property instance explanation still conceives God as instancing
properties with which he is not identical and upon which he depends
in some way.[89] Feinberg declares, "These philosophical problems plus
the biblical considerations . . . lead me to conclude that simplicity is not
one of the divine attributes."[90] Nevertheless, he is confident that he can
maintain God's aseity without ascribing to simplicity.[91]

Evangelical philosophers J. P. Moreland and William Lane Craig
declare the DDS to be "a radical doctrine that enjoys no biblical support and even is at odds with the biblical conception of God in various
ways."[92] Their criticism of the doctrine is more epistemologically sensi-
tive than the assessments of Nash or Feinberg. They dislike the rejection
of univocal predication that pervades historical accounts of the DDS. In
their opinion, to say that humans can only positively know God in an
analogical sense leaves us "in a state of genuine agnosticism about the
nature of God."[93]

Additionally, Moreland and Craig note four other "powerful objections" to the DDS. First, it "seems patently false" to insist upon the real
identity of all of God's attributes. Second, if God is identical with his
essence then he has no contingent knowledge or action and "all modal
distinctions [between necessity and contingency] collapse and everything becomes necessary." Third, Aquinas's denial that God stands in
any "real relation" to creatures implies that God could know nothing
other than he does even if some other possible world were the actual
world. Also, presuming that God knows contingencies, the DDS entails
that God himself is ontologically contingent inasmuch as it identifies
him with his knowledge. Moreover, if God lacks a real relation to the
world then the DDS makes "the existence or nonexistence of creatures
in various possible worlds independent of God and utterly mysterious."
Fourth, to identify God's essence with his existence "seems wholly obscure" insofar as it claims "that *exists* just exists." Following Christopher
Hughes's reasoning, existence as such is predicated of "things" but not
of itself. All said, Moreland and Craig conclude that Christians "have no

89. Ibid., 330–35.

90. Ibid., 335.

91. Ibid., 335–37. Feinberg's understanding of aseity is challenged below chapter 3.

92. Moreland and Craig, *Philosophical Foundations*, 524.

93. Ibid.

good reason to adopt and many reasons to reject a full-blown doctrine of divine simplicity."[94]

INITIAL RESPONSE

The outstanding common denominator in each of these serious and sophisticated arguments against the DDS is the strong commitment to ontological univocism. Each critic speaks as if God and creatures were "beings" in the exact same sense, reducing the Creator-creature distinction to a difference of degrees. God's is a higher existence and his attributes more perfect, but all told his are simply greater instances of the same sort of existence and attributes found in creatures. Given this outlook it is no wonder that the DDS appears incoherent to many modern philosophers and theologians. God, it would seem, could no more be identical with his existence and attributes than any creature could be really identical with its existence and attributes.

But it is precisely this ontological univocism that the DDS will not allow.[95] Though creatures bear the image of God's existence and attributes, their similarity to God is better understood as analogical than univocal. The manner in which God exists and possesses attributes is so radically unlike anything found in creatures that he cannot be classified together with them in a single order of being or as the highest link on a great chain of being. As the one who ultimately accounts for being in general, as its first and final cause, God does not stand within that general ontological order.[96] In this connection the various critics surveyed in the foregoing section seem to have gratuitously precluded the very ontological outlook in which the DDS is intended to make sense.

---

94. Ibid., 525.

95. It is worth observing that one discovers this same sort of ontological univocism in the thought of Duns Scotus and his followers. To this extent the Scotist version of the DDS appears open to many of the criticisms surveyed in the previous section. For Thomas Aquinas's denial of univocity between God and creatures see *ST* I.13.5.

96. Ontological commitments are often left unstated or unformulated by both philosophers and theologians. But, as Etienne Gilson observes, such commitments are inseparable from the position one takes on the question of God's simplicity: "since God is being *par excellence*, the notion of the divine simplicity will depend, for the theologian, on the particular ontology he will accept as a philosopher" (*Christian Philosophy*, 29). Reformed Christians should find this to be a sound observation regardless of whether or not they agree with Gilson on how one goes about acquiring a true philosophical knowledge.

One unfortunate corollary of this procedure is the forfeiture of divine absoluteness inasmuch as something other than God (e.g., abstract being, properties, necessary propositions, Platonic forms, or some other piece of abstracta) enters into the ontological account of his existence and essence.

I aim to show in subsequent chapters that denial of the DDS leads to the denial of God's absoluteness. The logical consequence of denying the DDS is that God is regarded as merely another being within the world, even if the most supreme instance of such being. Without a strong account of divine simplicity, the ultimate principle and explanation for the being and perfections of things in the world, yea even for God himself, must be sought outside of and back of God. This is, in effect, to offer a Platonic vision of the world in which even God possesses being and attributes through participation in ideal forms or universals. Plantinga and many other modern philosophers openly advocate this conception of reality.[97]

Furthermore, on their account, God may cause the world as its Creator, but he is not the *ultimate* sufficient explanation for many of those perfections that we discover in the world, such as truth, goodness, wisdom, justice, and the like. The ideal forms of those things exist eternally and independently of God. In contrast to the prevailing Platonism of the analytic philosophers, the following chapters of this study endeavor to uphold God's absoluteness by arguing that he alone is the final sufficient explanation for himself and all others things and that it is his simplicity that explains why this is the case.

Negatively, I aim to show that any denial or diminishment of God's simplicity must inevitably lead to the conclusion that God is dependent upon something other than himself and cannot be the ultimate sufficient explanation for himself or anything else. Positively, I aim to demonstrate that the DDS alone explains God's self-sufficient independence and his singular adequacy as the first cause of all other things. Both approaches are calculated to generate the conclusion of the Westminster Confession that God is "most absolute."

---

97. Plantinga's recognition of a "Platonic menagerie" is shared by numerous of his fellow analytic philosophers. See, for instance, Van Inwagen, "God and Other Uncreated Things," 3–20, and Wolterstorff, *On Universals*, 290–97.

2

Simplicity and the Models of Composition

IN ORDER TO UNDERSTAND how divine simplicity accounts for God's absoluteness it is first necessary to consider precisely what is meant by "simplicity." Though the doctrine has numerous positive implications for one's understanding of God's existence and essence (to be developed in subsequent chapters), it is formally articulated apophatically as God's *lack* of parts and denies that he is physically, logically, or metaphysically composite.[1] Non-composition, it is argued, must characterize God inasmuch as every composite is a dependent thing that cannot account for its own existence or essence and stands in need of some composer outside itself. To be composite is to be composed by another and to be dependent upon the parts that enter into the composition. Furthermore, composition signifies the capacity of a thing to change or even be annihilated. If God is to be understood as "most absolute" all such composition must be denied of him.

Reformed advocates of the DDS have traditionally followed Thomas Aquinas in his understanding that God alone is absolutely simple while every creature is more or less composite. Indeed, this matter of composition and simplicity is at the heart of the Creator-creature distinction. Nothing composite can be the reason for its own composition. "[E]very composite has a cause," Thomas argues, "for things in themselves different [i.e., parts] cannot unite unless something causes them to unite. But God is uncaused . . . since He is the first efficient cause."[2] Louis De

---

1. This apophatic approach to the DDS is found quite early in the Christian tradition. See, for example, the discussion of Basil of Caesarea's negative theology in Radde-Gallwitz, *Basil of Caesarea, Gregory of Nyssa, and the Transformation of Divine Simplicity*, 137–42, 154.

2. *ST* I.3.7.

Raeymaeker elaborates on this inability of composites to sufficiently account for their own existence:

> Every real structure of particular being consists in a real correlation, that is, in a harmony of transcendental relations, for instance, the correlation of the real principle of existence and the principle of essence, the hylomorphic structure, the composition of substance and accidents, etc. In each one of these structures the potential principle and the actual principle are really distinct, they are irreducible. Being distinct of themselves, they do not of themselves form a unity. Nevertheless, the principles are only conceived together, since they are correlative terms. Hence, there must be outside of them a real reason which makes them related, the one to the other, a reason which unites them; and since these principles have no reality outside of their correlation (for they are transcendental relations), this means that a reason is necessary to produce them. Consequently, everything composite is dependent on a cause.[3]

The principles, or parts, that enter into composition do not themselves explain *why* the composition exists; instead, they presuppose a composer. For our purposes it is observed that no composite entity can be "most absolute" inasmuch as it requires some entity prior to itself to account for the composition and is thus relative to that entity. Also, each composite thing must possess the capacity to come into existence from non-existence, go out of existence and, in most instances, change while in existence.

In book one, question three of his *Summa theologiae* Thomas identifies six varieties of composition that must be denied of God if his absolute simplicity is to be maintained: (1) bodily parts; (2) matter and form; (3) supposit and nature; (4) existence and essence; (5) genus and difference; and (6) substance and accidents.[4] These models of composition are understood as variations of the composition of act and potency. But the sense of "compositeness" in each model differs more or less based upon

---

3. Raeymaeker, *Philosophy of Being*, 255.

4. These models or some variation of thereof are also denied by many of Thomas's Roman Catholic and Protestant successors. See, for example: Giles of Rome, *Theorems on Existence and Essence*; Henry of Ghent, *Summa*, 28.1–6; Duns Scotus, *Treatise on God as First Principle*, 4.4–8; Cajetan, *Commentary on Being and Essence*; Perkins, *Workes*, I:11; Owen, *Vindicae Evangelicae*, XII: 70–72; Turretin, *IET*, 3.7.2–6; Brakel, *Christian's Reasonable Service*, I:96–99; Gill, *Body of Divinity*, I.4.3; and Bavinck, *RD*, II: 176.

what is being composed. Contiguous body parts, for instance, comprise a composition radically unlike that of genus and difference. The former is a physical composite while the latter is a logical one. Both of these senses of composition differ considerably from the metaphysical composition of form and matter or substance and accidents.[5] A grasp of each one of these kinds of composition is necessary for understanding what the DDS aims to affirm about God.[6]

Before considering each model we do well to summarize Thomas's reasons for denying them of God. He names several such motivations in *Summa theologiae* I.3.7: (1) every composite is posterior to its component parts and is in some way dependent upon them—but God is the *first being*; (2) every composite has a cause inasmuch as things differing within them cannot unite without a cause making them to unite—but God is the *first efficient cause*; (3) in every composite there must be potentiality and actuality in which one of the parts actuates the others or all of the parts are potential to the whole—but God is *pure act*; (4) in composites no one part can be identified with the whole and neither can the whole be predicated of any one of the parts and hence every composite "has something which is not itself"—but God "is absolute form, or rather absolute being" so that *in him there is nothing besides himself.*[7] Composition in God, as Thomas understands it, would jettison God's independent self-sufficiency, his uncausedness, his fullness of being, and his absolute self-identity. Expressed negatively, composition entails that the composite thing be a dependent effect that is in some sense in the process of becoming and is not wholly self-identifying. In short, *a composite being is a creature.*

---

5. For a brief summary of the differences between physical, metaphysical and rational composition see Dulles et al., *Introductory Metaphysics*, 46–47.

6. Aquinas recommends approaching the study of simple things by beginning with our knowledge of composite things: "We ought to get our knowledge of simple things from composite things and arrive at what is prior by way of what is posterior, so that the learning process will begin, appropriately with what is easier" (*De ente et essentia*, 1 [1]; cited hereafter as *DEE*). He is of the opinion that the simpler ontologically precedes the more composite though the composite is more readily accessible to the human intellect. Henry of Ghent concurs, writing, "And because what is composed is better known than what is simple . . . just as multiplicity is better known to us than unity . . . we must therefore bring out the simplicity of God from its contrary, namely from the composition of a creature, by removing it from God" (*Summa*, 28 [p. 177]).

7. *ST* I.3.7. A useful précis of these four reasons is found in Garrigou-Lagrange, *The One God*, 191–93.

In considering the various models of act-potency composition we are really observing various manifestations of creaturely dependence, finitude and relativity. Not every creature is characterized by every kind of composition; some are relatively simple, such as human souls and angelic spirits. But inclusion in just one of these categories is enough to demonstrate that the creature is non-absolute. Accordingly, if God is truly most absolute he must not exhibit any of these compositions.

After discussing Thomas's understanding of act and potency the remainder of this chapter follows the order of the models as they are discussed in *Summa theologiae* I.3. The only change is that the consideration of essence-existence composition has been moved to the end of the discussion since it is arguably the most significant for establishing the absolute distinction between God and all non-divine things.

ACT AND POTENCY

Although Thomas does not devote special place to act-potency composition in *Summa theologiae* I.3, it is clear that his affirmation of God as pure act and devoid of all passive potency informs his overall account of divine non-compositeness.[8] The concepts of act and potency were first

8. In summarizing his five ways for proving God's existence in *ST* I.2.3, Aquinas establishes that the first efficient cause of being must itself be pure act. He carries this conclusion over into his treatment of God's simplicity. The first way contends that anything in motion (broadly conceived as anything that changes whatsoever) must have previously been in potency to that motion and thus moved to that motion by some act external to itself. As Thomas states, "nothing can be reduced from potentiality to actuality, except by something in a state of actuality." What's more, "It is . . . impossible that in the same respect and in the same way a thing should be both mover and moved, *i.e.*, that it should move itself." An external agent already in act is required for the reduction of potency to act. Anything put in motion (i.e., anything in potency) is put motion by another and, as Thomas notes, "that by another again." But this chain of movers cannot go on infinitely or else there would be no first mover, that is, no ultimately sufficient reason for movement. Since the first mover is necessarily unmoved by another, and since all movement comes from some mover in act, that first mover must be *pure* act. If he possessed any potency we would have to look back of him for an account of his actuality. Thomas basically reproduces this same line of argumentation in his third way to argue that God is the necessary, self-sufficient and uncaused first being. There is no non-actuated possibility of being in the first being and thus he is pure act. Regardless of what one thinks of the apologetic merit of these arguments, they do seem to square soundly with the Christian account of God as the absolute Creator and source of being. On the impossibility of infinite regress see Owens, *St. Thomas Aquinas on the Existence of God*, 228–30. For an analysis of Thomas's conceptions of motion, change, and God as Unmoved Mover see Aertsen, *Nature and Creature*, 256–71.

employed by Aristotle to explain change and becoming in the material universe.[9] John Noonan remarks, "All physical reality outside God is essentially a mixture of becoming and being, of potential and actual. In fact, whether we are examining the constitution of physical or of metaphysical being, the nature of these concepts of act and potency must be understood before we can proceed very far in our investigations."[10] In a similar vein, Neo-Aristotelian philosopher David Oderberg observes,

> Things go out of existence and others come into being, and existing things lose characteristics and take on new ones. Reality is, as it were, constantly in a state of being carved up in new and different ways: bits of reality are constantly changing through the agency of other bits of reality . . . The only possible explanation for the fact that reality is able to take on new kinds of existence, whether substantial or accidental, is that there is some principle of potentiality inherent in reality.[11]

So, potency in a thing accounts for its ability to exist, become, and change while act is that by which the existence or change is brought about. A closer consideration of act, potency and change is in order.

Correlativity of Act and Potency

In the physical world potency is the ability or capacity for a thing to become either substantially or accidentally different than it is. An entity is in potency to whatever perfections it can acquire but presently does not possess in actuality. George Klubertanz explains: "Being in potency is the condition of not really having, but being able to acquire, some perfection."[12] Noonan offers some examples: "an acorn has potency to become an oak tree, an egg has potency to become a chicken, hydrogen and oxygen have potency to unite and become water."[13] No potency perfects itself or gives itself actuality; this comes to potency from a corresponding principle of act. Indeed, potency is only properly understood when conceived in composition with act: "It is . . . the correlative of act:

9. See Aristotle, *Physics* 190a32–192b2; 200b12–202b29; *Metaphysics* 1010a15–1010b1; 1011b34; 1042a32–1042b8. See also, Aquinas, *De Principiis Naturae* 1.1–7, and Elders, *The Metaphysics of Being of St. Thomas Aquinas*, 158–69.

10. Noonan, *General Metaphysics*, 35.

11. Oderberg, *Real Essentialism*, 62.

12. Klubertanz, *Introduction*, 88.

13. Noonan, *General Metaphysics*, 36.

the potency is for an act."[14] Paul Glenn summarizes: "For the potentiality of a thing is a capacity unrealized, unactualized, and hence it involves *lack* of perfection—and the word *perfection* suggests a 'thorough making' and a fulfillment,—which is given by actuality."[15]

Act perfects the potency in the sense of bringing it to completion in reality. Klubertanz again: "Being in act is the condition of really possessing some perfection or modification."[16] All actuality is the result of some reduction of potency to act (except in the case of pure act). Noonan distills the essence of this correlative relationship: "The relation between act and potency is one of the completing to the incomplete, the determining to the determinable, the perfecting to the perfectible. It is possible for a being to be in act and potency at that same time, but under different aspects. It may be a perfection in itself and thus an act, and still be capable of receiving another perfection and therefore be in potency for another act."[17] For instance, a scientist may *actually* understand Einstein's theory of general relativity while at the same time lack understanding of his theory of special relativity. He is in act with respect to knowledge of general relativity and in potency with respect to knowledge of special relativity at one and the same time and under the same conditions. But he cannot actually understand and not understand the theory of general relativity at one and the same time and under the same conditions. One cannot both instantiate and not instantiate the same perfection under the same conditions and in the same moment. Every changeable being is partly act and partly potency and is perfected as its potency receives actuality and thereby becomes real. No actual creature is ever *pure* actuality, but always possesses some kind of potency: "It is never merely *that which is*; it bears a real relation to *that which has been*,

---

14. Ibid.

15. Glenn, *Ontology*, 72–73.

16. Klubertanz, *Introduction*, 88.

17. Noonan, *General Metaphysics*, 36–37. It should be noted that Noonan's explanation here is basically restricted to the Aristotelian understanding of act and potency within the domain of physics. On Aristotle see Owens, *The Doctrine of Being in the Aristotelian* Metaphysics, 403–9. While Aquinas acknowledges this physical dimension of act and potency he also emphasizes a metaphysical aspect that seems to advance his conception of act and potency decidedly beyond Aristotle's (see the final section of this chapter). Specifically, Thomas goes beyond the Stagirite by construing potency as that which *limits* actuality. See the important article by Clarke, "The Limitation of Act by Potency."

and involves the possibility or even the forecast of *that which is to be* and *that which may be.*"[18]

It should be noted at this point that though potency and act are spoken of as if they were complete things or entities, they are in fact *principles*, which do not subsist by themselves (*per se*) as discreet beings. Klubertanz observes, "If act and potency were each a being, they could not be found combined within a single being (1 being + 1 being = 2 beings)."[19] As principles of a single complete being, act is *that by which* the being is (or is according to some modification) and potency is *that by which* a thing can be (or can exist according to some modification). But neither is properly understood as *that which is*; that designation belongs only to the subsisting thing itself.[20] Furthermore, it follows that neither act nor potency are intelligible *in themselves*. Again, Klubertanz is quite helpful: "[A]ct and potency are first learned together, in relation to each other. As we find them in immediate experience, neither act nor potency are absolute designations, but correlative intelligibilities: act is the act of a potency, potency is the potency to some act."[21] These principles, though not beings in themselves, are *really* distinct in the creature inasmuch as they are non-identical, their inseparability notwithstanding.

Kinds of Act and Potency

Aquinas identifies two distinct senses of act as well as two distinct senses of potency, which he calls "power":

> Now act is twofold; the first act which is a form, and the second act which is operation. Seemingly the word "act" was first universally employed in the sense of operation, and then, secondly, transferred to indicate the form, inasmuch as the form is the principle and end of operation. Wherefore in like manner power is twofold: active power corresponding to that act which is operation—and seemingly it was in this sense that the word "power" was first employed:—and passive power, corresponding to the

18. Glenn, *Ontology*, 64.

19. Klubertanz, *Introduction*, 129.

20. In some creatures *that which is* is identical with one or more of the principles *by which* it is. For example, Thomas regards angelic spirits as identical with their own substantial forms (see *ST* I.50.2). To this extent even some creatures are relatively simple. But the only *absolutely* simple being is that in which *that which is* is identical with the act of existence *by which* it is (see the existence-essence discussion below).

21. Klubertanz, *Introduction*, 126.

first act or the form,—to which seemingly the name of power was subsequently given.[22]

The principle of actuality is ordinarily first understood as an operation by which something is caused to exist or is modified to exist in a new way. But, as Thomas points out, operation presupposes an actually existing operator. Thus, the form of the operator by which the agent exists as an operator is the first actuality and its operation is the second actuality. Also, all operation is toward the end of supplying a new form (accidental or substantial) to something capable of being actuated by it. So, operators act by virtue of their form and for the purpose of supplying new form to something else. For example, a builder is in act secondarily when acting to give the form of a house to a pile of wood and nails (prior to this action the wood and nails are only potentially a house). This action of building the house is secondary to the builder's *actually being* a builder. "Builder" then is the form by which the builder performs the action of building. This is why Thomas says that form is the first act and operation is the second act.[23]

The principle of potency is also twofold in a manner corresponding to the twofold notion of act. There is an *active* potency (or power) that corresponds to the second act of operation. It is potency inasmuch as it is the *capability* of an existing thing to perform an act. Peter Weigel explains, "Active potency is the power in a substance to initiate and sustain an activity or operation that brings about a change, sometimes in another substance but almost always in the agent as well."[24] Thomas

22. Aquinas, *Quaestiones disputatae De potentia Dei*, 1.1. This is cited hereafter as *DP*. See also, *ST* I.25.1.

23. Paul Glenn elucidates the relation between first and second act: "A *first* actuality, or *actus primus*, does not presuppose another actuality in the order to which itself belongs. A *secondary* actuality, or *actus secundus*, does presuppose such a prior actuality. Thus, actual activity,—such, for instance, as vital activity in a man,—is an actuality; but it is not a *first* actuality, for it presupposes the actually existing human essence equipped for such activity. The man is capable of vital action in the *second* place, after his essence has been constituted in the *first* place" (*Ontology*, 65).

24. Weigel, *Aquinas on Simplicity*, 92. He says "almost always" because Thomas denies that God's actions are second acts (as they are in any creature) and thus that the actualization of his active potency brings about a change in him. When God performs an operation he does not move from potential agency to actual agency even if the temporal effects of his operation are moved from potentiality to actuality. Thomas believes that God does not have to be temporally indexed in order to be the efficient cause of temporal indexicals. Anyhow, the discussion of God's eternality is beyond the scope of this chapter.

describes it simply as, "the principle of acting upon something else."[25] One example of active potency is water's ability to dissolve salt by its power "to break the sodium-chloride bond due to the polarity in the water molecules."[26] Another is the digestive power of man by which he "lays hold of food and transforms it substantially into flesh and bone and tissue."[27] This is not the potency to receive act but, rather, the power to supply act.

It should be noted that the classical DDS does not deny that God possesses active potency in some sense. As Weigel informs us, "Active potency *is* attributed to God as the first efficient cause, but not in the same way in which creatures have it. Creatures change and become further actualized when they use their powers. God does not."[28] This is because the creature is ontologically correlative to those things upon which its active power operates so that effecting new forms of reality in others entails the appearance of a new relation in the creaturely agent. But Thomas rejects such correlativity between God and those things to which his active potency extends in operation: "We ascribe to God operation by reason of its being the ultimate perfection, not by reason of that into which operation passes. And we attribute power to God by reason of that which is permanent and is the principle of power, and not by reason of that which is made complete by operation."[29] The reason God actively operates is because all that is in him is perfect and thus actual (recalling that anything non-actualized is understood to be imperfect).[30]

---

25. *ST* I.25.1.

26. Oderberg, *Real Essentialism*, 63.

27. Glenn, *Ontology*, 70.

28. Weigel, *Aquinas on Simplicity*, 93.

29. *DP* 1.1. That "which is permanent" and is "the principle of power" is God's own essence. The possible effects of God's power do not determine its actuality in him, but rather its actuality in him determines those possible effects. That is because the actuality of his power is nothing other than his own essential actuality and his essence is entirely undetermined by anything non-identical with himself.

30. Thomas draws a careful distinction between God's act of operation and the ensuing effects: "God's power is always united to act, i.e. to operation (for operation is the divine essence): but the effects follow according as his will commands and his wisdom ordains. Consequently it does not follow that his power is always united to its effect, or that creatures have existed from eternity" (*DP* 1.1, ad 8). For more on God's relation to the world see chapter 4 below.

Thomas also identifies a *passive* potency that corresponds to the first act. It is this notion of potency that is utterly denied of God.[31] Aquinas defines it broadly as, "the principle of being acted upon by something else."[32] When act is received the principle of passive potency is reduced to act: "whatever is in passive potentiality can be reduced to act by the active power which extends over that potentiality."[33] Klubertanz notes that such passive potency can be found in wood or wax that are able to receive a shape other than the one they presently possess. These bits of matter depend almost entirely upon something outside of the matter itself for their shape. Also, anything at rest is in potency to local motion which depends upon some mover outside itself for its actuality. Another example would be that of a steak, which can become part of a living thing, such as a dog or a human, through the activity of digestion.[34]

Of course, these instances of passive potency are not each conceived as potency toward the same sort of new actuality. The change in the wood or wax, for instance, is *accidental* inasmuch as the elements remain substantially wood or wax. But the potency of the steak to be transformed into living matter is potency toward *substantial* change inasmuch as it would cease entirely to be a steak at the point of digestion. The only thing constant would be the primary matter that takes on the new substantial form of the human or animal body into which it is digested. In sum, "Passive potency is that disposition in the patient (or agent *qua* patient) that explains why the patient can be made actual, or can receive a different actuality, from what it had."[35] Paul Glenn illustrates this inherent possibility within an existent for either accidental or substantial change:

> That water, which is now actually cold, may become hot, is a potentiality resident in the water; it is *subjective* potentiality. That water may be presently changed substantially into hydrogen and oxygen is also a potentiality resident in the water as in its *subject*;

31. SCG I.16.

32. ST I.25.1. He elaborates upon the difference between active and passive potency: "Active power is not contrary to act, but is founded upon it, for everything acts according as it is actual: but passive power is contrary to act; for a thing is passive according as it is potential. Whence this potentiality is not in God, but only active power" (ST I.25.1, ad 1).

33. Ibid., I.105.1.

34. Klubertanz, *Introduction*, 124.

35. Weigel, *Aquinas on Simplicity*, 94. See also, Oderberg, *Real Essentialism*, 63.

more precisely, the potentiality in question resides in the *prime matter* which is the basic material constituent of water, which has here and now *the substantial form* of water, but which may undergo,—and hence is *subject* to,—the substantial change which will drive off the substantial form of water and, in the same instantaneous process, bring in the substantial forms of hydrogen and oxygen.[36]

The movement from cold to hot constitutes an accidental change while the movement from water to hydrogen and oxygen is a substantial change. A thing's passive potency is the metaphysical ground for predicating any change in it. It remains to consider how the correlative principles of act and potency enable us to account for becoming and change in non-divine things.

Kinds and Conditions of Becoming and Change

Anything composed of act and potency must be caused to exist by an agent extrinsic to it and must also be liable to change, improvement, dissolution, or annihilation. But according to classical Christian theism none of these is attributable to God. As pure actuality he can neither come into existence nor go out of it. Also, he cannot change accidentally or substantially in his existence. As the will and power of God account for creaturely coming-to-be and change from the divine side, act-potency composition helps us understand it from the creaturely side.

In the order of created being there are four types of change that are commonly identified: (1) local change; (2) quantitative change; (3) qualitative change; and (4) substantial change.[37] The first three are accidental changes while the fourth is substantial. Local and quantitative changes are fairly straight forward. Local change is the movement of some material body from one place to another or of one body part with respect to other parts of the same body, that is, local motion. Quantitative change pertains to the change of size in material bodies including augmentation (increase) or diminution (decrease) in mass, volume, or density. The third accidental change is qualitative change. Unlike changes of place and quantity, qualitative change is not restricted to corporeal beings. Peter Coffey notes, "Qualitative change is wider than material change, for it includes changes in spiritual beings, *i.e.*, in beings which are outside the

36. Glenn, *Ontology*, 67.
37. See Aristotle, *Physics* 224a21–226b17.

category of quantity and have a mode of existence altogether different from the extensional, spatial existence which characterizes matter."[38] Of course, material beings can also undergo qualitative alteration in their bodies. Glenn illustrates this sort of change: "[Change may be] from hot to cold, from sweet to sour, from light-colored to dark-colored, from ignorance to knowledge, from virtue to vice, from joy to greater joy."[39]

Substantial change "consists in the transition of a bodily thing (since spirits cannot be substantially changed) from one substantial state to another."[40] This involves the disappearance of one substantial form and the appearance of a new one in its place through a process of corruption and generation. Examples of substantial change include: "The change of a living body to a dead body; the change of lifeless food into living blood and tissue and bone and sinew; the change of oxygen and hydrogen into water and of water into these two elements; the change of coal into ashes and smoke."[41] The element that undergoes corruption and generation in substantial change is primary matter. Inasmuch as prime matter does not exist without some substantial form giving it shape, the transition from one form to another must occur in a single moment. Coffey remarks, "Substantial change is regarded as taking place instantaneously, as soon as the condition brought about by the accidental changes leading up to it become naturally incompatible with the essence or nature of the subject."[42] At that point the substantial form is shed and a new one

38. Coffey, *Ontology*, 69.

39. Glenn, *Ontology*, 87. Peter Coffey offers an intriguing critique of the atomist denial that qualitative change really occurs in material things: "If all material things and processes could be ultimately analyzed into configurations and local motions of space-occupying atoms, homogeneous in nature and differing only in size and shape, then each of these ultimate atomic factors would be itself exempt from intrinsic change as to its own essence and individuality. In this hypothesis there would be really no such thing as *substantial* change. The collection of atoms would form an immutable core of material reality, wholly simple and ever actual" (*Ontology*, 70–71).

40. Ibid.

41. Ibid., 87–88.

42. Coffey, *Ontology*, 68. Obviously substantial change is not immediately perceptible inasmuch as matter and form are not complete essences in themselves and our minds can only form (isomorphically) adequate conceptions of complete essences. Coffey explains: "The concepts of *material prima* and *forma substantialis* are concepts not of phenomenal entities directly accessible to the senses or the imagination, but of principles which can be reached only mediately and by intellect proper. They cannot be pictured in the imagination, which can only attain the sensible" (ibid., 72). More will be said below on prime matter and substantial form.

takes its place; the prime matter is never suspended between the two formal terms.

It is in considering the conditions of these various kinds of change that act and potency are shown to be indispensible concepts.[43] Paul Glenn identifies five things involved in every change:

> (1) *A thing to be changed* whether substantially or accidentally. This is called the *term from which* (or the *terminus a quo*) the change moves or takes its beginning. (2) *A thing resulting from the change*, and this is the *term to which* (or the *terminus ad quem*) the change moves and in which it finds its completion or fulfillment. (3) *An actual transition or movement* (called the *transitus*) in which the change essentially or formally consists. (4) *A substantial support* for the change, and this remains unchanged in the process. (5) *An agent or mover or motor-force* [not identical with (1) or (2)] which effects the transition.[44]

This process can be broadly applied to all varieties of change in the created order. The subject of (1) possesses the potential for actually becoming (2). This actuality is received in the occurrence of (3). If there were no potency toward (2) already present in (1) then no movement toward (2) would be possible. As for (4), the substantial support comes either from the thing itself (in accidental change) or from prime matter (in substantial change). Spiritual substances cannot undergo substantial change since they lack matter.

Given this conception of change it follows that neither creation nor annihilation are changes in the strict sense. Coffey explains: "In creation there is no real and positive *terminus a quo*; in annihilation there is no real and positive *terminus ad quem*; these therefore are not changes in the proper sense of the term."[45] In creation no subject undergoes accidental or substantial change, but rather enters existence as an entirely

---

43. Without the principles of act and potency one seems fated to endorse one of two extreme explanations of being and change. First, the position of Parmenides was to deny all becoming or change whatsoever on the basis that being can only be opposed to absolute non-being and thus cannot be determined in any way. Second, the position of Heraclitus was to deny all stability of being so that only becoming and evolution are the true reality. Aristotle's act-potency scheme was developed as a way to avoid absolutizing stability or change as the sole reality (though Aquinas discovers Aristotle's failure to account for why anything exists in the first place). On Parmenides, Heraclitus and Aristotle see the comments by Van Steenberghen, *Ontology*, 120–23.

44. Glenn, *Ontology*, 88. See also, Coffey, *Ontology*, 62.

45. Coffey, *Ontology*, 62.

and completely new being. Likewise, in annihilation no subject acquires a new accidental or substantial form, but, rather, goes out of existence altogether.[46] Even so, the concepts of act and potency are broad enough to help explain the metaphysics of creation and annihilation in addition to the metaphysics of change. The important thing to grasp in connection to the wide-ranging application of the act-potency composition scheme is that it can only apply to beings that are ontologically contingent and non-absolute in and of themselves. The ultimate sufficient reason for any such composition must be devoid of all like composition in itself. We proceed now to consider the various models of act-potency composition that are traditionally denied of God by the classical DDS.

BODILY PARTS

The first model of composition that Thomas denies of God in *Summa theologiae* I.3 is that which pertains to bodies. He prefaces his more philosophical arguments with a brief reference to the words of Jesus in John 4:24 in which he tells the Samaritan woman that God is spirit. Other biblical data may be added to this. In Luke 24:39, for instance, Jesus informs his disciples that a spirit does not have flesh and bones, by which we may understand that spiritual substances *qua* spiritual are necessarily incorporeal.[47] Furthermore, 1 Timothy 1:17 states that God is invisible, which cannot be said of any body. Stephen Charnock distinguishes between unseen and invisible: "If he be invisible, he is also spiritual. If he had a body, and hid it from our eyes, he might be said not to be seen, but could not be said to be invisible."[48] Apart from the express record of God's special revelation there are numerous other reasons to deny

---

46. Glenn, *Ontology*, 92. Glenn notes that although annihilation is within God's absolute power it does not appear to fall within his ordained power; that is, we have no reason to believe that God has in fact willed to exercise his power to annihilate.

47. Of course, some, such as Tertullian, do not understand Jesus to teach that God has no body whatsoever, but only that he does not have a body such as men possess. Tertullian's opinion is that God may possess a *spiritual* body. This position has been almost universally rejected in the history of the church and Thomas's arguments in *ST* I.3.1 are calculated to preclude *any* possibility of corporeity in God.

48. Charnock, *Existence and Attributes of God*, I: 185. Charnock uses the term "spiritual" interchangeably with "simple" and so most likely means to say that God's invisibility entails his simplicity and thus his incorporeity. Herman Bavinck treats God's incorporeity as an aspect of his spiritual nature, which follows, as he says, "very naturally" from the consideration of God's simplicity (*RD*, II: 182–87).

that the God of the Bible possesses a body. Thomas mentions three such reasons, the second being the most relevant to the question of simplicity.

The first reason he gives is that no body can be in motion unless put in motion by another; but God, as the unmoved First Mover is not put in motion by another and so cannot possess a body. The argument as it is appears in *Summa theologiae* I.3.1 seems somewhat underdeveloped.[49] Presumably, the reason for denying that the First Mover is corporeal is because all agents act according to their actuality.[50] Experience tells us that corporeal agents put other bodies in motion through the movement of their own bodies.[51] But if God were to do this then some mover outside of him must be found to account for his corporeal movement and he would not be the First Mover after all. The other problem with saying that the First Mover is corporeal is that all bodies are in potency to relocation through local motion. Garrigou-Lagrange comments, "[Any body can] be moved locally, and every moving body is moved at least as in potentiality for this, since it is by nature apt to be moved, and this suffices to distinguish it from the absolutely immobile first mover (this immobility not being that of inertia but of perfection)."[52]

The second reason Thomas gives for denying that God is a body is that every body is in potentiality "because the continuous, as such, is divisible to infinity."[53] Every body is extended in space and composed of continuous parts that are divisible from each other. This does not mean that the quantifiable parts are *actually* separated from each other; but

---

49. Immink notes, "The premises of this argument are obscure, but even the argument itself is not cogent. It only tells us that God cannot exercise the causality in a bodily fashion, but he still could be a body" (*Divine Simplicity*, 135).

50. See *SCG* II.20 [9].

51. Immink's criticism appears to be that Thomas has not proved that God cannot be an exception to this empirical observation about corporeal agents. Why might not God be the one corporeal being who moves other corporeal things purely by his intellect, sidelining the fact of his corporeity, as it were? This does seem to be a valid criticism of Thomas's natural theology at this point. Immink, of course, is not suggesting that God may have a body, but only that this argument in itself does not make an airtight case against it.

52. Garrigou-Lagrange, *The One God*, 172. "Immobile" carries a stronger sense than "unmoved" since it implies the *impossibility* of motion.

53. *ST* I.3.1. Stephen Charnock concurs: "If God had a body, consisting of distinct members, as ours; or all of one nature, as the water and air are, yet he were then capable of division" (*Existence and Attributes of God*, I: 184).

they are always in potency to such a division and are still numerically distinct from each other even when not actually divided.[54]

Thomas echoes Aristotle's arguments in *Physics* book VI when he insists that anything continuous is *infinitely* divisible. The Stagirite insists that "no continuous thing is divisible into things without parts."[55] He reasons to this conclusion by arguing that indivisibles (which are necessarily partless) cannot be contiguous with other indivisibles so as to be *one* with them or *together* with them. Contiguous parts form wholes by virtue of contact with other parts. But contiguous contact necessitates an extremity and indivisibles have no extremities (i.e., parts outside of parts) since nothing in it lies nearer or further from its exact center. For example, a line cannot be composed of so many points because points are by definition indivisible and without extension. Nothing without extension can be in real continuous contact with any other extensionless thing. Accordingly, really extended entities cannot be composed of extensionless parts such as indivisibles. Aristotle explains why indivisibles cannot be continuous: "[S]ince indivisibles have no parts, they must be in contact with one another as whole with whole. And if they are in contact with one another as whole with whole, they will not be continuous; for that which is continuous has distinct parts, and these parts into which it is divisible are different in this way, i.e., spatially separate."[56] Thus, he arrives at the following conclusion: "[I]t is plain that everything continuous is divisible into divisibles that are always divisible; for if they were divisible into indivisibles [i.e., not *infinitely* divisible], we should have [*per impossibile*] an indivisible in contact with an indivisible, since

54. This understanding is a mainstay in the medieval mereology upon which Thomas depends for much of his understanding of parts and wholes. On this complex subject see Arlig, "A Study in Early Medieval Mereology"; Henry, *Medieval Mereology*; Hovda, "What is Classical Mereology?"; and Simons, *Parts*.

55. Aristotle, *Physics* 231b10–11.

56. Ibid., 231b3–6. Aquinas comments on this passage: "The argument is as follows. Whenever anything touches another, either the whole of one touches the whole of the other, or part of one touches part of the other, or part of one touches the whole of the other. But since that which is indivisible has no parts, it cannot be said that part of one touches part of the other, or that part of one touches the whole of the other. And thus, if two points touch, it is necessary that the whole touches the whole. But a continuum cannot be composed of two parts of which the whole of one touches the whole of the other. For every continuum has distinct parts, one of which is here and the other there. And in those things that have position, the continuum is divided into diverse and distinction positions. But things which touch in respect to the whole are not distinct in place or position" (*Sententia super Physicam* VI.1.753).

the extremities of things that are continuous with one another are one and are in contact."[57] Aristotle applies this same reasoning to all varieties of continuous things including magnitude, time, and motion and concludes that each is infinitely divisible.

Understanding this bit of Aristotelian physics explains why Thomas cannot allow that God is a body. If he were he would be in potency to an infinite number of divisions and subdivisions and thus not *purely* actual. Consequently, he could not be regarded as the First Being who needs no further actuating principle back of him (as argued in the fourth way of *ST* I.2.3). The reason for this is because, in absolute terms, actuality is prior to potentiality even though potentiality is prior in all temporal things. In sum, if God were a body he would ever be in potency to division and thus require some unifying principle of actuality prior to himself. Put differently, no body can be strictly absolute, thus, God cannot posses a body and still be most absolute in being.

Thomas's third reason for denying that God has a body is based on the conclusion of his fourth way for proving God's existence in which he argues that God is the first and most perfect being and the lone sufficient cause for anything else that exists. But all living bodies have a principle of actuation by which they are animated. "Now it is impossible for a body to be the most noble of beings; for a body must be either animate or inanimate; and an animate body is manifestly nobler than any inanimate body. But an animate body is not animate precisely as body; otherwise all bodies would be animate. Therefore its animation depends upon some other thing, as our body depends for its animation upon the soul. Hence that by which a body becomes animated must be nobler than the body."[58] A key element of this argument is based on Thomas's act-potency scheme inasmuch as he points out that "what is" (the living body) is dependent upon "that by which" it is, that is, a principle of actuality not identical with itself. If God were a body then his body would have to be either animate or inanimate; but the body itself

57. Ibid., 231b15–18.

58. *ST* I.3.1. The Reformed theologian Stephen Charnock comes to basically the same conclusion based on the conception of graded perfection: "God were not the most excellent substance if he were not a Spirit. Spiritual substances are more excellent than bodily; the soul of man more excellent than other animals; angels more excellent than men. They contain in their own nature, whatsoever dignity there is in the inferior creatures; God must have, therefore, an excellency above all those, and, therefore, is entirely remote from the conditions of a body" (*Existence and Attributes of God*, I: 183).

is not sufficient to determine this and so needs some actuating principle outside itself to make it living. But as the absolutely perfect (complete) being God cannot be caused in any way.

MATTER AND FORM

The denial of form-matter composition in God follows naturally from the denial that God has a body. Thomas gives three reasons for denying such composition. First, all matter is in potency to act and God is pure act. Second, every form-matter composite owes its perfection and goodness to its form. Form, as the principle of actuality, causes matter to exist as this or that particular thing; it supplies the quiddity, or the "whatness" of the complete material being. The "goodness" of matter is conveyed to it by the form and therefore the matter is only good by participation in the form's perfections.[59] But whatever possesses its existence or quiddity by participation is dependent upon some perfection prior to itself and cannot be the first and best "good." But God is that first and best good, which is participated by all other beings but itself participates in none. Third, Thomas argues that every agent acts by its form and the first agent must be entirely identical with his form in order to be the first efficient cause. God is *essentially* form and so no matter can be conceived as a part of his essence as in all material beings.[60]

These arguments will undoubtedly appear more significant if brief consideration is given to Thomas's conception of substantial form and prime matter. Understanding of the composition of form and matter in material beings was originally arrived at through an analysis of becoming and change in the material world.[61] How can one natural being change into something else? In this change we must ask: what is lost, what is gained, and what remains? It was determined that what is lost and gained in substantial change—in which one complete thing becomes another complete thing—is substantial form and what perdures

59. Thomas assumes, in Aristotelian fashion, that "good" and "being" are convertible insofar as "being" is conceived as "one," "good," and "true" wherever it appears. On Thomas's understanding of "goodness" as a transcendental see *ST* I.5.3: "Every being, as being, is good. For all being, as being, has actuality and is in some way perfect; since every act implies some sort of perfection; and perfection implies desirability and goodness." See also, Wippel, *Metaphysical Thought*, 315–16, 530, and MacDonald, "The Metaphysics of Goodness," 31–55.

60. *ST* I.3.2.

61. See Aristotle, *Physics* 189b30–192b4.

is prime matter. Still, form and matter are not separate substances. They relate to each other as constitutive principles in one complete material being and not as complete subjects in themselves. George Klubertanz explains: "Primary matter and substantial form are not things or beings; they are not each, properly speaking, a substance. But they are principles of substance; *by them* a substance is respectively capable of substantial change, relatively indeterminate, and like other material substances, and, at the same time, actually of a given kind or species, determinate, and different from other kinds of material things."[62]

Consider first, then, the character of substantial form. David Oderberg provides a terse yet thorough description of how form functions in material substances:

> Now substantial form is *intrinsic* since it is a constituent solely of the substance. It is a *constituent* because it is a real part or element of it, though not on the same level as a substance's natural parts such as the branch of a tree or the leg of a dog. Rather, substantial form . . . is a radical or fundamental part of the substance in the sense of constituting it as the kind of substance it is. It is a *principle* in the sense of being . . . that *by virtue of which* the substance is what it is. It is *incomplete* in the sense that it does not and cannot, contra Platonism, exist apart from instantiation by a particular individual. In the specific case of material substances, i.e., substances that have a material element even though they may not be wholly material, this means the form cannot exist without correlative *matter* to individuate it. And form *actualizes the potencies of matter* in the sense of being the principle that unites with matter to produce a finite individual with limited powers and an existence circumscribed by space and time. Together with matter, it composes the distinct individual substance.[63]

In all immaterial beings—such as God, angelic spirits, and human souls after death—the substantial form is understood to be a complete substance in itself. But in any material substance the form cannot subsist apart from its composition with prime matter. Recall that a *principle* of being is not *that which is* but is only *that by which* a substance exists

---

62. Klubertanz, *Introduction*, 101. Raeymaeker points out that as principles the substantial form and prime matter are unintelligible apart from their union in the material being (*Philosophy of Being*, 168).

63. Oderberg, *Real Essentialism*, 66. Oderberg's entire discussion of substantial form as a valid concept for modern metaphysics (65–71) is worthy of careful consideration.

in the way it does. Thus, form is not the essence of a material thing, but, together with the matter, constitutes the complete essence.[64] Form determines matter into a genus and species and only then is the material individual's essence definable. No spiritual substance, least of all God, can stand in need of such determination in order to be an intelligible essence. The forms of spiritual substances are in themselves intelligible essences.

As substantial form functions as the act in material beings, prime matter functions as the corresponding potency. For the Christian theologian the notion of prime matter is more elusive than that of substantial form inasmuch as Christian theology can conceive of certain forms subsisting as complete beings without matter—specifically God, angelic spirits and disembodied human souls. This makes "form" seem somehow more accessible to the intellect and even definable. Prime matter, on the other hand, might appear as nothing more than "spooky metaphysics," as Oderberg whimsically puts it. But, Oderberg points out, prime matter is as crucial to one's analysis of material essences as is substantial form: "According to the hylemorphic theory, the unique substantial form of any material substance must be united to something to produce that substance, since in itself it is only an actualizing principle."[65] But what is this "something" that is actualized? What is that principle whereby substantial form is able to appear in a real sensible being? In saying that prime matter is this principle it is not suggested that prime matter is like bronze that can receive the form of a statue or wax that can be molded into the shape of a nose. In those instances the matter already possesses an actual shape or form prior to that of the statue or the nose. But as Oderberg observes,

> Prime matter *underlies* all these kinds of matter. It is a pure passive potentiality, without any form whatsoever, nor subject to any privation (i.e., it does not lack some form it *needs*, in the way that a blind person is deprived of sight), but is wholly receptive of any form whatsoever. It is the completely undifferentiated basic

64. See Aquinas, *DEE*, 2 [1] as well as the comments upon this text by Joseph Bobik in his *Aquinas on Being and Essence*, 67–80. See also, Bobik, *Aquinas on Matter and Form and the Elements*, 5–7, 24–33.

65. Oderberg, *Real Essentialism*, 71. Edward Feser describes Hylemorphism as the theory that "the ordinary objects of our [sensible] experience are composites of *form* and *matter*" (*Aquinas*, 13). It is derived from the Greek terms *hyle* (matter) and *morphe* (form).

material of the physical universe. It is not *something*, in the sense of something or other, but it is not nothing either. It is the closest there is in the universe to nothingness, since it has no features of its own but for the potential to receive substantial forms . . . It is changeless, but it is the *support* of all substantial change, and as such is subject to numerical identity, so that prime matter is conserved throughout substantial change.[66]

Since prime matter is not an essence it cannot be defined, but only described according to its function. Thomas declares that it is "the most incomplete of all beings."[67] It is that which undergoes alteration in all substantial material change but is not itself empirically discovered.

Oderberg contends for the notion of prime matter as a necessary component in any analysis of substantial change. In accidental change it is the subject itself that supports the changes: when a red wall is painted green the wall supports the change; in the ionization of an atom the atom itself supports the change; in local change it is the whole material subject that supports the change. But what supports the change in substantial changes? What changes, Oderberg asks, when a wall is hammered into a pile of fine dust or an atom of uranium-238 is transformed into thorium-234 as a result of alpha decay? For these sorts of changes there does not seem to be any substantial support but neither does it seem plausible to do away with the notion of support altogether when analyzing substantial change.[68] Prime matter, then, is understood to supply the needed support for substantial changes. It has no observable appear-

66. Ibid., 72.

67. *De Spiritualibus Creaturis*, art. 1. Thomas here uses "being" in a loose, improper sense. Unlike the substantial forms of spiritual beings there is no instance in which prime matter subsists without form.

68. Oderberg, *Real Essentialism*, 73. Oderberg strongly objects to proposals to do away with the notion that all change demands some underlying *support*. If one were to consistently apply this denial one must also deny the supports that undergo accidental change. But this flouts the most basic empirical observations. Oderberg challenges, "So the denier of a support for substantial change has to find an alternative metaphysical account of what is going on when one substance turns into a numerically distinct substance." The only alternative would be to claim that every instance of substantial change is really an instance of *creation* or *annihilation*. But in nature, he contends, there is no *pure* creation and annihilation. "Creation and annihilation, strictly speaking, are out of nothing and into nothing, respectively" (ibid., 73–74). Oderberg also refutes suggestions that sensible matter (i.e., secondary or proximate matter) itself may be sufficient to undergo substantial change (ibid., 74–76). See also, Aquinas, *DP* 3.2, and Raeymaeker, *Philosophy of Being*, 171.

ance and is incapable of any structural arrangement in itself. This is why Thomas thinks of it as pure potency. And because it is pure potency he strongly denies that any such thing could be rightly attributed to God.[69] Of course, denying form-matter composition in God is not in itself enough to distinguish him from all creatures; angelic spirits and human souls are also simple in this sense. God's simplicity is distinguished from theirs by virtue of his lack of supposit-nature, substance-accident, and essence-existence composition.

SUPPOSIT AND NATURE

Denying that God is composed of supposit and nature follows quite naturally from the denial that he is composed of matter and form. In material substances "individual matter" is added to the form as the principle by which a particular material creature is individuated. Thus, the formal nature alone (e.g., humanity, caninity, or equinity) is not itself identical with any particular subject that instantiates that nature (e.g., *this* man, *this* dog, or *this* horse). Something more than the formal nature or essence enters into the identity of any particular material being. In *Summa theologiae* I.3.3 Aquinas argues that in all composite subjects there is some real distinction between the subject itself and its essential nature or form and that God is identical with his nature.

"God is the same as His essence or nature," Thomas insists. This can best be understood in contrast with those subjects composed of form and matter in which "the nature or essence must differ from the *suppositum*, because the essence or nature connotes only what is included in the definition of the species; as, humanity connotes all that is included in the definition of man, for it is by this that man is man, and it is this that humanity signifies, that, namely, whereby man is man."[70] But the supposit as such is not definable and furthermore cannot be predicated of many individuals. J. L. A. West offers the following definition: "A supposit is an individual thing that can have properties predicated of it, and yet cannot be predicated of anything else." Furthermore, "a supposit is

---

69. For a detailed study of Thomas's understanding of substantial form and primary matter see Wippel, *Metaphysical Thought*, 295–375. See also, Maurer, "Form and Essence in the Philosophy of St. Thomas," 3–18, and Aertsen, *Nature and Creature*, 297–302, 324–36.

70. *ST* I.3.3.

not a part of something, like Socrates' hand or foot. Rather, a supposit is a whole that subsists through itself."[71]

The *nature* of any subject is that definable part of it that can be possessed in common with other supposits within the same species. But the supposit itself cannot be more than one particular individual. Consequently, it stands to reason that what makes the supposit a unique subject must be something in it in addition to its essence or nature. In material subjects the matter itself may be conceived as that which individuates: "Therefore this flesh, these bones, and the accidental qualities distinguishing this particular matter, are not included in humanity; and yet they are included in the thing which is a man. Hence the thing which is a man has something more to it than has humanity."[72] The human supposit is more than the human nature. No particular man is identical with humanity and, conversely, humanity is not identical with any one man. Humanity is *that by which* the human subject (i.e., what is) is human; it is that defining and formal part that locates man within the human species. But the formal principle alone is not a sufficient description of *this* or *that* man. In *Summa theologiae* I.3.3 Thomas reasons that in all subjects not composed of form and matter (and, thus, not individuated by particular bits of matter) the forms themselves must be identified as the subsisting *supposita*. "Therefore," he concludes, "*suppositum* and nature in them are identified. Since God then is not composed of matter and form, He must be His own Godhead, His own Life, and whatever else is thus predicated of Him."[73]

In consequence of these arguments Thomas concludes that in all material creatures there is a *real* distinction between supposit and nature. West elaborates: "A real distinction, or a distinction *secundum rem*, is to be understood in contradistinction to a conceptual distinction, or a distinction *secundum rationem*. This means that the supposit and nature pick out two aspects of one and the same thing that are not to be identi-

---

71. West, "Real Distinction," 87. See also, *ST* I.29.1, ad 2. Klubertanz offers a similar definition: "A supposit is a distinct, subsistent individual in a particular nature, whose property it is to be incommunicable." He adds, "A person is a rational supposit" (*Introduction*, 254).

72. *ST* I.3.3.

73. Ibid.

fied ontologically. This is to say that the distinction is an objective one; it is discovered, not imposed, by the intellect."[74]

Even though we apply to God the terms of "supposit" and "nature" we make only a *conceptual* distinction between these and do not suggest a real ontological distinction.[75] Moreover, in insisting upon this real distinction in material creatures Thomas does not mean to suggest that the distinction is between "thing" (*res*) and "thing" (*res*). Rather, these are two distinct aspects of one and the same *res* and do not properly exist apart from their composition in a subject.[76]

For all his arguments that every subject composed of matter and form must also be composed of supposit and nature, Thomas does not directly address the status of angelic spirits in either *Summa theologiae* I.3.3 or *Summa contra gentiles* I.21. Do angelic spirits, assuming that they are immaterial, exemplify any real distinction between supposit and nature? After all, are not angelic substances *pure* forms? Thomas is at best ambiguous on this question of a real supposit-nature distinction in angels. In *Summa theologiae* I.3.3 he states in plain terms that the form of any subject not individuated by matter is a subsisting supposit that cannot be distinguished from its essence. But this seems to suggest that particular angels, being immaterial, are identical with the very "angelness" by which they are angels. Yet, elsewhere he argues against such an understanding based on his view that all creaturely natures are caused: "in all creatures a nature constitutes a supposit. But nothing constitutes itself, so in no creature are supposit and nature the same."[77] Obviously,

74. West, "Real Distinction," 92.

75. Indeed, upon closer analysis, the classical tradition only applies these terms to God in an imprecise and accommodated manner. Insofar as "supposit" derives from the notion of "substance" it applies only analogically to God since one of the marks of any substance is to be in some species. But God is not in a species and so is not classified within the genus of substance. Still, he may be referred to as a "supposit" in the sense that a supposit is any subject that subsists *per se*. Substance or supposit is not a "thing" God is, but suggests only the manner or mode in which he subsists, that is, not in another. For the denial that God can be defined as a "substance," see Augustine, *De trinitate* VII: 10, and Aquinas, *DP* 7.3, ad 4. See also, West, "Real Distinction," 86–92. As with "substance," the term "nature" is also ascribed analogically to God. Richard Muller observes, "[Inasmuch as] '*natura*' indicates something that is given, imparted, or begotten, it cannot be applied to God: nature must always be in some sense, the work of a creator and is in created things only, as both containing and governing the thing whose nature it is" (*PRRD*, III: 209).

76. See West, "Real Distinction," 93.

77. Thomas Aquinas, *Quodlibet* 2.2.2. Here Thomas is answering the question, "Whether supposit and nature are the same in an angel?"

then, he believes that something more than material accidents contributes to the distinction between supposit and nature in creatures. Thomas reasons as follows: A thing's nature or substantial form supplies the structure of its intelligibility; it is that which locates the creature in a given species. For example, humanity accounts for man's intelligibility as a human. But the intelligible nature alone does not account for certain qualitative accidents that can be truly predicated of the supposit. The most outstanding of these "accidents" is the supposit's act of existence, which is not included within the intelligible structure of any creaturely nature: "Because such a substance is not its being, something outside the intelligible structure of the species is accidental to it, namely being itself and certain other characteristics which are attributed to the supposit and not to the nature. Thus in such a substance the supposit is not entirely the same as the nature." In conclusion, "A nature is signified as what constitutes, a supposit as what is constituted."[78] So, even in (non-divine) spiritual substances there is no real identity between the individual subject and the nature by which it is categorized and defined. In other words, *what is* (the supposit) and *that by which* it is (the nature) are really distinct in all creatures but really identical in God.

GENUS AND SPECIES

The classical DDS further denies that God can be categorized as a species in a genus.[79] If there is no real distinction between God and his divine nature then it follows that he is not *specified* by his divinity. That

78. Ibid. John Wippel observes a "shift" in the way Thomas applies the notion of supposit-nature composition. When the act of existence (*esse*) is not included in the *ratio* (notion) of a supposit (as in *ST* I.3.3) then certainly spiritual substances are thought of as simple since they lack all material accidents. But when a supposit is understood as including its act of existence (as in *Quodlibet* 2.2.2) then even spiritual substances, such as angels, are viewed as being composed of supposit and nature (those being really distinct in them). See *Metaphysical Thought*, 246–51.

79. Paul Glenn distils the basic sense of these conceptual categories: "An idea which expresses the essence of its inferiors [i.e., subjects] *incompletely* is called the *genus* (or, more specifically, the *generic idea*) of its inferiors. An idea which expresses the essence of its inferiors *completely* is called the *species* (or, more exactly, the *specific idea*) of its inferiors. The whole group of the inferiors of a generic idea is called *a genus*; the group of inferiors of a specific idea is *a species*" (*Ontology*, 29–30). It should be noted that metaphysical genera and species are not identical to biological genera and species. That is, some things that count as genera biologically (e.g., swans) are counted as a species metaphysically (see Oderberg, *Real Essentialism*, 279–80 n. 11).

is, unlike all non-divine beings, God is not defined within a species; his nature is not something he receives and by which he is located in some genus. In *De potentia* Aquinas observes that, "whatsoever is contained in a genus contains something in addition to the genus, and therefore is composite. But God is utterly simple. Therefore he is not contained in a genus." To this he adds an argument from God's infinity: "Moreover, whatsoever is contained in a genus can be defined, or else comprised under something that is defined. But this cannot apply to God since he is infinite."[80] In *Summa theologiae* I.3.5 Thomas gives three reasons for denying that God is composed of a genus and specific difference.

First, a species is constituted of genus and specific difference. The specific difference is related to the genus as act is related to potency. Indeed, genus-species composition is simply a *conceptual* (or logical) act-potency composition similar to the way that form-matter composition is a *metaphysical* act-potency composition. As a principle of potency no genus subsists independent of some species. The genus animality, for instance, is always discovered in some particular *species* of animal that is marked out by a specific difference. Thus, humans are animals that differ from all others precisely in their rationality. The existence of the rational animal (or any other species of animal) is what causes the genus "animality" to actually exist. Thomas argues that since God needs no additional actuality in order to exist he cannot be in any genus as a species. This line of reasoning is nicely summarized in the words of Henry of Ghent: "[W]hat is composed from genus and difference does not have perfect being in act except through a difference that determines it in the being of the genus, which is of itself imperfect and in potency, as is seen from the nature of genus and species . . . If, therefore, God were composed from genus and difference, he would have being that is determined and contracted, and he would not be simple and absolute."[81]

Thomas's second reason for denying genus-species composition in God is based on his argument in *Summa theologiae* I.3.4 that God's existence and essence are identical. Since God is being itself (*ipsum esse*) he would have to be in a genus called "being" if he were in any genus at all. God's identification of himself in Exodus 3:14 as "I AM" makes it impossible that there should be some more basic identity in him than his own act of existence. But being is not a genus since genus refers to the

80. *DP* 7.3.

81. Henry of Ghent, *Summa*, 28.3.

essence of a thing and "to be" is not the essence of anything but is always added to an intelligible essence that is already classified in a species and genus. Thus, being characterizes any actual essence or species whatsoever and cannot itself account for differences in kind found among existing things. But such sortal distinctions are precisely the function of the genera.[82] All genera are themselves diversified by the specific differences of the species that exemplify them. But, Thomas argues, being can only be distinguished or contrasted to nonbeing and nonbeing is not a specific difference; therefore, being is not a genus and God, as pure act, is not in a genus.[83]

Thirdly, Thomas contends that no member of a genus can be pure act since everything in a genus is a species of one variety or another. And in every member of every species there must be a real distinction between its particular act of existence (*esse*) and its common nature (*essentia*). If this were not so there would be no way to distinguish, for example, a man from a horse or this man from that man. Inasmuch as existence and quiddity do not differ in God, he cannot be a member of any species and so cannot be in a genus. Thomas's words in *Summa contra gentiles* I.25 [4] nicely express this argument: "[W]hatever is in a genus differs in being from the other things in that genus; otherwise, the genus would not be predicated of many things. But all the things that are in the same genus must agree in the quiddity of the genus, since the genus is predicated of all things in it in terms of what they are. In other

82. Wippel explains that things participate in being (*esse*) differently than a species participates in genus. Genus falls within the definition of what the species is. But being does not fall within the definition of any creature since being is neither a genus nor a difference. *Esse* is participated by a thing in a manner such that it is not included in the essence of the thing. So the question of *whether* a thing is (*an est*) is different from the question of *what* a thing is (*quid est*) (*Metaphysical Thought*, 106).

83. In *DP* 7.3 Thomas seems to offer a slightly different form of this argument when he insists that the being of any particular thing is proper to that thing and distinct from the *being* of any other thing. Each thing's "act of existence" is entirely its own act and is not possessed in common with anything else (though the being-in-general, or *esse commune*, in which particular beings participate, presumably is common to all existents) and therefore cannot constitute a specific difference or a genus. So, on the one hand, as that in which all beings participate, "being" is too general to count as a genus; but, on the other hand, no individual act of existence is general enough to function as a genus or specific difference. All told, there does not seem to be any fundamental conflict between Thomas's two ways of arguing that "being" cannot be a genus. See also, *SCG* I.25 [3] and [6]. For more on Thomas's conception of how genus relates to being see Wippel, *Metaphysical Thought*, 157–61.

words, the being of each thing found in a genus is outside the quiddity of the genus. This is impossible in God."

Thomas is aware that denying the conceptual composition of genus and specific difference in God places him beyond all definition. But any being that is "pure act" or "being itself" must be the principle of all being whatsoever and so cannot be reduced to some specific class of being. As the source of all genera God cannot be contracted into a particular genus by some specific difference. His absolute being transcends all such definitional composition. In this vein, Herman Bavinck aptly remarks: "For precisely because God is pure being—the absolute, perfect, unique, and simple being—we cannot give a definition to him. There is no genus to which he belongs as a member, and there are no specific marks of distinction whereby we can distinguish him from other beings in this genus. Even the being he has, so to speak, in common with all creatures does not pertain to him in the same sense as it does to them (univocally), but only analogically and proportionately."[84]

SUBSTANCE AND ACCIDENT

The denial of all act-potency composition in God further entails the denial that he is composed of substance and accidents.[85] Many modern theologians find this denial somewhat troublesome inasmuch as denying accidents in God seems to deny that he possesses any genuine freedom. The thought is that any free choice or action on God's part constitutes an accidental divine property. I shall defer discussion of this important matter at this juncture in order to take it up more fully in chapter 7. It is important for our present purposes to understand why Thomas and his heirs deny that God could possess an accidental property or attribute.

In *Summa theologiae* I.3.6 Aquinas builds upon his denial of genus-species composition in God and indicates that God is not a "subject" or substance in the ordinary sense since his essence is not composed of some genus and specific difference. Inasmuch as every accident is

---

84. Bavinck, *RD*, II: 121. Neither Aquinas nor Bavinck intends to suggest that God cannot be truly known, described or distinguished from non-divine beings, but only that he cannot be properly defined by some particular *differentia* or comprehended as he is in himself.

85. For an historical introduction to the notions of substantial and accidental being, see Elders, *The Metaphysics of Being of St. Thomas Aquinas*, 239–68. See also, te Velde, *Participation and Substantiality*, 36–40.

received in some substance, God cannot possess accidents because he is not a "subject" properly speaking. Thomas tenders three further arguments to make his case. First, substance is to accidents as potency is to act since every subject is, in some sense, made actual by its accidents; but there is no passive potency in God. Second, because God's essence is pure act (existence and essence being identical in him) nothing can be superadded to it. Pure and unreceived being is necessarily incapable of having further actuality added to it, even accidental actuality. Unlike creatures composed of existence and essence, God cannot be further determined in his existence. Third, any accident (even those essential accidents, such as risibility in humans) must be caused to be by the constituent principles of the subject and so posterior to the essence of that being. But as first cause and "absolute primal being" nothing in God can be the result of causation. He cannot be composed of prior and posterior actuality inasmuch as no aspect of his actuality is caused to be.[86]

Space does allow for a complete analysis of Thomas's metaphysics of substance and accidents, but a few key aspects of his thought in this connection must be noted.[87] A substance is defined according to its essence (genus plus specific difference) whereas an accident is defined in part by the substance in which it inheres (i.e., by something outside itself). In this regard the substance functions somewhat like a genus in the definition of an accident. Thomas elaborates: "The manner of definition differs in accidents and substances. Substances are not defined by something outside their essence: wherefore the first thing included in the definition of a substance is the genus, which is predicated essentially of the thing defined. Whereas an accident is defined by something outside its essence, namely by its subject, on which it depends for its being. Hence in its definition the subject takes the place of the genus."[88]

<hr/>

86. Thomas offers similar arguments in *SCG* I.23.

87. For an extended study of Aquinas on this topic see Wippel, *Metaphysical Thought*, 197–294; Hart, *Thomistic Metaphysics*, 172–82; Owens, *Elementary Christian Metaphysics*, 143–209; and Renard, *Philosophy of Being*, 199–215, 241–48. For modern expositions of accidents that basically accord with a traditional Thomistic outlook see Oderberg, *Real Essentialism*, 152–76, and Gorman, "The Essential and the Accidental," 276–89.

88. *DP* 8.4, ad 5. Thomas does point out, though, that substances do differ from genera in that they remain identically the same when their accidents are removed; no genera remains identically the same when its difference is removed. "This is because an accident does not complete the essence of its subject as a difference completes the essence of a genus" (ibid.). Put differently, if there were no species there would be no

Aquinas considers a substance to be a complete being in itself (*ens per se*) whereas accidents only have their being through the substances in which they inhere. Substance is not self-subsistent being, but, rather, as Thomas defines it, "a thing whose quiddity is competent to have being not in a subject."[89] It possesses its own discreet act of existence (*esse*). An accident, on the other hand, is defined as, "a thing to which it belongs to be in something else."[90] Its act of existence is thus posterior and subsequent to its receiving subject. A substance's *esse* is the primary act by which the thing is or is not; its accidents are that by which a thing is this or that accidentally. The first indicates the essential order of existence and the latter the accidental order.[91] Joseph Owens characterizes the existence of accidents as *inesse* ("being in") as opposed to the *esse* of substantial or essential existence, which we might call the "first act" of a thing's existence.[92] Thomas's denial of accidents in God amounts to claiming that God is not composed of a plurality of acts or distinct operations. Nothing that is identical with the *esse* by which it is (which is only true of God) can receive any additional determination of being. But all creaturely substances are able to receive such accidental determination.

It should also be noted that Thomas speaks of divine "substance" in an analogical and accommodated sense. Inasmuch as a substance is that which subsists, God is properly called a substance. But a substance is also conceived of as that which "stands under" in support of accidents. Thomas clarifies his position: "Although nothing subsists but the individual substance which is called a hypostasis, it is not said to subsist for the same reason as it is said to substand: it is said to subsist as not existing in another, and to substand inasmuch as other things are in it. Hence if there were a substance that exists by itself without being the subject of an accident, it could be called a subsistence but not a substance."[93]

---

genus, but if there were no accidents a substance's essence would still remain the same. On Thomas's somewhat elastic use of the notion of genus see Maurer, "St. Thomas and the Analogy of Genus," 19–31.

89. *DP* 7.3, ad 4. In truth this is more of a description than a proper definition since substance is a genus and definitions are properly derived from some composition of genus and specific difference. See Wippel, *Metaphysical Thought*, 233–34.

90. *Scriptum super libros Sententiarum*, IV.12.1.1, quoted in Wippel, *Metaphysical Thought*, 234.

91. See the discussion in Raeymaeker, *Philosophy of Being*, 130–33.

92. Owens, *Elementary Christian Metaphysics*, 159.

93. *DP* 9.1, ad 4. See the discussion on Thomas's two ways of conceiving substance

God is like a substance inasmuch as he is a complete being *per se* and does not exist by inherence in some other subject. But he is not a substance in the sense of being classified within a logical or natural genus (substance being the most common genus) or standing under any accidents.[94]

Finally, in every creaturely subject there are accidents that inhere in it as intrinsic properties flowing from the principles latent in its essence. Essential properties are not themselves identical with the essence and theoretically can be removed without doing violence to the essence itself. For instance, risibility is not of the essence of humanity, but it invariably flows from the principles of every human essence such that it is regarded as an intrinsic essential property of humanity. But essential properties are concomitant with an essence and are neither the essence as such nor constituents of the essence (since only genus and specific difference are constituents of creaturely essences). Thus, even essential properties are regarded as accidents in some sense.[95] All accidents are *caused* to be by some principle and are received by another. If God were to possess any accidents they would be caused in him by something outside himself and he would not be the first cause or else he would be the cause of them himself. But if he caused himself to have accidents then he would have to be composed of act and potency since, as Wippel points out, "a subject must receive an accident under one aspect and serve as the cause of that

in Aertsen, *Nature and Creature*, 61–64. Turretin offers similar conclusions in *IET*, 3.23.4–5.

94. Gregory Doolan argues that the notion of substanding is only characteristic of substance when it is considered as a logical or natural genus, but not of substance as an absolute perfection. As an absolute perfection substance signifies nothing more than something "existing in itself" (*existere per se*) and thus may be properly ascribed to God. In so doing, we simply remove from the notion of substance those features that obtain only according to its creaturely mode. Of course, the fact that God is *properly* conceived as a substance does not change the fact that we still speak of the "divine substance" analogically. See Doolan's important essay, "Substance as a Metaphysical Genus."

95. See ST I.77.1, ad 5. For a compelling argument to the effect that *every* property is an accident of some sort see Oderberg, *Real Essentialism*, 156–62. A real distinction between essence and property is thought to follow from the real distinction between substance and accident. Oderberg explains: "For a substance is constituted by its essence, and properties are a species of accident. No property of a thing is part of a thing's essence, though properties flow from the essence" (*Real Essentialism*, 156–57). I shall make recourse to this argument again in chapter 5 below to show the inadequacy of the "property account" of the DDS.

accident under another aspect."[96] But the first cause must be pure act and utterly incapable of all passive potency. Such radical actuality in God is established in Thomas's argument that in him there is no composition of essence and existence.

ESSENCE AND EXISTENCE

In denying that God is composed of essence and existence Thomas makes his most important contribution to the DDS.[97] Having already established that God must be identical with his own essence (see discussion of supposit-nature composition above) Thomas proceeds in *Summa theologiae* I.3.4 to argue that he is also identical with his own act of existence (*esse*). Thomas begins by considering two possible objections to the real identity between God's existence and essence. First, if God's essence and existence are the same then it would appear that nothing can be added to God. But the being to which no addition may be made is the universal being (*esse commune*) that is predicated of all things. But, denying pantheism, God cannot be identical with being in general and so there must be some real distinction between his existence and essence. Second, since we can have an adequate knowledge *that* God exists but not an adequate knowledge of *what* he is it follows that God's existence is not the same as his essence, that is, his nature or quiddity. Before answering these two objections Thomas provides three reasons for denying any essence-existence composition in God.[98]

First, whatever a thing has in addition to its essence (such as necessary and accidental properties or existence) must be caused either by

96. Wippel, *Metaphysical Thought*, 270.

97. An enormous body of literature has emerged over the past century expositing and expounding Aquinas's conception of the real distinction between existence and essence in creatures and their real identity in God. Some representative treatments include: Gilson, *Being and Some Philosophers*, 74–189; Owens, *St. Thomas Aquinas on the Existence God*, 52–96; Sweeney, *Christian Philosophy*, 441–516; Wippel, *Metaphysical Themes*, 107–61; Wippel, *Metaphysical Thought*, 132–94; Elders, *The Metaphysics of Being of St. Thomas Aquinas*, 170–89; Twetten, "Really Distinguishing Essence from *Esse*," 40–84; MacDonald, "The *Esse/Essentia* Argument," 141–57; Clarke, "What is Really Real?" 61–90; Thomas, "The Identity of Being and Essence in God," 394–408; Kopaczynski, *Linguistic Ramifications of the Essence-Existence Debate*; Oderberg, *Real Essentialism*, 121–30. Additionally, this aspect of Thomas's thought is treated in nearly all of the standard Thomistic metaphysical textbooks such as those by Coffey, Glenn, Noonan, Klubertanz, Renard, and Hart.

98. In addition to *ST* I.3.4 see also, *SCG* I.22 and *DP* 7.2.

the constituent principles of that essence or by some outside agent. If existence differs from the essence then it is either caused by the essence itself or by some exterior agent. Now, it cannot be caused by the essence of the thing inasmuch as nothing can be the sufficient cause of its own existence (since it must first *be* in order to be an efficient cause of existence). So it must be caused by something not identical with itself. But this cannot be said of God since he is the absolute first cause of all existence. Second, every essence is made actual by an act of existence. In this relation essence functions as the principle of potency and existence as the principle of act whereby the essence is caused to exist in reality; but as pure act God cannot be subject to act-potency composition. Third, anything that possesses existence but is not existence itself (*ipsum esse*) must possess it by participation. But the first being, which God is, cannot *be* by participation and so he must exist by his own essence. Since existence is essential in God and since essence cannot be the cause of its own existence it follows that these two are identical in God. God is not only his own Godhead, but is also that act whereby he exists.

Thomas answers the objection respecting being in general (*esse commune*) by identifying two kinds of "being" to which nothing can be added (see *SCG* I.26). The divine *esse* can have nothing added to it because it is fully and infinitely actual and subsistent in itself. Thus, it is God's nature, as fullness of being, to be impervious to any further specification according to quiddity or to accidental actuality. The *esse commune*, which is predicated of all creatures, can have nothing added to *it* because it is the most common and indeterminate aspect of any creature and cannot subsist by itself. The reasons for denying the possibility of addition to being are strikingly different in these two utterly dissimilar notions of *esse*. In answer to the second objection Thomas notes that the "existence" that we understand of God is a "proposition effected by the mind" in an act of judgment and is not the "act of essence" itself.[99] Thus, even in knowing *that* God exists we do not comprehend that *esse* as it is in itself.

In identifying essence and existence in God Thomas radically distinguishes God from every creature. A key component of his position is his insistence that in every non-divine thing there is a real distinction between *esse* and *essentia*. For all the differences that one may identify among different kinds of creatures the one thing they all share in com-

99. *ST* I.3.4, ad 1 and 2.

mon is that their existence is received; that is, it is not of their essence to exist. Consider Aquinas's words from *Summa theologiae* I.12.4: "Now the mode of being of things is manifold. For some things have being only in this one individual matter; as all bodies. But others are subsisting natures, not residing in matter at all, which, however, are not their own existence, but receive it; and these are the incorporeal beings, called angels. But to God alone does it belong to be His own subsistent being." Even the simplest of creatures, the angelic spirits, do not possess their existence as belonging properly to their essence. *Esse* is never ascribed to any creature substantially or essentially. John Wippel reminds us: "Being (*ens*) is predicated of God alone essentially, and of every creature only by participation; for no creature is its *esse*, but merely has *esse*." Thomas points out that whenever anything is predicated of an entity by participation, "something else must be present there in addition to that which is participated."[100] Existence is participated and essence is the "something else" that does the participating.

The distinction between the two is real although it is not a distinction between two things (*res*) or beings (*ens*), but between two constituent principles. Louis De Raeymaeker explains: "À propos of every being two questions are raised: '*Is* it?' and '*What* is it?' These questions are as irreducible as their answers. To one who asks what is man we do not answer by saying that men actually exist; and to one who asks if men exist it is not at all opportune to answer that man is a rational animal. This adequate opposition ought to make us conclude to a real distinction."[101]

The difficulty, of course, is that we speak of *esse* and *essentia* as if they were complete things or substances. We speak of each as though it were a subsisting thing in itself. This is due to the limitations of language and should not obscure the fact that the real composition in view is that between *principles*. Gerald Phelan explains the difficulty:

> However scrupulous one may be to exorcise . . . essentialism by due distinctions and refinements, the impression still remains, in spite of all protests to the contrary, that *something* called *esse* is given by a Being called Creator to a being called creature; *something* called *esse* is shared by God and creatures; *something else* called *essence* is distinct from *esse* in creatures, but not in the Creator. In other words, the very words we use, being gram-

---

100. Wippel, *Metaphysical Thought*, 105.
101. Raeymaeker, *Philosophy of Being*, 102–3.

matically nouns or substantives, it is difficult to avoid thinking
that what they designate are things or substances with a nature
of their own.[102]

Phelan further elaborates on the real distinction: "No *ens* is its essence any more than it is its *esse*. Essence is not a substance, an *id quod*;
essence is that in (or of) a substance by which the being (*esse*) of the
substance is measured, limited, determined, defined."[103] The creature
as a "being" (*ens*) or actual substance is what exists *after* the principle
of essence (as potency) has received the principle of existence (as its
actuality). In fine, that which is (the existing creature) is not identical
with that *by which* it exists (*esse*) or that *by which* it is what it is (*essentia*). Furthermore, neither are the principles identical with each other.
Thomas's entire argument in *Summa theologiae* I.3.4 is that such distinctions between God's essence and existence are impossible inasmuch as
there can be nothing prior to God in the way that *esse* and *essentia* are
prior to the complete *ens* in any created thing. If there were such priority
to God then he could not be the first cause of all things and would himself need some extrinsic agent back of him to account for his actuality. I
shall have occasion to discuss further implications of the real identity of
essence and existence in God in chapter 4 below.

CONCLUSION

The models of composition considered in this chapter each point to
some aspect of non-absoluteness and dependence characteristic of every
composite being. Every composite thing is posterior to its parts inasmuch as its constituent parts are either really or conceptually separable
from it and prior to it, even if only logically prior. The parts together
account for and identify the composite in some sense. Their actuality
in the composite grounds the intelligibility of the subject. Furthermore,
the various models of composition do not themselves account for the
actuality of the composite. No composition is necessary in and of itself;
each presupposes a composer. It follows that none of these models can
apply to the God of the Bible inasmuch as he is the absolute Creator
and is before all things. Indeed, in Thomas Aquinas's own explanation of
why God cannot be composite he repeatedly returns to the theological

102. Phelan, *Selected Papers*, 87–88.
103. Ibid., 92.

commitments of God as the absolute first cause of all being and as pure act since God cannot be caused to be in any way whatsoever.

In placing this discussion of the models of composition prior to the following treatment of the theological rationale for the DDS it is not my intention to suggest that understanding these models serves as a pre-amble to faith or as the philosophical *basis* for theological commitment. Rather, the placement has been purely for the purpose of clarifying the DDS's own claims about simplicity and parts. Without this understanding of what is meant by simplicity and composition some are liable to be confused by the theological function ascribed to this doctrine in later sections.

The motivation for the doctrine of divine simplicity does not lie solely in the consideration of the inadequacy of composites to account for themselves. Rather, the positive impetus for the doctrine is derived from the contemplation of what it means for God to be self-sufficient, one, infinite, immutable, and eternal. We turn to a consideration of these theological motivators in the next chapter.

3

Simplicity and the Theological Rationale
for Divine Absoluteness

THE DOCTRINE OF DIVINE simplicity is not plainly revealed in
Scripture, but is arrived at by rational reflection upon a host of
biblical data and other more clearly revealed doctrines about God. This
does not suggest that it is an unbiblical doctrine, but only that its cognitive realization is by way of contemplation upon the good and necessary
consequence of other pieces of classical Christian dogmata (see WCF
1.6). Gerrit Immink observes, "The doctrine itself is not revealed by
Scripture but is used to secure God's aseity and otherness, and this aseity
and otherness is certainly taught by Scripture."[1] Simplicity is indispensible for the traditional understanding of doctrines such as God's aseity,
unity, infinity, immutability, and eternity.

These doctrines—divine aseity, unity, infinity, immutability, and
eternity—are considered in this chapter insofar as they represent some
of the strongest accounts of the Creator-creature distinction upheld by
the classical Christian tradition. Reformed theologians tend to classify
these with God's "incommunicable" attributes. It is my contention in
this chapter that it is the DDS that supplies the strength of absoluteness
in each of these doctrines. Without simplicity these dogmatic claims
would not be sufficient to distinguish God absolutely from his creation.
Indeed, absolute simplicity is the theological rationale underlying each
of these claims. It is not my intention to offer a general survey of these
doctrines, but to consider precisely how each requires that the orthodox
Christian maintain a strong account of divine simplicity.

---

1. Immink, *Divine Simplicity*, 35. Of course, the DDS is bound up with numerous
other doctrines in addition to aseity and otherness.

ASEITY

Both critics and adherents of the DDS have rightly noted the strong theological support divine simplicity derives from the doctrine of divine aseity.[2] The doctrine of aseity maintains that God is entirely self-sufficient and does not depend on anyone or anything for his existence and essence; that is, he is *a se* (of or from himself).[3] Aseity is often articulated negatively by denying that God is caused to be in any way whatsoever and positively by affirming that he is, in himself, the fullness of being. Herman Bavinck captures both emphases: "But as is evident from the word 'aseity,' God is exclusively from himself, not in the sense of being self-caused but being from eternity to eternity who he is, being not becoming. God is absolute being, the fullness of being, and therefore always eternally and absolutely independent in his existence, in his perfections, in all his works, the first and the last, the sole cause and final goal of all things."[4] By identifying God with the being by which he exists, Bavinck clearly employs the notion of divine simplicity to account for God's aseity and independence. In this section I shall consider the claims of the doctrine of aseity that God is neither caused by another nor by himself and attempt to show how such an assertion requires that God be absolutely simple in his existence and essence.

2. See Plantinga, *Does God Have a Nature?* 28–35, and Brower, "Simplicity and Aseity," 106–8.

3. Edith Stein delineates two ways of understanding self-sufficiency: "'Selfsufficiency' can mean being by itself, *in se, non alio esse* [being in itself, not in another]. This is true of any finite person. Or 'selfsufficiency' may mean to be through itself or from itself—*a se, non ab alio esse* [from itself, not from another]. This applies only to an uncreated person, not to any created person" (*Potency and Act*, 127). Every complete substance is self-sufficient in the sense that it possesses complete being in itself and does not, like an accident, derive its act of existence through inherence in some other substance. This is existence *in se*. But all creaturely existence *in se* is still dependent upon God and thus is not to be confused with God's unique self-sufficient existence which is not only *in se*, but also *a se*. Stein elsewhere speaks of the existential "unselfsufficiency" of every non-divine thing, even relatively simple things (see ibid., 47–49).

4. Bavinck, *RD*, II: 152. Although aseity and independence are not strictly identical notions, they are often considered together when discussing God's existence and essence. We should be careful, though, not to articulate aseity *solely* in terms of God's independence from creation; its primary positive sense should be drawn from God's own name, "I AM," by which he reveals his fullness of being, life, power, and glory. It is this divine fullness that obviates any need for dependence upon something *ad extra*. For a more detailed argument along these lines see Webster, "Life in and of Himself," 109–13.

In chapter 6 of his *Monologium* Anselm offers a classic account of God's absolute self-sufficiency: "But, in no wise does the supreme Nature exist through another, nor is it later or less than itself or anything else. Therefore, the supreme Nature could be created neither by itself, nor by another; nor could itself or any other be the matter whence it should be created; nor did it assist itself in any way; nor did anything assist it to be what it was not before."[5]

Anselm's claims are fairly straightforward in denying both that God is caused by another and that he is self-caused. He maintains that every existing thing exists *through* something or other. But the notion of "existence through" seems to suggest existence through a cause and thus dependence of some sort: "For, what is said to exist through anything apparently exists through an efficient cause, or through matter, or through some other external aid, as through some instrument. But whatever exists in any of these three ways exists through another than itself, and it is of later existence, and, in some sort, less than that through which it obtains existence."[6]

Yet Anselm affirms that, although the supreme Nature exists through itself, it is not the cause of itself. For all non-divine things, "existence through" indicates existence through a cause because *that which is*, the subject, is not-identical to *that by which* it is. All non-divine things have their existence and their essence by participation in something other than themselves.[7] But God does not derive existence through participation in some cause *ad extra* and, furthermore, nothing is self-participated. Thus, to say that God exists through himself is not to make a claim about divine self-causation, but, rather, a claim about the sufficient condition for God's existence.

God alone is the absolute sufficient condition for the existence of non-divine things; they exist through him. Likewise, he is the absolute sufficient condition for his own existence; he exists through himself. But, while the existence of creatures through God is necessarily understood as effects existing through a cause, God's existence through himself cannot possibly be conceived in this way. Self-existence is neither self-

---

5. Anselm, *Monologium*, 6. For a treatment of Anselm's aseity doctrine and how he ultimately grounds it in his understanding of divine simplicity see Morreall, "The Aseity of God in St. Anselm," 35–44.

6. Ibid.

7. See *Monologium*, 7, 13, and 14.

causation nor self-dependence.[8] Of the notion that God is self-caused, John Webster remarks, "When pressed, the concept soon shows itself incoherent and dogmatically precarious. At a purely formal level, it seems to suggest that God in some way precedes himself as his own cause."[9] Dogmatically, self-causation is dubious as well, since, as Webster observes:

> Talk of God as his own cause cannot easily cohere with teaching about divine eternity or immutability, since it appears to introduce an actualist concept of God's "coming-to-be" as the result of some causal process . . . Further, it imperils divine simplicity, introducing distinctions between cause and that which is caused or between potentiality and act, which, by attributing potentiality to God, undermines the all-important identity of essence and existence in God . . . By suggesting that God produces himself, it seems to require the possibility of God's nonexistence as a kind of background to his being.[10]

8. John Webster notes that there is a long history of adherence to divine self-causation that runs through the patristic and medieval Christian tradition. He cites Jerome's commentary on Ephesians 3:15 where he describes God as "himself the origin of himself and the cause of his own substance" (Heine, *The Commentaries of Origen and Jerome on St. Paul's Epistle to the Ephesians* (Oxford, 2003), 158, cited in Webster, "Life in and of Himself," 117). Such opinions are by far the minority report among classical Western Christians.

9. Webster, "Life in and of Himself," 117–18. Many who would reject the language of self-causation are more comfortable describing aseity as a doctrine about God's self-dependence or self-reliance. See, for instance, John Feinberg, *No One Like Him*, 239–40. These somewhat ambiguous notions are also subject to Webster's criticism of self-causation if they imply that God *assists* himself to be. Of course, they may just be inexact ways of affirming that God depends upon nothing outside himself.

10. Ibid., 118. Many of Webster's concerns are also well expressed in the words of Stephen Charnock: "Nothing can act before it be . . . For anything to produce itself is to act; if it acted before it was, it was then something and nothing at the same time; it then had a being before it had a being; it acted when it brought itself into being. How could it act without a being, without it was? So that if it were the cause of itself, it must be before itself as well as after itself; it was before it was; it was as a cause before it was as an effect. Action always supposeth a principle from whence it flows; as nothing hath no existence, so it hath no operation: there must be, therefore, something of real existence to give a being to those things that are, and every cause must be an effect of some other before it be a cause. To be and not be at the same time, is a manifest contradiction, which would be, if anything made itself" (*Existence and Attributes of God*, I: 46). Noting that many sound theologians have described God as *causa sui* (cause of himself), Cornelius Van Til explains how this might be understood in an orthodox sense: "God may be said to be *causa sui* if by *causa* is meant the reason for and meaning of his existence" (*Introduction to Systematic Theology*, 327–28). Thus, "cause" may by conceived more

To maintain that God exists *a se*, then, is merely to say that God himself is the sufficient ontological condition and explanation for his existence and essence.[11] *But this still leaves the question of precisely what it is about God that accounts for his aseity.* Or, is aseity simply the stopping point of all inquiry? George Joyce observes, "The real significance of the notion *Ens a se* is to deny that God is, like creatures, caused by another. He is conceived as self-existent in the sense of 'unoriginated.'" "But," he hastens to add, "it still remains for us to ask what is the internal constitutive, in virtue of which He is unoriginated and needs no cause. And to reply to this question we must fall back on our concept of Him as subsistent existence—as the Being whose existence is His nature."[12] In other words, the reason God is *a se* is because he is absolutely simple. It is God's identity with his existence and essence that ensures that he is *wholly* non-derived and sufficient in himself.

Stephen Charnock argues that God's independence is rooted in his simplicity:

> We can conceive no other of God, if he were not a pure, entire, unmixed Spirit. If he had distinct parts, he would depend upon them; those parts would be before him; his essence would be the effect of those distinct parts, and so he would not be adequately and entirely the first being; but he is so (Isa. xliv. 6): 'I am the first, and I am the last.' He is the first; nothing is before him. Whereas, if he had bodily parts, and those finite, it would follow, God is made up of those parts which are not God; and that which is not God, is in order of nature before that which is God. So we see that if God were not a Spirit he could not be independent.[13]

Although Charnock's chief concern historically is to refute the Socinian insistence that God is a corporeal being, his reasoning respect-

---

modestly as sufficient reason, and need not necessarily suggest an act-potency relation as is found between cause and effect. But, inasmuch as "cause" ordinarily suggests the production of some effect, it seems advisable to dispense with the idea of divine self-causation as an explanation of aseity.

11. For a helpful exposition of the difference between sufficient reason and efficient causality see Maritain, *Preface to Metaphysics*, 99–101. Maritain criticizes Descartes for confusing these two. Undoubtedly, this same confusion leads many modern theologians to infer that divine aseity as sufficient explanation must entail God's self-causation.

12. Joyce, *Principles of Natural Theology*, 297.

13. Charnock, *Existence and Attributes of God*, I: 186. Charnock often uses "Spirit" as a shorthand reference for simplicity.

ing God's simplicity applies, as he says, "to any composition" in God, including those models of composition considered in the previous chapter. The basic logic is that if God were composed of parts he would, in some sense, depend upon those parts inasmuch as those parts would be indispensible to the explanation of his existence and essence. If God were not identical with all those things ascribed to him (i.e., simple) then something less than the Godhead would be necessary to explain and account for God's being and nature. It will not do to reverse the order and simply insist that God is prior to the parts of which he is essentially and existentially composed, for then one would fall into the notion of divine ontological self-causation. Moreover, one cannot deny simplicity and still preserve aseity by insisting that the various parts in God are, after all, *divine* parts so that his dependence upon them is not injurious to his absolute self-sufficiency. Unless these divine attributes are themselves identical with the Godhead they are something less than and other than God himself and cannot, per aseity, be the reason for God's essence and existence.

Aseity insists that God is that by which he is and it grounds this claim in the DDS.[14] Divine simplicity is the sufficient ontological condition for regarding God as *a se* and it prevents aseity from becoming a doctrine of divine self-origin, self-causation, or even self-reliance. It is the DDS that suffuses the doctrine of God's aseity with the absoluteness of being and proscribes the possibility of regarding it as a doctrine about divine self-control.[15]

---

14. Not all adherents to divine aseity agree. John Feinberg, for instance, believes that even if one denies the DDS divine aseity can be upheld on the basis of God's necessity (*No One Like Him*, 335–36). But "necessity" tells us nothing ontologically about God that demands he be regarded as *a se* inasmuch as it does not tell anything about how God relates to his existence and essence. Not all necessity arises from the same ontological conditions. Thomas even identifies a version of "absolute necessity" that applies to spiritual creatures which, as creatures, cannot possibly be regarded as *a se* (see SCG II.30). *Bare necessity lacks the ontological strength that absolute simplicity supplies to the doctrine of aseity.* Harm Goris points out, "In Aquinas' view, the notion of necessity does not by itself exclude the dependence upon a cause" (*Free Creatures of an Eternal God*, 303). Patterson Brown observes that Thomas regards divine necessity as a consequence of divine simplicity ("St. Thomas' Doctrine of Necessary Being," 89).

15. Inasmuch as Alvin Plantinga denies divine aseity it is no surprise that he rejects divine simplicity as well; he has no need for it theologically. It should be noted that part of the reason he denies aseity is because he thinks of it as a doctrine about God's control over his nature. Yet, Plantinga contends that God does not control those aspects of the "Platonic menagerie" (i.e., abstract properties) that together form the divine nature

UNITY

Numerous passages of Scripture affirm that God is one.[16] Deuteronomy 6:4 is the *locus classicus* for the inspired account of God's unity: "Hear, O Israel: The LORD our God, the LORD is one." Undoubtedly it is the singularity and uniqueness of God that is in the foreground of most of the biblical texts affirming his oneness. Scripture is unequivocally monotheistic in both the Old and New Testaments.[17] But the many passages that affirm God's oneness do not, on the face of them, convey anything about the metaphysics of divine unity, so to speak. They do not address the ontological conditions by which God is one. Even so, they do point us toward this ontological account of God's unity by insisting or implying that God's singularity is unique and absolute. Not only is he one, but he is one in such a way that there could not possibly be another (consider Deut 32:39; Isa 37:16; 44:8). He does not exist in an actual or potential series with other deities. This raises the question of *why* it is that God's divine being and essence cannot possibly be shared by another. The strength or absoluteness of this unique singularity is drawn from another aspect of his unity, namely, his simplicity.

Traditionally, Christian orthodoxy has differentiated between two aspects of God's unity: his unity of singularity and his unity of simplicity.[18] The former is ontologically accounted for by the latter. Rudi te

---

(such as omnipotence, justice, and wisdom); therefore the "sovereignty-aseity intuition" is wrong in his opinion. Those properties, as Plantinga sees it, are eternal and necessary truths and their existence, as abstractly independent of God, is not within his control (see *Does God Have a Nature?* 80–84). The problem with Plantinga's view extends beyond his commitment to Platonism; he also misunderstands the motive for aseity. It is not a doctrine about God's *control* of his nature; it teaches, rather, that God's nature needs no reason or explanation beyond itself. Taking aseity to teach that God is in control of his existence and essence seems to treat it as merely a special instance of divine sovereignty. But God's sovereignty is concerned with how he relates to other things, not how he relates to himself. Immink aptly remarks, "[I]t would be outrageous to understand God's sovereignty in terms of control over *his own nature*" (*Divine Simplicity*, 83; emphasis his). For a further critique of Plantinga along these same lines see Stump, Review of *Does God Have a Nature?*" 616–22. In answer to Plantinga's question—Does God have a nature?—the simplicity proponent does not say that God *has* a nature in the way that created things participate in universals; rather, God just *is* his nature and is thus *a se*.

16. Frequently cited passages include: Deut 6:4; Rom 3:30; 1 Cor 8:6; Gal 3:20; and 1 Tim 2:5. All Scripture citations not found in passages quoted from other authors are taken from the English Standard Version.

17. See Bavinck's remarks in *RD*, II: 170–73.

18. Among those who plainly affirm this distinction are: Aquinas, *ST* I.11.3; Leigh,

Velde writes, "There can be but one single God, because what it means to be God—utterly simple and most perfect—excludes the possibility of multiplication and division. It is therefore impossible that there should be many Gods."[19] To affirm, without qualification, that God is one does not necessarily establish his singularity as unique or absolute. After all, oneness and unity are generally ascribed to anything that exists. Thomas Aquinas clearly expresses this convertibility of oneness and being:

> "One" does not add any reality to "being"; but is only a negation of division; for "one" means undivided "being." This is the very reason why "one" is the same as "being." Now every being is either simple or compound. But what is simple is undivided, both actually and potentially. Whereas what is compound, has not being whilst its parts are divided, but after they make up and compose it. Hence it is manifest that the being of anything consists in undivision; and hence it is that everything guards its unity as it guards its being.[20]

For something to be is for it to be unified either simply or compositely.[21]

W. Norris Clarke points out that even composite beings are "one" inasmuch as they actually exist. He propounds a negative thought experiment to make this point:

> Let us see if we can think of some real being that is not in fact internally unified, not an undivided whole, but is made up of parts that are divided off from each other, not joined together, not cohering together as a unity. In such a case there is no longer any objective ground for calling it *this* being, an "it," but only a multitude of *thises* and *thats*. There is no *something* that exists in the singular. Furthermore, if we examine each of these parts in turn and if to be this part does not require it to be one, then each part immediately breaks down into a multiplicity of further parts, of *thises* and *thats*. Each of these in turn breaks down into

---

Systeme, 189–90; Bavinck, *RD*, II: 170; and Berkhof, *Systematic Theology*, 61–63. See also the historical account in Muller, *PRRD*, III: 241–46.

19. te Velde, *Aquinas on God*, 84. See also, Henry of Ghent, *Summa* 25.3.

20. *ST* I.11.1. Benignus elaborates: "Unity, like truth and goodness, is convertible with being; whatever is, is one. The concept of unity adds the notion of indivision to the concept of being, but what is signified by the two concepts is the same reality. Thus being and one are the same *in re* but differ *in ratione*" (*Nature, Knowledge, and God*, 522). See also, Smith, "God One and Indivisible," 54–61; Gilson, *Elements of Christian Philosophy*, 145; Raeymaeker, *Philosophy of Being*, 61; Henry of Ghent, *Summa* 25.1.

21. For a thorough treatment of being and unity see Glenn, *Ontology*, 107–44, and Elders, *The Metaphysics of Being of St. Thomas Aquinas*, 81–94.

many parts, and so on in an endless regress; there is no way of stopping the disintegration until we reach an "infinite dust," so to speak, of pure multiplicity, where nothing holds together to be a distinct something at all. But pure multiplicity with no inner cohesion at all is indistinguishable from pure nothingness, no-thing-ness.[22]

Clarke does a fine job showing that unity is required in order for something to actually exist. The important thing to understand from this passage, though, is that unity alone is not enough to distinguish God from all other existing things. Inasmuch as oneness is as common as being we will only be able to express the uniqueness and supremacy of God's unity by identifying the uniqueness of his mode of existence.

How is it, then, that God's singularity is distinguished from and superior to the singularity of all other beings? Thomas answers this question by observing that the form of God's nature, unlike things in a genus and a species, is entirely incommunicable on account of his simplicity:

[I]t is manifest that the reason why any singular thing is "this particular thing" is because it cannot be communicated to many: since that whereby Socrates is a man, can be communicated to many; whereas, what makes him this particular man, is only communicable to one. Therefore, if Socrates were a man by what makes him to be this particular man, as there cannot be many Socrates, so there could not in that way be many men. Now this belongs to God alone; for God Himself is His own nature, as was shown above [*ST* I.3.3]. Therefore, in the very same way God is God, and He is this God. Impossible is it therefore that many Gods should exist.[23]

This passage assumes that in every creature there is a real distinction between the supposit and its nature (see our discussion in the previous chapter). The reason there can be many men and yet also singular, individual men is because that by which any man is a human is really distinct from that by which the same man is this *particular* individual. Accordingly, as Socrates' humanity is communicable to many, there are many humans; but Socrates' Socrates*ness*—that which makes him Socrates and not Plato or anyone else—is entirely incommunicable to

22. Clarke, *The One and the Many*, 61–62.

23. *ST* I.11.3. See also, Wippel, *Metaphysical Thought*, 486, 495; Garrigou-Lagrange, *The One God*, 300–304; Boedder, *Natural Theology*, 91–92.

others. Thus, Socrates is "one" man, but he stands in a series with others who are no less human than he. God, on the other hand, is one in a radically different sense inasmuch as he is wholly identical with his divine nature. He does not stand in a series of deities because that which makes him *this* God is identical with that by which he is God. Just as there cannot be many instances of *this* God, so there cannot be many gods.

It follows from all this that God's supreme unity of singularity (monotheism) is ontologically explained by his perfect unity of simplicity. God is not only one because he is undivided, but because he is indivisible.[24] It is the *indivisibility* of divine simplicity that ensures that God is supremely and absolutely one. Other sorts of unity that we discover in creation—such as collective, potential, and abstract (or ideal) unities—fail to set God's unity apart from that of creatures.[25] Indeed, instances of relatively simple unity may be found among creatures, such as angelic spirits and disembodied human souls; but, inasmuch as these are still composed of supposit and nature, substance and accident, and existence and essence, they do not approach God's absolute simplicity or his absolute unity. Thomas appeals to God's identity with his own existence in order to distinguish his unity from that of all other undivided things:

> Since "one" is an undivided being, if anything is supremely "one" it must be supremely being, and supremely undivided. Now both of these belong to God. For He is supremely being, inasmuch as His being is not determined by any nature to which it is adjoined; since He is being itself, subsistent, absolutely undetermined. But He is supremely undivided inasmuch as He is divided neither actually nor potentially, by any mode of division; since He is altogether simple, as was shown above [*ST* I.3.7]. Hence it is manifest that God is "one" in the supreme degree.[26]

24. Clarke reminds us that, "'undivided' does not mean 'indivisible,' but only that which at present is *actually undivided*, though it may be *potentially divisible* into parts" (*The One and the Many*, 61).

25. For an older, yet still useful discussion of how the concepts of collective, potential, and abstract unity are inadequate explanations of God's oneness see Driscoll, *Christian Philosophy*, 211–23. Driscoll rightly observes: "It is not sufficient to say that God is a unity. We could not draw any definite conclusion therefrom, nor could we from the phrase, as it stands, form a real and definite conception. There are various kinds of unity. To be exact we must distinguish [between them]" (ibid., 211).

26. *ST* I.11.4. Oneness of the "supreme degree" refers to the unique exclusiveness of God's unity. In *SCG* I.42 [8] Thomas grounds the unique oneness of God in his non-composite existence and essence: "[I]f there are two beings of which both are necessary

Divine existential simplicity is ultimately the ontological reason why the biblical writer can affirm, "the LORD is God in heaven above and on the earth beneath; there is no other" (Deut. 4:39). The exclusive singularity of God, affirmed throughout Scripture, prompts the ontological conclusion that his unity is rooted in his absolute simplicity.

INFINITY

As with God's aseity and unity, the DDS is also integral to the traditional Christian explanation of God's infinity.[27] Divine infinity is often articulated negatively as the opposite of finitude and positively as God's plentitude of being and nature. Etienne Gilson locates finitude in the "metaphysical composition of categorical being,"[28] and Benignus Gerrity explains it in terms of the mutual contraction of a creature's parts: "whatever is limited, is limited by virtue of the limitations imposed upon it by the subject in which it is; thus all forms of corporeal being are limited because they are received in matter, and even immaterial forms are limited if they are received in a limited subject; as for example, intelligence and freedom, though unlimited essentially, are limited in man."[29]

Thomas notes, "everything that according to its nature is finite is determined to the nature of some genus."[30] We are prohibited from saying that a subject found in a genus is infinite inasmuch as it is the nature

---

beings, they must agree in the notion of the necessity of being. Hence, they must be distinguished by something added either to one of them only, or to both. This means that one or both of them must be composite. Now . . . no composite being is through itself a necessary being. It is impossible therefore that there be many beings of which each is a necessary being. Hence, neither can there be many gods." Divine non-composition is the linchpin of this argument inasmuch as it provides the ontological conditions for absolute necessity. Thomas adds, "the proper being of each thing is only one. But God is His being, as we have shown [SCG I.22]. There can, therefore, be only one God" (*SCG* I.43 [17]). See the informative discussion of God's oneness in Aertsen, *Medieval Philosophy and the Transcendentals*, 367–69.

27. It is not my intention in this section to consider the numerous implications of God's infinity for our understanding of various other attributes (such as his immensity, omnipresence, omnipotence, omniscience, and eternity), but to restrict the consideration to the role of simplicity in accounting for God's infinite being and nature. For a broader discussion of divine infinity see Sweeney, *Divine Infinity in Greek and Medieval Thought*, and Muller, *PRRD*, III: 325–64.

28. Gilson, *Being and Some Philosophers*, 229–30.

29. Benignus, *Nature, Knowledge, and God*, 517.

30. *SCG* I.43 [4].

of a genus to lack the perfections unique to other genera; no one genus contains the perfections of every other genus. Putting it in broader
terms, Thomas explains that everything composed of act and potency is
inherently terminated or limited in its perfection: "[E]very act inhering
in another is terminated by that in which it inheres, since what is in another is in it according to the mode of the receiver . . . [A]n act is all the
more perfect by as much as it has less of potency mixed with it. Hence,
every act with which potency is mixed is terminated in its perfection."[31]

Creaturely finitude can be construed in just as many ways as creaturely composition can. A corporeal entity's form, for instance, is limited
by matter and its prime matter is always contracted by some substantial
form.[32] A thing's genus reduces it to a certain class of being so that it
cannot exemplify the properties unique to other genera. Accidents are
limited by the substances in which they inhere (for example, although
the form of intelligence is potentially infinite in itself, it is always limited by the subject possessing it). Most importantly, a creature's act of
existence (*esse*) is limited by its essence since contraction to a particular
essence restricts it from functioning as the act of existence for any other
being.[33] It is the varieties of metaphysical composition that account for
the finitude of non-divine things and stand in sharp contrast to the ontological conditions necessary for divine infinity.

If God's infinity is to be conceived as positive perfection it must be
differentiated from the older Greek concept of infinity as imperfection
or incompleteness.[34] Indeed, many Christian theologians have derived

31. Ibid., I.43 [5] and [7]. See the foregoing chapter on act-potency composition.

32. Aquinas explains how matter and form operate to make each other finite when
composed: "Matter indeed is made finite by form, inasmuch as matter, before it receives
its form, is in potentiality to many forms; but on receiving a form it is terminated by
that one. Again, form is made finite by matter, inasmuch as form, considered in itself,
is common to many; but when received in matter, the form is determined to this one
particular thing" (*ST* I.7.1).

33. See Weigel's discussion of Thomas's teaching that *esse* is not self-limiting in,
Aquinas on Simplicity, 156–60.

34. Norris Clarke explains: "In classical Greek thought, including both Plato and
Aristotle, perfection was habitually identified with the finished, the well-defined or
determinate—i.e., the finite or limited—typified by intelligible form. The infinite was
identified with the indeterminate, the unfinished, the chaotic, the unintelligible, typified by unformed matter. Even the linguistic term in Greek for perfection came from
limit, end (*teleios*, 'perfect,' from *telos*, 'end' or 'limit')" (*The Philosophical Approach to
God*, 127). For a detailed analysis of the pre-Plotinian Greek position on infinity see
chapters 1–8 in Sweeney, *Divine Infinity*, 1–165. For the Greeks, the concept of infinity

the biblical motivation for divine infinity from passages that teach God's immeasurable greatness.[35] Infinity conceived as the *limitlessness* of God's perfection does not denote that God is ever in potency toward a further intensification of being, but rather that he eternally subsists as the fullness of being and perfection in himself.[36] It is only when infinity is applied to the categories of finite and composite being that it is conceived as passive potency, openness, and incompleteness.

Maurice Holloway observes that God's infinity follows from his pure actuality: "since God's being is completely in act, there can be nothing potential or limiting within it."[37] Infinity is the negative way of expressing God's perfection and indicates that "there is no limit or term to his Being."[38] Consequently, God cannot be composed of parts since discreet parts, whether physical or metaphysical, necessarily delimit one another. Any act that is received (whether this act is understood as matter, form, nature, species, accident, existence, or whatever else may function as an

---

requires a potency or openness toward perfection which can never be fully actualized. In this sense an infinite cannot be a complete and subsistent being since it is by definition incomplete. The infinite is, in the Greek mind, like prime matter, a pure potency and never actually existent as such. It is thought of merely in terms of the extension of what is by nature finite. Against the Greek notion, Richard Muller points out that Aquinas, the medieval doctors, and the Protestant scholastics, "define divine infinity not as the endless extension of the categories of finite being, but as the transcendence of those categories" (*PRRD*, III: 330).

35. Standard passages include: Job 11:7: "Can you find out the deep things of God? Can you find out the limit of the Almighty?"; Psalm 145:3: "Great is the LORD, and greatly to be praised, and his greatness is unsearchable"; 1 Kings 8:27: "But will God indeed dwell on the earth? Behold, heaven and the highest heaven cannot contain you"; Isaiah 40:13: "Who has measured the Spirit of the LORD, or what man shows him his counsel?" Some of these passages speak of God's infinity affirmatively, some negatively, and some comparatively in relation to creatures. See Muller, *PRRD*, III: 327; Turretin, *IET*, 3.8.5; Brakel, *Christian's Reasonable Service*, I: 94; and Leigh, *Systeme*, 170–71.

36. James Thornwell explains God's infinity by the absence of act-potency composition: "[I]t is obvious that the entire distinction between the possible and the actual could have no existence as regards the absolutely infinite; for an unrealized possibility is necessarily a relation and a limit" (*Collected Writings*, I: 114).

37. Holloway, *Introduction*, 243. Holloway is representative of both the medieval and Protestant scholastics in his characterization of God's perfection as his complete actuality: "Since the Being of God is completely in act, he is completely perfect; absolutely nothing is lacking in his Being" (ibid., 242). George Joyce concurs, noting that the implication of affirming that God is *actus purus* is that "He contains within Himself all perfection—all reality" (*Principles of Natural Theology*, 317).

38. Holloway, *Introduction*, 242. See also, Wippel, *Metaphysical Themes II*, 123–51.

act) is limited, contracted, or shaped, as it were, by its receiving principle or subject. But such limitation is wholly absent in one whose act of being is not received in any way, as Thomas indicates: "an act that exists in nothing is terminated by nothing . . . But God is act in no way existing in another, for neither is He a form in matter, as we have proved, nor does His being inhere in some form or nature, since He is His own being . . . It remains, then, that God is infinite."[39] God's existence in nothing is a crucial notion for understanding his existence and essence as positively and absolutely infinite, for existence in something—form contracted by matter or existence bounded by essence—would mean that God is intrinsically limited and finite.

Aquinas enhances the strength of this position through a discussion of the relative infinity of non-divine self-subsistent forms: "If, however, any created forms are not received into matter, but are self-subsisting, as some think is the case with angels, these will be relatively infinite, inasmuch as such kinds of forms are not terminated, nor contracted by any matter. But because a created form thus subsisting has being, and yet is not its own being, it follows that its being is received and contracted to a determinate nature. Hence it cannot be absolutely infinite."[40] All non-divine self-subsisting forms fall short of absolute infinity because that which is most formal in them, existence, is contracted by essence and is not self-subsistent that is, no creature is subsistent being itself even though spiritual natures may be self-subsistent forms. Thomas explains: "Now being is the most formal of all things, as appears from what is shown above [*ST* I.4.3, obj. 3]. Since therefore the divine being is not a being received in anything, but He is His own subsistent being as was shown above [in *ST* I.3.4], it is clear that God Himself is infinite and perfect."[41] As God is identical with his own act of being, per the DDS, he is identical with that which is most formal in him. He is not only self-subsistent form, but also subsistent being itself (*ipsum esse subsistens*) and this ensures that his infinity is absolute while the infinity of other self-subsistent forms is only relative. Holloway summarizes the argument: "Now that which is most 'formal' in a thing is its act of existing. Not in the sense that 'to be' is a form, but in the sense that everything in a

39. *SCG* I.43 [5]. See also, Charnock, *Existence and Attributes of God*, I: 185–88, and Renard, *Philosophy of Being*, 36.

40. *ST* I.7.2. See also, Wippel, *Metaphysical Thought*, 153.

41. *ST* I.7.1.

being is related to the act of existing as potency to act, and that existence itself cannot receive anything. Existence says simply act and in no sense potency. Now the 'To Be' of God is not received in anything. God is subsistent Being. And unreceived Being is simply infinite."[42]

The DDS teaches that there is no metaphysical space, as it were, between God and his act of existence. It follows, then, that since subsistent existence is unlimited and non-contracted, the absolute infinity of God is ontologically explained by his absolute simplicity. Though the doctrine of divine infinity may give rise to the contemplation of simplicity in the order of theological discovery, it seems to be simplicity that provides the ontological conditions for God's absolutely infinite mode of life and perfection and sets it apart from all relatively infinite creaturely forms.[43]

IMMUTABILITY

God's immutability seems to be an entailment of his infinity. Anything actually infinite in being and perfection can neither lose a perfection it already possesses and remain infinite nor receive any additional act of being since it lacks no actuality; thus, it cannot undergo change either by augmentation or diminution. As absolutely simple and infinite God is ontologically unsuited to any change whatsoever.

Divine immutability enjoys more explicit biblical affirmation than doctrines such as divine aseity and infinity.[44] Many of the supporting

42. Holloway, *Introduction*, 244. *Esse* is called a "form" only improperly and analogically; it relates to essence as proper form relates to matter, that is, as act to potency. J. L. H. Thomas suggests that in referring to being as "form" Aquinas means only that existence is the *formality* "which confers validity or status upon some situation or state of affairs." He concludes, "The Thomist distinction between being and essence can, then, be approached via the distinction between state [corresponding to essence] and status [corresponding to existence]" ("The Identity of Being and Essence in God," 402). That by which God's state possesses the status of existence is nothing other than the state (i.e., the Godhead) itself.

43. See chapter 4 below for a further discussion of God as *ipsum esse* and for the denial that God is identical with being in general.

44. Texts customarily cited include: Mal 3:6: "For I the LORD do not change"; Isa 41:4: "I, the LORD, the first, and with the last; I am he"; Isa 14:27: "For the LORD of hosts has purposed, and who will annul it? His hand is stretched out, and who will turn it back?"; Heb 1:11–12: "they will perish, but you remain; they will all wear out like a garment, like a robe you will roll them up, like a garment they will be changed. But you are the same, and your years will have no end"; Jas 1:17: "Every good gift and every perfect gift is from above, coming down from the Father of lights with whom there is no variation or shadow due to change." These passages are merely representative of a

passages tend to focus on the constancy and faithfulness of God to
do what he has promised to do, that is, upon his ethical immutability.
Nevertheless, even ethical immutability requires an ontological explanation rooted in the very being and essence of God.[45] How do God's
existence and essence provide a metaphysical foundation such that we
can be assured that he will be faithful to his promises? Put differently,
what is it about God that makes his word infinitely surer than even that
of other relatively reliable promise makers? The answer is found in God's
ontological immutability, which is inextricably entailed in his simplicity.

The medieval schoolmen and Protestant scholastics were keen to
express mutability in terms of act-potency composition and immutability as the absence of such composition (see the discussion of the kinds of
act and potency in chapter 2). Thus, when Thomas seeks to explain that
God is "altogether immutable" his first two arguments appeal to God's
lack of potency and his unique identity as pure act:

> God is altogether immutable. First, because . . . [the] first being
> must be pure act, without the admixture of any potentiality, for
> the reason that, absolutely, potentiality is posterior to act. Now
> everything which is in any way changed, is in some way in poten-
> tiality . . . Secondly, because everything which is moved, remains
> as it was in part, and passes away in part; as what is moved from
> whiteness to blackness, remains the same as to substance; thus in
> everything which is moved, there is some kind of composition to

---

host of others. See discussions in: Brakel, *Christian's Reasonable Service*, I: 100–102;
Leigh, *Systeme*, 179–82; Turretin, *IET*, 3.11.3; Bavinck, *RD*, II: 153; Berkhof, *Systematic
Theology*, 58–59; Muller, *PRRD*, III: 313–15.

45. Richard Muller considers the objection that the Bible only teaches God's ethical
immutability and therefore it is concluding too much to say that he is absolutely immutable in his being and essence. He notes, "The question is whether theology must
. . . stop short of drawing ontological and essentialist conclusions from texts which
speak of the ethical, moral intentional, and volitional constancy of God or whether
theology must move beyond an affirmation of that constancy to a doctrine of essential immutability." Muller finds ontological immutability indispensible to ethical immutability: "if God can become something that he was not, then the constancy of the
promises and, indeed, the laws made prior to the change cannot be guaranteed either
in or subsequent to the change" ("Incarnation, Immutability, and the Case for Classical
Theism," 30). He adds, "Ethical, intentional constancy . . . must have an ontological
basis. The constancy of the divine purpose, the consistency of the God who is what he
is and will be what he will be, must also indicate a consistency, an immutability of the
divine being" (ibid., 32).

be found. But . . . in God there is no composition, for He is altogether simple. Hence it is manifest that God cannot be moved.[46]

Even Thomas's third argument, based on divine infinity, presupposes
God's lack of potency since God, as infinite, comprehends "all the plentitude of perfection of all being" and cannot stand open to the reception
of a further act of being: "He cannot acquire anything new, nor extend
Himself to anything whereto He was not extended previously."[47] In every
mutable thing there is found some actuality as well as passive potency
toward some other accidental or substantial form of being. Indeed, the
composition of act and potency is the ontologically sufficient condition
for all change, with passive potency as the key principle.

Thomas further appeals to the act-potency schema in order to contrast the *absoluteness* of God's immutability with the relative immutability of certain creatures found in the universe.[48] Mutable things, Thomas
observes, are called such in two ways: both by some passive potency for
change in them and by some active power that exists in another. Prior
to its actual existence the potency for any creature's existence does not
reside in some created power, but belongs, rather, to the active power
(or potency) of God by which he is able to produce them in existence.
Inasmuch as creatures depend upon God's will for their entrance into
existence it follows that his active power preserves them in that existence
and can, if he wills, be removed so as to reduce them again to non-being.
This is not the mutability of change, properly speaking, but of potential
annihilation. The existence of any non-divine thing depends for its origin and preservation upon the active potency that is in another, namely,
God. As producible in existence creatures are changeable and mutable
in a fundamental sense.[49]

46. *ST* I.9.1.

47. Ibid. See the summary of *ST* I.9.1 in Holloway, *Introduction*, 265–66, and in
Dodds, *Unchanging God of Love*, 99–103.

48. See *ST* I.9.2.

49. Michael Dodds points out that this existential mutability is due to the non-
identity of existence and essence in creatures, that is, to their composite existence: "In
the creature existence is always distinct from essence. Its essence (what it is) does not
explain its existence (the fact that it is). Since its essence does not account for its existence, it must depend on another for existence. Considered in itself, it could cease to
exist. In this sense all creatures are mutable, and God alone (upon whom all creatures
depend and who depends on no other) is immutable" (*Unchanging God of Love*, 126).
See also, Weigel, *Aquinas on Simplicity*, 104–8.

But there is also mutability in the creature according to a passive potency that is found in the creature itself. This is the potentiality for accidental change in all creatures, and for substantial change in material beings. Thomas writes, "I call that power passive which enables anything to attain its perfection either in being, or in attaining to its end."[50] But, Thomas is quick to point out that respecting this intrinsic passive potency, not all creatures are equally mutable (since not equally imperfect or composite); indeed, some are relatively immutable. Material beings seem to be most mutable since they can change not only accidentally, but also substantially. One aspect of their passive potency is the potency of prime matter, which is intrinsically oriented toward non-being inasmuch as material substances can lose their substantial forms and thereby cease to be what they are substantially.[51] Of course, material beings are also changeable accidentally, which is not potency toward non-being as much as toward new forms of accidental being.

Immaterial entities, such as angelic spirits and human souls, differ from material creatures in that their passive potency is not naturally oriented in any way toward non-being (as is the case with prime matter). As self-subsisting forms, spiritual creatures are immutable in a peculiar sense. Holloway explains: "While it is true that these spiritual forms are related to their act of existing as potency to act, they nevertheless cannot suffer the privation of this act of existing. For existence (*esse*) comes through the form, so that nothing can lose its act of existing unless it loses its form. And since a form cannot 'lose itself,' angels and human souls are naturally incorruptible. There is within them no passive potency for non-being. Thus these creatures are unchangeable according to their substantial being."[52]

Following Thomas, Holloway locates the spiritual creature's potency toward non-being in the power of God that preserves it in existence

50. *ST* I.9.2.

51. The natural potency toward non-being that is unique to material substances is toward a *relative* non-being according to the order of substantial form, not toward absolute existential nothingness. Prime matter is such that it can potentially lose the act of existence it possesses through its form and acquire a whole new act of existence through the reception of another substantial form. When this happens we say that one whole being is replaced with another being, although the prime matter itself has remained as the support and thus this is a genuine *change* in being and not an annihilation of it. See the discussions in above in chapter 2 on prime matter and substantial change.

52. Holloway, *Introduction*, 267–68.

and thus outside of the creature itself.[53] Self-subsisting forms cannot be lost and replaced by new forms—as occurs in the substantial change of material creatures—since there is no matter there to support such a change. A spiritual creature's loss of form would be nothing other than absolute annihilation and not properly a change. Thomas discovers that spiritual forms are less mutable than those existing in matter inasmuch as they seem to be more in act. Actuality comes to any being through its form and those beings that are nothing but form appear to have their actuality in a higher or stronger degree.

Spiritual substances are still essentially mutable in two important ways, as Thomas observes: "one as regards their potentiality toward their end; and in that way there is in them a mutability according to their choice from good to evil . . . ; the other as regards place, inasmuch as by their finite power they attain to certain fresh places."[54] It turns out, then, that even the most immutable of creatures still possess passive potency toward accidental, qualitative, and local change in actuality and are thus composed of potency and act. Thomas concludes that, "since God is in none of these ways mutable, it belongs to Him alone to be altogether immutable."[55] In other words, he is immutable because he lacks every variety of passive potency and because he does not depend upon an outside power for his act of existence. Again, it is divine simplicity that accounts for the absoluteness of God's immutability and sets him apart from even the relative immutability found in some creatures.[56]

53. Garrigou-Lagrange distinguishes between the "real potency for non-existence" in material beings and the "logical potency for non-existence" in spiritual beings (*The One God*, 273).

54. *ST* I.9.2. Holloway points out that immaterial substances may also change in respect to their acts of knowledge and love (*Introduction*, 268). We may add that they change in respect to their temporal (or *aeviternal*) moments as well.

55. Ibid.

56. Stephen Charnock summarizes this argument: "If God were not a Spirit, he were not immutable and unchangeable. His immutability depends upon his simplicity. He is unchangeable in his essence, because he is a pure and unmixed spiritual Being. Whatsoever is compounded of parts may be divided into those parts, and resolved into those distinct parts which make up and constitute the nature. Whatsoever is compounded is changeable in its own nature, though it should never be changed" (*Existence and Essence of God*, I: 187). In like manner, Henry of Ghent states: "Since, therefore, on account of the simplicity of the divine essence, because of which it cannot enter into composition with something else, or something else with it . . . it is utterly immutable by a change of some variation that can occur in its substance" (*Summa* 30.4). Michael Dodds writes, "Since in him [God] essence and to-be (*esse*) are one, he is absolutely

In addition to ensuring that God is absolutely immutable in his being and essence, the DDS also makes certain that the doctrine of divine
immutability is not misunderstood as teaching that God is somehow
cold, inert, and lifeless. Many critics of the classical account of immutability dismiss it on precisely these grounds. Karl Barth, for one, is concerned that classical immutability quickly devolves into a "pagan idea"
insofar as its unmoved mover seems to be nothing but a pure *immobile*:

> If it is true . . . that God is not moved either by anything else or by
> Himself, but that, confined as it were, by His simplicity, infinity,
> and absolute perfection, He is the pure *immobile*, it is quite im-
> possible that there should be any relationship between Himself
> and a reality distinct from Himself—or at any rate a relationship
> that is more than the relation of a pure mutual negativity, and in-
> cludes God's concern for this other reality . . . The pure *immobile*
> is death. If, then, the pure *immobile* is God, death is God . . . And
> if death is God, then God is dead.[57]

It is uncertain who in the orthodox Christian tradition actually concludes that for God to be unmoved means he is the "pure *immobile*"
in the way that Barth understands *immobile*. He equates *immobile* with
lifelessness and inactivity. Anyhow, Barth seeks to remedy the supposed
problem of classical immutability by proposing instead that God exemplifies "a holy mutability": "There is such a thing as a holy mutability in
God. He is above all ages. But above them as their Lord . . . and therefore
as One who—as Master and in His own way—partakes in their alteration, so that there is something corresponding to that alteration in His
own essence. His constancy consists in the fact that he is always the same
in every change."[58]

But Barth goes wrong in assuming that the classical Christian
understanding of immutability implies an inactive immobility. In fact,
quite the opposite is true. God is unmoved not because he lacks life and
action, but because he is identical with his life and actuality and therefore cannot be determined to any further actuality of life than he already

---

simple, transcending all composition required for change" (*Unchanging God of Love*,
143–44).

57. Barth, *Church Dogmatics*, II/1: 494 [§31.2].

58. Ibid., II/1: 496 [§31.2]. See the useful discussion in McCormack, "The Actuality
of God," 231–32.

has.[59] *Pace* Barth, God's simplicity, infinity, and perfection do not "confine" him, but rather ensure that he is absolutely unconfined in his actuality. God would only be confined if he were in potency to further act of being, which Barth suggests he is when he urges that God partakes *essentially* in the alteration of the ages. This implies that God must possess some principle of non-being (i.e., passive potency) in order to partake essentially in the changes that come with the passage of time. For Barth, God is above all change according to his divine Lordship over creation, but not according to his being and essence, which changes along with creation. It is a Barthian maxim that God's being is in his becoming.

Contrary to Barth's skepticism, though, it is the DDS that infuses the doctrine of immutability with the notion of *dynamic liveliness* and *absolute actuality* so that to say God is *immobile* in no way suggests that he is inactive. A thing can be considered *immobile* in two senses: either (1) because of its radical paucity of act or (2) because it possesses act so perfectly and completely that it cannot possibly be moved to receive further actuality. Thomas Weinandy illustrates the difference between these two ways of accounting for immobility:

> One should not be misled into thinking that God's immutability is like the immutability of a rock only more so. What God and rocks appear to have in common is only the fact that they do not change. The reason for their unchangeableness is for polar-opposite reasons. The Rock of Gibraltar does not change or changes very little because it is hardly in act at all, and the change that it does undergo is mainly from outside causes—wind and rain. God is unchangeable not because he is inert or static like a rock, but for just the opposite reason. He is so dynamic, so active that no change can make him more active. He is act pure and simple.[60]

It seems that the pure *immobile* would only be "death" if it were like the immobility of a rock, dominated by passive potency. This is precisely

---

59. Process theist Burton Cooper seems to miss Thomas's insistence upon God as *actus purus* when he charges that Thomas endorses "an ontology of rest rather than of change" (*The Idea of God*, 44). In truth, these are false alternatives and the classical Christian tradition endorses neither. It insists, rather, upon the conception of God as pure act and thus rejects both the inactivity of rest and the incomplete activity of change. Insofar as some orthodox theologians do attribute "rest" to God (e.g., Augustine and Bavinck) their meaning is simply that he does not possess his existence and essence through the restless process of acquisition; this is not the rest of the inert and non-dynamic as Cooper imagines.

60. Weinandy, *Does God Change?* 78–79.

what the DDS disallows of God when it denies that he is composed of act and potency and insists instead that God is existence itself. Weinandy responds frankly and insightfully to the tendency of some scholars to equate immutability with inactivity:

> What the critics consistently fail to grasp is that God's immutability is not opposed to his vitality. Nor need one hold together in some dialectical fashion his immutability and his vibrancy, as if in spite of being immutable he is nonetheless dynamic. Rather, it is precisely God's immutability as *actus purus* that guarantees and authenticates his pure vitality and absolute dynamism. Thus, when the critics assert that because Aquinas and the tradition believe God to be immutable they espouse a static and inert conception of God, they but demonstrate their own lack of understanding.[61]

In the final analysis divine simplicity furnishes the logic of immutability with its denial of act-potency composition and establishes the absoluteness of God's immutability over against all relatively immutable spiritual substances. It further ensures that this immutability is really the unchangeableness of an absolute life and activity.[62]

ETERNITY

Classical Christian theism typically regards God's atemporal eternity as an aspect of his infinity and immutability, which themselves are established by the DDS, as I have been arguing in this chapter.[63] Wilhelmus

61. Weinandy, *Does God Suffer?* 124. Michael Dodds agrees with Weinandy: "Far from implying . . . that God is somehow static or inert, immutability directly signifies that God, as subsistent *esse*, is pure dynamic actuality" (*Unchanging God of Love*, 159). See also, Franks, "The Simplicity of the Living God," 275–300.

62. This section has not addressed the question of how it is that God freely wills and knows certain things while remaining wholly immutable and even simple. How could God be, per simplicity, identical with his *free* knowledge and *free* will? I have reserved these intriguing questions for discussion in chapter 7. Arguably, the question of divine freedom is the most challenging for the classical affirmation of God's simplicity and immutability.

63. It is not within the scope of my purpose here to make the case for the atemporal understanding of divine eternity. My argument in this section assumes the correctness of the view that God's eternity is successionless. Contemporary proponents of divine atemporality include: Helm, *Eternal God*; Leftow, *Time and Eternity*; Stump and Kretzmann, "Eternity," 219–52. Opponents include: Wolterstorff, "God Everlasting," 181–203; Feinberg, *No One Like Him*, 375–436; DeWeese, "Atemporal, Sempiternal, or Omnitemporal," 49–61; Swinburne, *The Christian God*, 137–44.

à Brakel makes the connection between simplicity and eternity explicit: "God's Being is eternity and eternity is God's Being. It is not fortuitous as time is in relation to the creature. There can be no chronology within the Being of God since His Being is simple and immutable."[64] Louis Berkhof defines eternity as "that perfection of God whereby He is elevated above all temporal limits and all succession of moments, and possesses the whole of his existence in one indivisible present."[65] Boethius famously describes divine eternity as "the whole, simultaneous and perfect possession of boundless life."[66] Eternity in these descriptions is characterized both by indivisible unity and limitless life and existence. As has been shown above, these notions of divine indivisibility and unboundedness are ontologically rooted in divine simplicity. Eternity, then, is derived from the consideration of how an absolutely simple God (with the concomitant notions of his infinity and immutability) must relate to time.

Aristotle notes that, though time is not synonymous with motion, it is inextricably bound up with it. Time is the "number of movement in respect of the before and after."[67] Anything measured by time must possess some term from which it moves and another at which it arrives: "Those things therefore which are subject to perishing and becoming—generally, those which at one time exist, at another do not—are necessarily in time."[68] Temporal things must be composed of parts—that is, of act and potency—in order for them to move from one term of existence to another. Movement is change and as such requires act-potency composition in order to occur. For this reason Bavinck notes that, "One who says 'time' says motion, change, measurability, computability, limitation, finiteness, creature."[69] It is the essence of time, then, to measure (or "number") the succession of a thing's movement (recalling that movement is broadly conceived as any change whatsoever, physical or otherwise). But this cannot apply to any immovable thing: "In a thing that does not move but which always has itself in the same manner," Holloway points out, "there is not present this part following that part.

---

64. Brakel, *Christian's Reasonable Service*, I: 92.

65. Berkhof, *Systematic Theology*, 60.

66. Boethius, *Philosophiae Consolationis*, V, 6 [10–11].

67. Aristotle, *Physics* 220a25. This description of time is universally accepted by the medieval and Reformed scholastics.

68. Ibid., 221b28–30.

69. Bavinck, *RD*, II: 163.

There is no before and after, no succession. Therefore, just as the notion
of time consists in numbering or observing of what is before and after, or
of what is successive in motion, so in like manner the notion of eternity
consists in the apprehension of the uniformity of that which is entirely
without motion."[70] Two things are indispensible to our conception of
time: (1) a plurality of terms reducible to a term of act (from which) and
a term of potency (to which); (2) a succession of motion between these
terms. It is by denying these two things of God that we approach the
notion of divine eternity.

In *Summa theologiae* I.10.2 Thomas considers a striking objection
to God's eternity: it would seem that God is not eternal since he is immeasurable and eternity is a measure of some duration in being. Thomas
answers with an appeal to divine simplicity: "Eternity is nothing else
but God Himself. Hence God is not called eternal, as if He were in any
way measured; but the idea of measurement is there taken according to
the apprehension of our mind alone."[71] By insisting that God is identical with his eternity, Thomas affirms that the standard of God's unique
successionless life and existence is nothing other than God himself. This
can be summarized by saying that God is the measure of God's eternity.
He does not stand *in* eternity but rather is identical with the eternity by
which he is eternal. It follows that eternity is not a realm of duration that
stands shoulder to shoulder, as it were, with time as merely a different
species in a genus called "measures of duration."[72] It is, rather, the exis-

---

70. Holloway, *Introduction*, 269–70. He rightly says that we "apprehend" the mo-
tionless uniform being rather than "comprehend" it. Without movement in a thing our
minds cannot begin to measure or close on it, as it were. Brian Davies writes, "For
Aquinas . . . our concept of time is parasitic on our recognition of change" (*Thought of
Thomas Aquinas*, 106).

71. *ST* I.10.2, ad 3.

72. Cornelius Van Til argues that time is, in some sense, a replica of eternity. But
eternity, unlike time, is not a realm or atmosphere that stands over against its "subject"
(God), somehow defining him from the outside: "Thinking of the infinity of God in
relation to time . . . we therefore think of the fullness of internal activity of which the
movement in the temporally conditioned universe is a created replica . . . God is the
self-predicator. God is life in himself. Plato's god had the idea of life standing above him;
the Christian God knows no definitory principles over against himself" (*Introduction
to Systematic Theology*, 336). This last statement suggests that God's eternity is not some
defining realm in which he stands, but rather that, as self-predicator, God is identical
with his eternity.

tence and essence of God considered as his complete, undivided, and unchanging life.

As identical with God's dynamic unchanging life, his eternity comprehends instantaneously and simultaneously all of his creative actions in time. Accordingly, Jacques Maritain informs us that "eternity is not a kind of divine time which precedes time. It is a limitless instant which indivisibly embraces the whole succession of time."[73] It can only do this by being ontologically unconditioned by time, standing ontically apart from and above it. Thomas remarks, "For, since time lies within motion, eternity, which is completely outside motion, in no way belongs to time. Furthermore, since the being of what is eternal does not pass away, eternity is present in its presentiality to any time or instant of time."[74] He offers the following illustration:

> Let us consider a determined point on the circumference of a circle. Although it is indivisible, it does not co-exist simultaneously with any other point as to position, since it is the order of position that produces the continuity of the circumference. On the other hand, the center of the circle, which is no part of the circumference, is directly opposed to any given determinate point on the circumference. Hence, whatever is found in any part of time coexists with what is eternal as being present to it, although with respect to some other time it be past or future. Something can be present to what is eternal only by being present to the whole of it, since the eternal does not have the duration of succession. The divine intellect, therefore, sees in the whole of its eternity, as being present to it, whatever takes place through the whole course of time. And yet what takes place in a certain part of time was not always existent.[75]

It is significant that Thomas characterizes God as a "point" in this illustration since a point is entirely non-extended in strict mathematical terms; that is, points are partless. As lacking parts (i.e., simple) God need not turn away from one moment of time on the circumference in order to be *wholly* present to another.[76] Rather, his partlessness enables him to

73. Maritain, *Existence and the Existent*, 113–14.

74. SCG I.66.7.

75. Ibid. In this passage Thomas is primarily concerned to explain how an eternal God can have comprehensive knowledge of all time as well as being ontologically present to things in time while not himself temporal.

76. It is also significant that God is "positioned" at the center of the circle. This indicates that God's simultaneous presence to all temporal things does not demand the

be simultaneously present to all moments of time in the completeness of his being and essence.

In sum, it is divine simplicity that provides the ontological conditions for explaining God's non-successive eternity as well as for explaining how it is that his eternity enables him to comprehend within it his temporally conditioned effects (i.e., creation). When Thomas appeals to divine immutability as the reason for insisting that God alone is eternal (*ST* I.10.3) we may safely deduce that just as the DDS fixes the absoluteness of God's immutability it fixes the absoluteness of his eternity. Lacking all act-potency composition, God cannot possibly be subject to movement and movement is the required condition for a thing to be genuinely temporal.[77]

CONCLUSION

From the discussion in this chapter it appears that those doctrines that are traditionally understood to establish an absolute Creator-creature distinction are dependent upon the DDS for their strength of absoluteness. It is God's simplicity that promotes these doctrines of aseity, unity, infinity, immutability, and eternity to their status as genuinely incommunicable divine attributes. In this way the theological function of the DDS can be understood as that by which God is rightly regarded as most absolute. In chapters 4 and 5 I will further examine the implications of divine simplicity for the absoluteness of God's existence and attributes respectively.

---

difficult proposition that one temporal thing is really present to another at some other location on the circumference.

77. Thomas holds that spiritual substances are not strictly temporal, but are "*aeviternal*" (*ST* I.10.5). This unique type of successive existence corresponds to the relative immutability of the spiritual substances. *Aeviternal* things are not substantially subject to time (even as spiritual substances are not, in themselves, subject to substantial change). It follows that in the strict sense of Aristotle's *Physics* they are not properly subject to motion at all. Joyce explains the difference between temporality and *aeviternity*: "Temporal duration consists in continuous change. *Aevum* is in itself changeless, though connected with changes in the accidental determinations of the subject: and, further, these changes are not continuous but discrete." He adds, "Yet though *aevum* differs fundamentally from time, it differs even more radically from eternity . . . 'Aeviternal' existence is not inclusive of past and future. For a spirit the past is past, and the future has not come. To coexist with a temporal event, that event must be awaited. Only the Infinite transcends the differences of time" (*Principles of Natural Theology*, 326–27).

4

Simplicity and God's Absolute Existence

THE ABSOLUTENESS OF GOD'S existence stands over against the contingent existence of all non-divine things. Indeed, this divine existential absoluteness has traditionally been reached by comparing God's
existence with that of his creatures and removing from our conception
of him everything suggestive of imperfection, dependence, and correlativity. Not only do these features conflict with the attributes considered
in chapter 3, but they also are unbefitting for one who is regarded as
having created the world *ex nihilo*.

Thomists and Reformed theologians have traditionally held that
only an absolute being sufficiently explains and causes the phenomenon
of "being in general."[1] Moreover, the cause of being in general cannot
itself be an instance of such general being without thereby being conceived as existentially self-caused. But such an explanation of the world's
existence easily falls foul of the problem of infinite regress. To stave off
such an illogical and unchristian conclusion classical theologians have
frequently maintained that God is both pure act (*actus purus*) and is
subsistent being itself (*ipsum esse subsistens*). Though these notions are
incomprehensible to the human mind, they consistently represent the
claims of divine simplicity and seem to be a ready answer to the question
of how it is possible that anything exist at all. The conception of God
as *actus purus* and *ipsum esse subsistens* effectually places God beyond
the creaturely mode and order of being, thus upholding his absolute

---

1. This is true whether one is speaking of "being in general" as *ens commune* or as
esse commune. It is important to differentiate between these two as between subsisting
things in general and the principle by which all created subsisting things exist. Even
so, this distinction does not negate the fact that the explanation for both must be an
absolute subsistent being who is neither classified within *ens commune* nor exists by
participation in *esse commune*.

transcendence, while at the same time explaining how such a creaturely order could possibly come to be in the first place.[2] Existential absoluteness alone can ground all existential contingency and becoming.

Not surprisingly, many modern philosophers and theologians object to such a peculiar notion as God being identified with being itself. Christopher Hughes and Anthony Kenny charge that identifying God with existence or being results in the loss of God's richness and fullness. Being is too "thin" and uninteresting a notion to meaningfully identify the God of the Christian tradition. Kenny concludes that identifying God's existence with his essence is just so much "sophistry and illusion"[3] and that identifying him as subsistent *esse* "seems to be equivalent to an ill-formed formula."[4]

It is my contention in this chapter that to just the extent that these critics diminish the identity of God (including his essence) with his existence they diminish the absoluteness of his existence. Consequently, they also considerably weaken the argument for how it is that God can be the sufficient reason for the existence of the universe and its pluriformity of perfections. Any ontological distinction drawn between God and that whereby he exists (his *esse*) results in the conception of him as yet another instance of being in general, even if one continues to argue that he is the greatest and most perfect existent.

This chapter unfolds through three sections. First, the absoluteness of God's existence is considered by way of contrast with the creaturely composition of existence and essence. Special focus upon Thomas's teaching of the "real distinction" between a creature's *esse* and *essentia* serves to set in sharp relief the real identity of *esse* and *essentia* in God. Second, the understanding of God as *ipsum esse subsistens* is considered

2. Aquinas explains that as *ipsum esse subsistens* God comprehends in himself the perfection of all things: "Since therefore God is subsisting being itself, nothing of the perfection of being can be wanting to Him. Now all created perfections are included in the perfection of being; for things are perfect, precisely so far as they have being after some fashion. It follows therefore that the perfection of no one thing is wanting to God" (*ST* I.4.2). As *ipsum esse subsistens* God's act of existence supplies the idea or exemplar forms after which anything whatsoever is created. Thus, the very feature by which God absolutely transcends creatures, his identity with his own act of existence, is also the feature that enables him to be the absolutely sufficient Creator and reason for the world's existence and its plurality of perfections.

3. Kenny, *Aquinas*, 60.

4. Kenny, *Aquinas on Being*, 193. For Hughes's objections along these same lines see the relevant discussion in chapter 1.

as the natural consequent of the identity of his existence and essence. The non-abstract sense of *ipsum esse* as predicated of God is contrasted to the more abstract notion of *ipsum esse* as it refers to "being in general" (either as *ens commune* or *esse commune*). Third, being in general and the being of God are shown to stand in absolute contrast, constituting two entirely different orders of being and yet not entirely inaccessible to each other. Accordingly, it is denied that God can be located on a single chain of being with non-divine things and affirmed that, as God's proper effect, the existence of creatures is analogical to his own existence.

REAL DISTINCTION BETWEEN *ESSE* AND *ESSENTIA* IN CREATURES

Giving expression to the absoluteness of God's existence is more easily done by comparing him with creatures than by attempting to depict that existential absoluteness baldly and abstractly. For this reason, Thomas Aquinas and many who follow him have seen fit to express God's absoluteness in terms of the identity of his existence with his essence and to contrast this with the creature's composite mode of being.[5] The basic metaphysical contours of essence-existence composition (in creatures) and identity (in God) have already been briefly sketched in chapter 2 above. This section intends to elaborate upon the conclusions established there, particularly as they relate to creaturely contingency.[6]

In order to understand why Thomas insists upon distinguishing between being and essence in creatures and identifying them in God it is expedient first that we have a firm grasp of what is meant by terms such as "being" and "essence." In brief, "being" can be understood in two distinct (though related) senses. First, it can denote an existent as a whole subsisting entity. It is in this sense that we identify rocks, plants, unintelligent animals, and humans as *beings*. In Latin this sense of "being" is rendered as *ens* and is indicative of complete subsisting entities

5. For a brief introduction to Thomas's unique metaphysics of existence see Thibault, *Creation and Metaphysics*.

6. Jacques Maritain defines contingent being as "being which does not contain in itself the ground of its being, its sufficient reason" (*Preface to Metaphysics*, 131). See also Jan Aertsen's discussion of Thomas's twofold conception of the creature's contingency: (1) as *creature* it is contingent because it depends upon God's will for its existence, and (2) as a *nature* it is contingent because it depends upon the principles of which God has constituted it and by which its continuance in nature is preserved (*Nature and Creature*, 239–48).

as they exist in reality.[7] Second, "being" can also signify a constituent *within* a complete subsisting entity that accounts for its actuality in the real world. This sense is typically denoted by the Latin term *esse* and indicates the *principle* of a being's existence rather than its existence as an actual entity; this is "being" understood as that *by which* anything that is exists.[8] Finally, "essence" (*essentia*), as the term itself suggests, derives from the notion of being and signifies that which possesses *esse*. Like *esse*, it is also regarded as an internal constituent and *principle* of a complete being (*ens*), not subsisting as an existent in itself. It functions as that *by which* a being is *what* it is.[9] In sum, the three terms, each applying to the same substance, possess roughly the following distinct connotations: *ens* denotes the subsisting thing itself (entitativeness); *esse* indicates that *by which it is* (isness); and *essentia* signifies *that by which it is what it is* (whatness).[10]

When Thomas contends for the "real distinction" between creaturely being and essence he is primarily thinking of *esse* and *essentia*, not *ens* and *essentia*. For our present purposes it should be observed that he makes this observation about the real distinction (though never treating it *ex professo*) not merely as a bit of metaphysical speculation, but in an attempt to demonstrate that the observation *that* creaturely essences exist is not sufficient to explain *why* they exist. Inasmuch as a creature's essence does not explain the fact of its existence we must presume that its existence is somehow not an intrinsic feature of its essence, but is really distinct from it. This being so, creaturely essences are regarded as existentially contingent. Thomas moves rather fluidly from this observation to the conclusion that only one whose existence is identical with

7. It bears pointing out that *ens* can also be applied to accidents, which, although they are beings in a secondary sense, are still *complete* beings within their category. *Ens* applies primarily to those entities classified in the category of substance and secondarily, yet still properly, to those entities found in all the other categories.

8. Many Thomists prefer to render this principial sense of being with the verbal expression "to be" in order to differentiate it from the connotations of actual subsistent being latent in the term *ens*.

9. In creatures essences *qua* essences don't subsist; they only exist in particular beings (*ens*) after they have received their principle of actuality, *esse*.

10. A useful summary of these key terms is found in Kossel, "Principles of St. Thomas's Distinction between the *Esse* and *Ratio* of Relation," 29–30. See also the informative discussion in Elders, *The Metaphysics of Being of St. Thomas Aquinas*, 190–217. On the structure and role of *ens* in Thomas's thought, see te Velde, *Participation and Substantiality*, 200–206.

his essence (i.e., existentially simple) can be regarded as an absolute or non-contingent being.

In *De ente et essentia* Aquinas famously makes the case for the real distinction in creatures by insisting that the *fact* of their existence is not necessary to one's knowledge of their *whatness*:

> Everything that does not belong to the concept of an essence or quiddity comes to it from outside and enters into composition with the essence, because no essence can be understood without its parts. Now, every essence or quiddity can be understood without knowing anything about its being. I can know, for instance, what a man or a phoenix is and still be ignorant whether it has being in reality. From this it is clear that being is other than essence or quiddity, unless perhaps there is a reality whose quiddity is its being.[11]

The Angelic Doctor is quick to point out that any constituent part of a being (such as *esse* in any *ens*) is either from the essence of the being itself or comes to it from the outside. Now, if *esse* and *essentia* are really distinct in each creature the only explanation for its *esse* is either that it was caused by the essence or it came to the creature from "an extrinsic principle." His argument thus proceeds: "Now being [i.e., *esse*] itself cannot be [efficiently] caused by the form or quiddity of a thing . . . because that thing would then be its own cause and would bring itself into being, which is impossible."[12] It is a short step from this conclusion about the creature's inability to account for the fact of its existence to the conclusion that its "extrinsic principle" of existence must be a perfectly simple agent in which *esse* and *essentia* are identical:

> It follows that everything whose being is distinct from its nature must have being from another. And because everything that exists through another is reduced to that which exists through itself as to its first cause, there must be a reality that is the cause of all being for all other things, because it is pure being. If this were not so, we could go on to infinity in causes, for everything that is not pure being has a cause of its being, as has been said.[13]

---

11. *DEE*, 4 [6]. The man-phoenix argument in itself does not yield a real distinction, but only a logical one. I am grateful to Professor Gregory Doolan for pointing this out to me.

12. Ibid., 4 [7].

13. Ibid. See the helpful comments in Bobik, *Aquinas on Being and Essence*, 172–75.

Obviously, the hinge of this whole argument is the plausibility that the distinction between a creature's *esse* and *essentia* is indeed *real*.[14]

Thomas again utilizes this contrast in his commentary on Lombard's *Sentences* in an attempt to exposit the existential uniqueness of God's name ("He Who is") in Exodus 3:14:

> [I]n everything that is, it is possible to consider its quiddity, through which it subsists in a determinate nature, and its *being* [*esse*], through which it is said of that which actually is, the name "thing" (*res*) is imposed on a thing from its quiddity . . . [T]he name "He Who is" or "a being" (*ens*) is imposed by the very act of *being* [*ipso actu essendi*]. But although it is the case in any created thing its essence [*essentia*] differs from its *being* [*esse*], the thing is properly denominated from its quiddity and not from the act of *being*, e.g., a man from humanity. In God, however, His very *being* is His quiddity: and so the name that is taken from *being* properly names Him and is His proper name, just like the proper name of man, which is taken from his quiddity.[15]

No creature is named from its *esse* inasmuch as all things are named from their essence and it is not the essence of any creature to be.[16] Existence does not enter into the essential identity of any non-divine thing. Inasmuch as Thomas reads Exodus 3:14 to name God from his *esse*, he concludes that God's very essence must be identical with his existence.[17] In this passage Thomas does not attempt to prove the real dis-

---

14. Leo Sweeney offers numerous arguments for why this distinction in creatures is real and not merely mental in his, *Metaphysics of Authentic Existentialism*, 70–75.

15. *Scriptum super libros Sententiarum*, I.8.1.1.

16. Part of the difficulty that we have in separating our conception of creaturely essences from their acts of existence stems from the fact that all essences, though not existing necessarily or by definition, are truly *oriented* toward *esse*. Recalling that essence corresponds to potency and existence to act, Maritain reminds us that "it is of the very essence of potency to be referred to act and to be knowable only through the act to which it is referred" (*Preface to Metaphysics*, 110). Thus, we can only conceive (intellectually) of essences as existing although existence does not belong properly to the essences as such. For instance, we may conceive of the essence of the dodo bird, which, as now extinct, does not *actually* exist but to which we supply hypothetical (mental) existence in order to represent the essence to our minds.

17. Gilson rightly notes that the Exodus 3:14 passage is not properly making a metaphysical or philosophical claim, but rather serves as the biblical warrant for such claims: "No hint of metaphysics, but God speaks, *causa finita est*, and Exodus lays down the principle from which henceforth the whole of Christian philosophy will be suspended" (*The Spirit of Medieval Philosophy*, 51).

tinction between essence and existence in creatures, but instead simply presupposes it as background to his exposition of the divine essence as identical with the divine existence. Theologically, Thomas's point seems to be that God's very name, "I AM," conveys his existential absoluteness over against the creature's contingency. Both God and creatures are named from their essences, but only God's name includes his very act of existence.[18]

But what are we to make of the Thomistic real distinction? Theologically, it is readily agreeable to the orthodox Christian outlook to insist that no creature exists essentially, that is, through its essence. If it did so exist then we should have no need to look back of or outside of its essence for any principle or explanation of its actual existence. Its essence alone would suffice to reveal to us both *what* it is and *whereby* it exists. But the doctrine of creation *ex nihilo* closes off such an explanation since it teaches that God is the ultimate sufficient and efficient cause of all creaturely existence. So, the more perplexing question for the Christian is: What are we to make of the real distinction *metaphysically*? This question has already been partially answered in chapter 2, but a few additional observations now need to be made.[19]

David Oderberg defends the real distinction doctrine by noting, "No essence can *exist* apart from its actual instances, but that is not the same as saying that its existence just consists in the existence of its actual

---

18. Thomas makes the same argument in *SCG* I.22 [10]: "This sublime truth Moses was taught by our Lord. When Moses asked our Lord: 'If the children of Israel say to me: what is His name? What shall I say to them?' The Lord replied: 'I AM WHO AM . . . You shall say to the children of Israel: HE WHO IS has sent me to you' (Exod. 3:13, 14). By this our Lord showed that His own proper name is HE WHO IS. Now, names have been devised to signify the natures or essences of things. It remains, then, that the divine being is God's essence or nature." Gilson observes, "There is no treatise on being in the Bible, but everyone remembers the famous passage of *Exodus*: III, 14 . . . Now, no Christian needs to draw from this statement any metaphysical conclusions, but, if he does, he can draw only one, namely, that God is Being" (*Being and Some Philosophers*, 30).

19. For a historical analysis of some medieval friends and foes of Thomas's real distinction doctrine see Wippel, "The Relationship Between Essence and Existence in Late-Thirteenth-Century Thought," 131–64. Many of the medieval critics who thought they were rejecting Thomas's real distinction were really rejecting Giles of Rome's distorted explanation of Thomas. Giles took the real distinction between essence and existence to be a distinction between two *things* (*res*) and not between two principles (as Thomas actually taught). See the appropriate clarifications in the final section of chapter 2 above, especially those offered by Raeymaeker and Phelan.

instances."[20] To demonstrate this point he considers Thomas's assertion that we can know a thing's essence (e.g., of a man or a phoenix) and yet be entirely ignorant of its actual existence. Does this in fact *prove* the real distinction between existence and essence? After all, do we not frequently grasp essences while not grasping them in their *entirety*? This does not mean that those parts of the essence we do not grasp are really distinct from the essence, does it? Why should a thing's existence be an exception? Oderberg maintains that we have not grasped a thing's essence if we implicitly or explicitly exclude from it any of its constituents; at best our grasp would be incorrect and at worst non-existent. By neglecting to include a thing's essential constituents in our consideration of it we actually forfeit any claim to know its essence. Oderberg illustrates: "I cannot grasp the essence of whales correctly if I think of them as fish, and not at all if I think of them as land-dwelling creatures."[21] But what then of a being's existence? Do we surrender knowledge of its essence if we do not include the fact of its existence? Oderberg states, "In the case of existence in respect of contingent things, the answer is surely that I do not misconceive any such thing if I exclude existence from it. Hence existence cannot be of the essence of contingent things."[22]

Oderberg also defends the real distinction against the modern notion that anything that is true of a thing must be a characteristic or property of that thing. This argument is frequently used by philosophers to repudiate the real distinction doctrine. The reasoning is that if something truly exists then existence must be one of that thing's characteristics. But this does not follow. If we understand *esse* as that by which an essence is made to *actually* exist then existence is to essence as act is to potency. But just as the passive potency (*qua* potency) is not identified as partially act, so also essences cannot be conceived of as including existence within them. Oderberg draws on the Thomistic metaphysics of act-potency to make his point:

> Just as form actualizes potentiality to produce a substance, so existence can be thought of as actualizing form itself. Form actualizes matter; existence actualizes form. These are not really separable, since when the former happens the latter by that very

20. Oderberg, *Real Essentialism*, 122.

21. Ibid., 123.

22. Ibid. Oderberg's confidence here is partially attributable to his immanent realist approach to the knowledge of essences. See ibid., 81–85.

fact obtains, and vice versa. But they should be thought of as really distinct acts, and existence should be described (not defined) as . . . the *last* actuality of a substance. (For non-substances, existence is had derivatively from the actualization of the forms of the substances on which the non-substances are ontologically dependent.) Hence existence is not a part of essence, nor identical with essence, nor a characteristic of existing things. Yet it is still true of them.[23]

That which makes the essence to be cannot itself be part of the essence. To the extent that one insists upon either fully or partially identifying existence and essence in creatures, the contingency of the creature has been replaced by a measure of existential absoluteness.

John Wippel further strengthens the argument for the real distinction doctrine by identifying its critical component in Thomas's conclusion that there cannot be more than one being whose essence is identical with its act of existence. Wippel contends that it is not necessary to understand that such a being is none other than the God of the Bible in order to appreciate the power of this insight for prompting the conclusion of real distinction in creatures.[24] Following his suggestion (in *De ente et essentia* 4) that an exception to the real distinction may occur in one whose quiddity is its being, Thomas immediately notes that such a reality "must be unique and primary."[25] He gives three reasons for this, observing that a being is only multiplied: (1) by the addition of some difference as when a generic nature is multiplied in a species through the addition of specific difference; (2) by the reception of some form in different parts of matter such that a single form is thereby found in

23. Ibid., 124–25.

24. Wippel argues that the actual existence of such an existentially simple being is not necessary for the force of the argument to render the conclusion of the real distinction. The fact that any instance of the real identity of existence and essence could only be singular is sufficient to show that entities found in multiplicity (including angels) must be instances of beings whose essence and existence are really distinct. If this were not so the essences could not show up in multiples or even hypothetical multiples. Accordingly, Wippel writes, "If he [Thomas] has successfully shown that it is impossible for there to be more than one being in which essence and existence are identical, then he can conclude to factual otherness of essence and existence in all other entities" (*Metaphysical Themes*, 115). Wippel's argument for the immediate purpose of proving the real distinction in creatures seems sound, though it is not necessary that we also argue, as he does elsewhere, that creaturely being is itself intelligible whether or not one acknowledges God. That is a different matter altogether.

25. *DEE*, 4 [6].

various material individuals; and (3) by the distinction between what is
separate and what is received in something.[26] From these rules restrict-
ing multiplication Thomas concludes that nothing that is identical with
its existence can be multiple:

> Now granted that there is a reality that is pure being, so that be-
> ing itself is subsistent, this being would not receive the addition
> of a difference, because then it would not be being alone but be-
> ing with the addition of a form. Much less would it receive the
> addition of matter, because then it would not be subsistent, but
> material, being. It follows that there can be only one reality that
> is identical with its being. In everything else, then, its being must
> be other than its quiddity, nature, or form.[27]

As Wippel sees it, this is enough to establish metaphysically the
real distinction in everything other than the one who is "pure being."
The argument in summary is that, "If it is impossible for there to be
more than one being whose essence is its *esse*, then it follows that in
all other beings essence and existence are not identical. And this follows whether or not that single exception has already been assumed or
proven to exist, or whether it is simply regarded as a possibility."[28] Of
course, Thomas does not think that an existentially simple God is merely
possible, rather he is absolutely necessary to account for the fact of any

26. Ibid. The third point, though Platonic in its overtones, is basically the claim
that a single form can only be one in its separated mode and multiple only insofar as
it is participated and received by substances not identical with itself. Forms in their
separate, non-participated mode cannot be multiple. Now, if we improperly allow *esse*
to be regarded as a form (for the sake of argument) it stands to reason that only one
thing can possibly be identical with *esse* itself. All other existents must have their *esse*
("to be") through participation. In Platonic expression we would say that inasmuch as
only one thing can be any form *itself* (e.g., wisdom itself, goodness itself, truth itself, and
the like) so also "being" *itself* can only be one. See the useful summary by Joseph Bobik,
Aquinas on Being and Essence, 171. Of course, as a modified Aristotelian, Thomas does
not believe that forms (understood as universals) subsist in themselves.

27. *DEE*, 4 [6].

28. Wippel, *Metaphysical Themes*, 117. In the context Wippel is particularly inter-
ested to refute Joseph Owens's claim that God's existence must first be proved for one to
arrive at the metaphysical doctrine of the real distinction. Though Wippel acknowledges that in some places Thomas does argue in this order, from God as subsistent *esse* to
the real distinction of existence and essence in all non-divine things, he is unconvinced
that this knowledge is absolutely necessary to the discovery of the real distinction. In
other words, the existential contingency of all creatures is knowable simply upon the
rational conclusion that there can be only one being in which existence and essence are
identical. See also, Wippel, *Metaphysical Thought*, 150–57.

instance of contingent existence whatsoever. Though such a conclusion is required to ultimately account for existence in contingent things, it is not prerequisite to the demonstration of the real distinction between their essence and existence.

So what is the importance of affirming the real distinction doctrine in our attempt to establish the absoluteness of God's existence? Oderberg answers that, "by grasping the real distinction we make room for the very idea of contingency, for in contingent things no essence *must* be actualized."[29] Additionally, the real distinction doctrine makes metaphysical space for the notion of an absolute being whose essence *is* his existence. "Theists identify this being as God, and it is traditionally held that God is *pure actuality*, i.e., a being that has no potentiality in its constitution, this absence being the root cause of its unlimited and infinite nature."[30] Forfeiture of the real distinction doctrine eradicates any possibility of expressing metaphysically the absoluteness of God's existence and the non-absoluteness of the creature's existence.

Having considered the real distinction as the metaphysical framework for explaining creaturely contingency, it is fitting that we should turn now to the consideration of the real identity of God's essence and existence (i.e., existential simplicity) as the framework by which his ontological non-contingency is explicated. In the Christian tradition this real identity has frequently been expressed by saying that God is subsistent being itself (*ipsum esse subsistens*).

GOD AS *IPSUM ESSE SUBSISTENS*

Thomas Aquinas is well known for his insistence upon God's identity with his act of being: "*being* must be the essence or nature of God."[31] Indeed, Thomas insists that it is this identity with being that most fundamentally distinguishes God and sets him apart from all other beings. Contrary to creatures, which are individuated by their bits of matter or respective essences and not by their acts of existence, God is individuated by his *esse* and not by some principle of reception or contraction as in the case of composite beings: "God's being is individualised and distinct from every other being by the very fact that it is self-subsistent

29. Oderberg, *Real Essentialism*, 125.

30. Ibid. Oderberg uses "cause" here to signify sufficient ontological condition.

31. *DP* 7.2.

being, and is not something additional to a nature that is distinct from its being. Now every other being that is not subsistent must be individualised by the nature and essence that subsists in that being: and of such beings it is true that the being of A is distinct from the being of B by the fact that it is the being of another nature."[32] The self-subsistent and non-contracted manner of God's *esse* is what supplies the "difference" that in all finite existents is supplied by their respective essences. Thomas accordingly declares, "Now God is act both pure and primary."[33] This rather grandiose claim that God is primarily distinguished by his identity with being (or act) is also endorsed by Herman Bavinck in a striking passage:

> God is the real, the true being, the fullness of being, the sum total of all reality and perfection, the totality of being, from which all other being owes its existence. He is an immeasurable and unbounded ocean of being; the absolute being who alone has being in himself. Now, this description of God's being deserves preference over that of personality, love, fatherhood, and so forth, because it encompasses all of God's attributes in an absolute sense. In other words, by this description, God is recognized and confirmed as God in all his perfections.[34]

Impressive as these assertions are, we are still faced with the challenge of explaining them. Critics of this Thomistic tendency to identify God as *ipsum esse subsistens* find such an identification to be philosophically absurd as well as uninformative and uninteresting. After all, Thomas himself admits that "being" is the most common of features as it is found without exception in every single existent.[35] How could

32. Ibid., 7.2, ad 5.

33. Ibid., 1.1.

34. Bavinck, *RD*, II: 123. This real identity of God's *esse* and *essentia* is also implied in the Second London Confession of Faith (2.3) when it states that God "is not divided in nature and being." The implication of God's identity with his *esse* for all the other perfections ascribed to him will be considered in chapter 5. For a further explication of the preferred status accorded to "being" in naming God, see Aertsen, *Medieval Philosophy and the Transcendentals*, 364–67.

35. For instance, in *ST* I.65.3 Aquinas suggests that being is the *most* general or universal principle to be found in a thing: "Now the underlying principle in things is always more universal than that which informs and restricts it; thus, being is more universal than living, living than understanding, matter than form." The reason "being" is more universal than living is that even those non-living entities such as rocks and cars can still be said to *be* even if they cannot be said to *live*. Upon analysis it is *being* that is discovered without exception in everything that is.

this possibly serve to meaningfully identify God and set him apart from all other beings? Furthermore, is it even coherent to speak of *esse* as self-subsistent?

Anthony Kenny faults Thomas's depiction of God as *ipsum esse* precisely because *esse* appears too universal to meaningfully identify God. He points to Thomas's affirmation of the commonness of being in *De potentia* 7.2 when arguing for God as the proper cause of being: "different causes having different natures and forms must needs have their respective different proper effects: so that if they have one effect in common, this is not the proper effect of any one of them, but of some higher cause by whose virtue they act . . . Now all created causes have one common effect which is *being*."[36] In the context Thomas's point is that one common effect, such as the *being*, which is found in all existents, cannot have multiple proper causes; each effect has only one *proper* cause that produces its effects in similarity to its own nature. Kenny's criticism, though, disregards Thomas's greater point about effects and their proper causes and focuses instead on the fact of being's commonness. He concludes that inasmuch as being seems to be the common attribute possessed by anything with substantial or accidental form it "seems to be the thinnest possible kind of predicate; to be, so understood, is to have that attribute which is common to mice and men, dust and angels." He adds, "This attribute, being common to every substance, could hardly constitute the particular essence of any subject."[37] It would appear nothing so common could meaningfully differentiate one thing from another, much less God from creatures.[38]

Kenny further argues that naming God as *ipsum esse* seems very much like a failure to predicate anything at all. This follows from his assumption that existence is not a first-level predicate or concept, but a second-level concept.[39] Thus, it always points to the factuality (or *is-ness*) of some thing's quiddity. The *whatness* is the first-level concept and the *thatness*, signified by "is," belongs to second-level predications. For

---

36. *DP* 7.2.

37. Kenny, *The Five Ways*, 92. See also, Kenny, *Aquinas on Being*, 121.

38. For a sympathetic explanation of how and why Thomas names God from common transcendentals such as "being," "one," "good," and "true" see Aertsen, *Medieval Philosophy and the Transcendentals*, 372–78.

39. For an example of Kenny's commitment to existence as a Fregean second-level concept see his discussion in *Aquinas on Being*, 195–204. For a nuanced response consult Klima, "On Kenny on Aquinas on Being," 567–80.

this reason, identifying God as "He who is" or "He is" just seems to be an incomplete sentence. Kenny would ask, "He who is *what*?" Without some addition to the affirmation of being the predication remains non-sensical. Thomas's attempt to make God's *esse* a meaningful concept is logically and linguistically misguided, according to Kenny. "Aquinas," he tells us, "in order to prevent God's *esse* from being the applicability of a quite uninformative predicate, turns it into the applicability of a predicate which is no predicate at all."[40] Whenever we say that something "is F" we simply intend to indicate that it is specified in some particular way. But Thomas, in saying simply that "God is," does not at all mean to say that he is a *kind* of thing.[41] But without the specification of some particular kind, Kenny wonders how "God is" can possibly be a meaningful sentence, much less the name of God. "So interpreted," he opines, "the incommunicable name [He who is] seems to be just an ill-formed formula."[42] Underlying Kenny's objection, as will be noted below, is his commitment to a univocal notion of being as predicated in the same way of anything whatsoever.[43]

Yet another difficulty that Kenny has with identifying God as *ipsum esse subsistens* is that it appears to be applied to God both concretely *and* abstractly: "God does not just be, he is being."[44] He is aware that Thomas affirms this somewhat enigmatic notion in order to uphold the denial that God possesses any accidents. But it seems that identifying God with *esse* abstractly, far from distinguishing God from the world, makes him almost totally unidentifiable. Indeed, it seems to suggest that God is the

40. Kenny, *The Five Ways*, 94. Elsewhere he writes, "[I]f a sentence containing a predicate after 'is' indicates the subject to be in a certain way, then a sentence containing 'is' with no addition indicates the subject to be in no way. Once again, the consideration of pure *esse* seems to lead us to a void" (*Aquinas on Being*, 112).

41. It should be observed that this is precisely what Thomas's DDS suggests when it is denied that God is composed of genus and species.

42. Kenny, *The Five Ways*, 94. This is exactly the charge taken up by Christopher Hughes when he remarks, "it seems clear that nothing subsistent could be just existent" (*On a Complex Theory*, 21). The logic of Kenny and Hughes is that *substances* or *things* subsist and "to be" is merely a second-level predicate indicating the thing's *actual* subsistence. To Kenny, "God is" is just an incomplete sentence.

43. Consider Kenny's assessment of the predicate for existence, "*x* is F": "Such a predicate, we might say, seems to be the totally uninformative highest (but minimal) common factor of all predicates: but being, so understood, would be too thin and universal an attribute to be the essence of anything" (*Aquinas*, 57).

44. Kenny, *The Five Ways*, 94.

most universal of the Platonic ideas. Kenny remarks, "What all men call 'God', on this account, is the Platonic idea of Being."[45] But this "idea" must surely hold true for all substances. Thus to identify God with being abstractly is "at best uninformative and at worst unintelligible."[46]

The challenges issued by Kenny (and echoed by Christopher Hughes) against the real identity of God's essence with his act of existence can be met with a number of considerations. First, we should not lose sight of the fact that Thomas derives this conclusion that God is *ipsum esse subsistens* from the affirmation that God is entirely identical with *that by which* he exists; that is, that God is his own ontological sufficient condition. Indispensible to this existential self-sufficiency is the affirmation that God is pure act (*actus purus*), for only if God is pure act (i.e., without passive potency) can it truly be said that his existence is uncaused and unreceived.[47] From this we may readily conclude that "to be" is not predicated of God in exactly the same way as it is of the creature.

Kenny and Hughes tend to speak of *esse* as though it were exactly the same in everything to which it is attributed. They simply take *esse* to be "an on/off property" that a thing either has or does not have.[48] Inasmuch as *esse* in creatures always points to the existence of some particular essence or *differentia*, they reason, it must function in exactly that same way for God. If "to be" did not refer to some additional principle of differentiation then God would not be *this* or *that*. But, of course, this is precisely what the doctrine of God's simplicity maintains. Rudi te Velde explains: "God is not a *particular* being among others, not even the highest one: He *is* his being. One cannot speak of God as if He were 'this' but not 'that' . . . God is not one amidst others, particularized within the common space of being, but He is 'being itself' (*ipsum esse*). The way of *simplicitas* leads ultimately to the identity in God of essence and being."[49]

---

45. Ibid., 95.

46. Ibid.

47. Aquinas states in *SCG* I.22 [7]: "Being, furthermore, is the name of an act, for a thing is not said to be because it is in potency but because it is in act. Everything, however, that has an act diverse from it is related to that act as potency to act; for potency and act are said relatively to one another. If, then, the divine essence is something other than its being, the essence and the being are thereby related as potency and act. But we have shown that in God there is no potency [*SCG* I.16], but that He is pure act. God's essence, therefore, is not something other than His being."

48. Hughes, *On a Complex Theory*, 27.

49. te Velde, *Aquinas on God*, 79. By insisting upon the real identity of God's *esse* and *essentia* Christian thought transcends the ordinary metaphysical conception of

Undoubtedly, this is where Kenny and Hughes break with Thomas. For them, God *is* one being among others, whereas for Thomas God is the cause of being and so cannot be counted among those beings in general. He is existentially distinguished from all other existents not by this or that, but by the fact that in him existence is self-subsistent and is not something received and marked off by an essence.

Given that God is pure act it follows that denominating him "*ipsum esse*" must carry a different sense than when we speak of *ipsum esse* generally, that is, of *esse commune*. The difference between the "being itself" that is God and the "being itself" that is the general being common to all non-divine things is that God's *esse* is a *self-subsistent act of existence* while the *esse* commonly attributed to creatures does not subsist in itself. God is not abstract being, "but being that is fully determinate in itself and subsistent, and from which all other things derive their being. As *ipsum esse per se subsistens*, God is formally determined as the cause of all beings."[50] And as the cause of being God cannot be an instance of *esse commune* unless he is existentially self-caused, which is impossible.

This twofold sense of *esse* (divine and creaturely) also allows us to deny that *ipsum esse* is too abstract to be identical with God. Indeed, insofar as *esse commune* is considered as *ipsum esse* it must be in an abstract sense since there is no such thing as *esse commune per se subsistens*.[51] In non-divine things it is a principle by which complete created substances are said to be; but as an intrinsic principle of the subsisting creaturely being (*ens*) it does not subsist in itself. In God, though,

---

esse. As Maritain informs us, "Metaphysics uses the concept of existence in order to know a reality which is not an essence, but is the very act of existing" (*Existence and the Existent*, 34). Robert Sokolowski argues that Thomas's introduction of *ipsum esse subsistens* is evidence that in his thought "Aristotelian metaphysics has given way to the metaphysics of *esse*" (*The God of Faith and Reason*, 108). For a terse explanation of the *ipsum esse subsistens* formula as employed by Aquinas, see te Velde, *Participation and Substantiality*, 119–25.

50. te Velde, *Aquinas on God*, 81.

51. *Esse commune* considered in itself is abstract because it can only exist *per se* in the intellect. That is to say that in creation one never discovers *esse* subsisting *per se*, but always subsisting *per aliud*. The *esse* that is common to all creatures is contracted and limited by the essence of each creature in which it is found and only actually exists in that contracted and composite relationship. In this sense its commonness is much like that of an Aristotelian universal, which never subsists *per se*. Thomas states in *SCG* I.26 [5], "that which is common to many is not outside the many except by reason alone." See also, Knasas, *Being and Some Twentieth-Century Thomists*, 241–44.

esse is not a principle in the proper sense, but is simply the Godhead itself considered as its own sufficient reason for existing.[52] Te Velde emphasizes that in God *ispum esse* "is not abstract, but most concrete and fully determined; God is not merely being without essence but being that has fully and completely 'essentialized,' and, as such, God possesses the whole infinite fullness of being."[53] God's *esse* is not like the abstract simple *esse* of composite entities, which is only actualized in composition with an essence really distinct from it. Rather, God is the personal, self-subsistent simple *esse* because of the real identity of his essence with his existence. Te Velde clarifies this non-abstract notion of *ipsum esse*:

> This impression of abstractness, with its connotations of being inert, static, and lifeless, may be partly due to the fact that the received picture of Thomas's conception of God is particularly dominated by the doctrine of divine simplicity without taking sufficiently into account how the idea of simplicity is intrinsically qualified by the idea of perfection and subsistence. What Thomas tries to think by means of the formula *ipsum esse per se subsistens* is, in fact, the most concrete; not concreteness as a result of the fact that a simple form is received into something else, a material substrate, but the full *concretio* of being itself which is, as it were, "individualized" and distinguished from everything else by the fact that it subsists through itself.[54]

Finally, in addition to the twofold sense of *esse* and the non-abstractness of God as *ipsum esse*, it should be observed that God is identified as *ipsum esse subsistens* because he is the proper cause of being in general; being is his proper effect. This is the very point that Thomas makes in *De potentia* 7.2 and that Kenny virtually ignores in his consideration of that passage.[55] The underlying maxim is that all effects preex-

---

52. The reason for denying that God's *esse* is a *principle* of his being is that, as Aquinas states, "a principle is naturally prior to that whose principle it is" (*SCG* I.26 [4]). But nothing is prior to God and God cannot be prior to himself. Therefore, the divine *esse* is not a principle of his being but rather just is God in his actual subsistence.

53. te Velde, *Aquinas on God*, 81.

54. Ibid., 84.

55. Even when Kenny does acknowledge that Thomas is arguing for the likeness between the nature of a cause and its proper effect, he seems unwillingly to adjust his critique to Thomas's causal argument. Thus, even after noting Thomas's denial that God's *esse* is the *esse* that is common to creatures, Kenny still insists that the reason why God can differ from common *esse* "is only by being the Platonic Idea of that *esse*" (*Aquinas on Being*, 121). But Platonic Ideas are not the efficient causes of anything and

ist eminently in their proper causes. Rather than posing a problem for the *ipsum esse subsistens* doctrine, though, the commonness of being among creatures actually *demands* just such a conception of God insofar as he is the first efficient cause of all creaturely existence.

It is observed in *De potentia* 7.2 that as one agent causes this *to be*, another agent causes that *to be* and their common effect is being while their proper effects differ as this from that. But, this multitude of improper causes does not sufficiently explain the common effect of being because no effect can have more than one proper cause. Thomas concludes, then, that there must be some "higher cause" back of the various proximate causes to which being belongs as its proper effect. Moreover, the nature or essence of this proper efficient cause of *esse* must itself be *esse* inasmuch as any agent's proper effect is always a likeness or reproduction of its own nature: "Now the proper effect of any cause proceeds therefrom in likeness to its nature."[56] Thomas clearly expresses this point when he states, "it belongs to the nature of action that an agent produce its like, since each thing acts according as it is in act. The form of an effect, therefore, is certainly found in some measure in a transcending cause, but according to another mode and another way."[57] Thus, for Aquinas, every agent must actually *be* the form of the effects it causes to exist; every cause produces something that in some way is like itself. This raises the question posed by John Wippel: "How does [Thomas] justify this?"[58]

---

cannot possibly correspond to what Thomas means when he argues that God is *ipsum esse* on account of being the proper efficient cause of *esse commune*. Kenny fails to genuinely engage the question in the context of efficient causality and thus seems to talk past Thomas when he maintains that Thomas's doctrine amounts to nothing more than identifying God with a Platonic Idea.

56. *DP* 7.2. See te Velde's discussion on being as God's proper effect, in *Participation and Substantiality*, 176–81.

57. *SCG* I.29 [2]. See also, *ST* I.45.5. Etienne Gilson notes that the manner in which all creaturely forms preexist in God is "under the mode of intelligible being, that is, in the form of ideas" (*The Christian Philosophy of St. Thomas Aquinas*, 126). See chapter 6 below for a discussion on how all created things can preexist as ideas in God and yet God still be absolutely simple.

58. Wippel, *Metaphysical Thought*, 517. Undoubtedly, many will find these metaphysical niceties of Thomas's argument somewhat perplexing at first, maybe even overly speculative. But, as Wippel shows, Thomas's view of proper causes and effects fits quite naturally with his act-potency metaphysics.

The key to Thomas's claim that causes produce only things in their own likeness is his insistence that agents act only as they themselves are in act. No agent can produce an effect without being in act itself. "Moreover," Wippel explains, "it seems evident that if an agent is to communicate something to an effect, it must actually have or at least virtually possess what it is to communicate to its effect."[59] Importantly, he adds, "It is clear that Thomas is here thinking of principle agents, not of purely instrumental ones."[60] In sum, then, an efficient cause cannot give a form to an effect that it does not itself possess in some actual way. Now, non-divine agents only cause the *esse* in their various effects insofar as they are the *instrumental* causes of those things; but God causes all *esse* as the *principle* cause and so is himself *esse* in a manner transcendent to the *esse* of his effects.[61]

All told, the notion of God as *ipsum esse subsistens* follows negatively from the denial of any real *esse-essentia* distinction in him and positively from the affirmation that, lacking all passive potency, he is pure act. This identity of God is entailed in the DDS and serves to distinguish the absoluteness of God's existence from the contingent existence of all composite and non-divine things. It remains, then, to consider more specifically the difference between being in general and the being of God.

BEING IN GENERAL AND THE BEING OF GOD

The distinction between the being of God as *ipsum esse subsistens* and the being of the world as *ens commune* (and as existing by *esse commune*) is radically unlike the distinction between this and that being within the world itself. The Christian doctrine of creation *ex nihilo* "urges a distinction between the whole and God."[62] This being so, God cannot be

---

59. Ibid., 518.

60. Ibid. See also, Gilson, *The Christian Philosophy of St. Thomas Aquinas*, 122–23, and Aertsen, *Medieval Philosophy and the Transcendentals*, 390–91.

61. Barry Miller has recently sought to defend the notion of God as *ipsum esse subsistens* by suggesting that he is the "limit case" of existence to which the whole series of existents points but which is not itself an instance of existence as it is found in the common order or scale of being. The sophistication of this argument demands more attention than the scope of the present chapter allows. See Miller, *A Most Unlikely God*, as well as, *The Fullness of Being*, 137–52.

62. Sokolowski, *The God of Faith and Reason*, 46.

thought of as the highest existent within *ens commune*.[63] As existentially simple, his existence is most absolute and so cannot be measured as though it were relative to other existents. To attempt such a comparison, as so many modern analytic philosophers and Perfect-being theologians are wont to do, is to conceive God as one being among others. Robert Sokolowski contends that such an existential univocism is really an extension of the pagan notion of God: "The pagan sense of the divine is that of the best, highest, greatest, most powerful and most necessary beings within the whole or within the world."[64] Against the pagan notion of God as a being within the world, Sokolowski informs us that the Christian understanding of God is not defined "by contrast to other beings in the world, but in contrast to the world as the whole."[65] Put differently, God's existence is not the existence of the biggest thing around, but the existence of the one who causes anything to be around at all.

Distinguishing God's existence from the existence of the world requires an expression of his existence as entirely non-correlative. If God's *esse* were measured or assessed as some particular within *ens commune*, and from which we could simply abstract the notion of *esse commune*, he could hardly be thought of as most absolute in his existence. As the preceding sections have argued, it is God's real identity with his own act of being—that is, his simplicity—that both accounts for the possibil-

---

63. Edith Stein maintains, "The moment we mention being we must distinguish between the being of God and creature" (*Potency and Act*, 9). K. Scott Oliphint agrees, remarking, "[W]e cannot simply posit existence without at the same time saying whether it is God's existence that we are positing or something that exists because created by God" (*Reasons for Faith*, 110). It is crucial in this connection to note that Aquinas does not conceive of God as the proper subject of metaphysics, which investigates being in general, but as the principle cause of being in general and thus of metaphysics itself. Metaphysics contemplates God as the principle and cause of common being, but not as one of those beings. Jan Aertsen is instructive on this point: "The subject of first philosophy is not the first, transcendent being, but *ens commune* and that which is consequent upon being. The divine is studied by the science of being insofar as it is the cause of the subject, that is, the universal cause of being" (*Medieval Philosophy and the Transcendentals*, 375). On *esse commune* as applicable only to the creaturely realm, see te Velde, *Participation and Substantiality*, 188–94. Te Velde insists that the commonness of *esse commune* itself is enough to indicate that it pertains only to creatures: "The addition of *creatures* [to *esse commune omnibus*] is logically redundant, since to have being in common with many other things, each according to a distinct essence, is precisely what it is to be a creature" (*Participation and Substantiality*, 194).

64. Sokolowski, *The God of Faith and Reason*, 46.

65. Ibid., 47.

ity of the actual coming to be of all non-divine existents and for the entirely non-derived and non-contingent manner of his own existence. This notion of existential absoluteness can be unfolded by considering: (1) that God is not in a series of being with any creature; (2) that the order of God's existence and the order of the world's existence are really two distinct orders; and (3) that the relation between God and non-divine things is analogical and not univocal. These observations should go some distance in undermining the assumed univocism latent in the thought of the modern critics of the DDS surveyed in chapter 1.

God not in a Series with Creatures

Consider, then, that God is not to be counted as existing in an ontological series with any creature. As the absolute cause of all creaturely being, God himself cannot be numbered as one of those things appearing within being in general. Being in general, whether thought of as *ens commune* or *esse commune*, is fundamentally a *caused* being and God is the sufficient ontological reason for its actuality.[66] In the Nicene Creed Christians confess belief in one God who is "Maker of heaven and earth, and of all things visible and invisible."[67] This making, or creation, is particularly God's making of things to be, or to exist. It is existence *qua* existence that is caused in creation and not merely the causation of a thing to be this or that. Creation is a complete coming-to-be and not properly a change in some preexisting subject or matter.[68]

66. In *DP* 3.16, ad 4 Thomas affirms that God is the cause of being *qua* being and in *ST* I–II.66.5, ad 4 he states that "universal being" is God's "proper effect." We can only conclude that, for Thomas, God is not one of those beings discovered within *ens commune* inasmuch as he is neither self-caused nor is any aspect of his existence or essence an "effect."

67. Biblical support for this assertion is found in Colossians 1:16: "For by him all things were created, in heaven and on earth, visible and invisible, whether thrones or dominions or rulers or authorities- all things were created through him and for him."

68. See James Anderson, *The Cause of Being*, 1–30. Etienne Gilson helpfully distinguishes between the Christian conception of God as the cause of the world and the Greek conception of divine causation: "On the Greek side stands a god who is doubtless the cause of all being, including its intelligibility, efficiency and finality—all, save existence itself; on the Christian side a God Who causes the very existence of being. On the Greek side we have a universe eternally informed or eternally moved; on the Christian side a universe which begins to be by a creation. On the Greek side, stands a universe contingent in the order of intelligibility or in the order of becoming; on the Christian side a universe contingent in the order of existence. On the Greek side, there is the immanent finality of an order interior to beings; on the Christian side the

Now, the way in which each particular being within *ens commune* relates to God, as its ultimate efficient cause, is traditionally said to be through "participation."[69] No non-divine being ultimately exists by virtue of itself, assuming that its *esse* and *essentia* are really distinct, but, rather, through the existence of that first cause by which its essence and existence are composed. Thomas explains:

> Now it has been shown above [*ST* I.3.4] when treating of the divine simplicity that God is the essentially self-subsisting Being; and also it was shown [*ST* I.11.3, ad 4] that subsisting being must be one . . . Therefore all beings apart from God are not their own being, but are beings by participation. Therefore it must be that all things which are diversified by the diverse participation of being, so as to be more or less perfect, are caused by one First Being, Who possesses being most perfectly.[70]

The fact that all existents participate in God's *esse* does not entail that God's *esse* is the universal *esse commune*. Although he is *ipsum esse*, God is not that formal *esse* that is received by finite beings. Invoking his conclusion that only in one being could existence and essence be identical, Aquinas maintains, "If . . . the divine being were the formal being of all things, all things would have to be absolutely one."[71] This distinction between the being of God and creatures is made even more explicit in *De potentia* 7.2: "God's being which is his essence is not universal being,

---

transcendent finality of a Providence who creates the very being of order along with that of the things ordered" (*The Spirit of Medieval Philosophy*, 81). See also, Gilson, *The Christian Philosophy of St. Thomas Aquinas*, 121. It should be observed that though God as first cause of being is set apart from all pagan notions of causation, this does not mean that his proper name is, as Descartes held, "Author of Nature." Inasmuch as creation is a free act of God it is better to retain "He who is" as his proper name; in this way his proper name is not derived from nature. Gilson makes this argument in *God and Philosophy*, 89.

69. For a thorough study of Aquinas's doctrine of participation see te Velde, *Participation and Substantiality*. See also te Velde, "God and the Language of Participation," 19–36; Aertsen, *Medieval Philosophy and the Transcendentals*, 379–81; Aertsen, *Nature and Creature*, 83–86, 116–27; Elders, *The Metaphysics of Being of St. Thomas Aquinas*, 218–30.

70. *ST.* I.44.1. In saying that God possesses being "most perfectly," he means only that God alone possesses *esse* without any potential for further determination to being.

71. *SCG* I.26 [3].

but being distinct from all other being: so that by his very being God is distinct from every other being."[72]

Creatures participate in *esse* in two distinct ways: they participate formally in *esse commune* and causally (or imitatively) in God's own *esse*. Accordingly, the creature does not participate in the divine *esse* by receiving *ipsum esse subsistens* as its intrinsic principle of existence; rather the creature participates in God's *esse* as a produced likeness of it. In this sense God can be thought of as the *esse* of all things, but with the important qualification that he is "not '*esse essentiale*' but the '*esse causale*.'"[73] In causing the *esse* of creatures by his act of creation God produces an imperfect likeness of his own perfect act of existence. Consequently, both *ens commune* and *esse commune* are themselves characterized by participation in their efficient cause, God himself.[74]

But, as *ipsum esse subsistens*, God cannot possibly be an instance of participated being and so cannot be classified within that being in

---

72. *DP* 7.2, ad 4.

73. Phelan, *Selected Papers*, 90. Due to this creational bond of creatures to God Rudi te Velde warns against conceiving the distinction between God and creatures too abstractly (see his "God and the Language of Participation," 19–20). W. Norris Clarke argues that this causal bond of being serves to establish our ability to speak of God analogically. Thus, he prefers the expression "causal participation": "There is only one bridge that enables us to pass over the cognitive abyss between ourselves and God and talk meaningfully about Him in our terms: the bridge of causal participation, or more simply of efficient causality, taken with all its implications. If God were not the ultimate causal Source of all the perfections we find in our world, we would have no way of talking meaningfully about Him at all. It is the causal bond which grounds all analogous predication about God" (*The Philosophical Approach to God*, 78–79). Thomas Aquinas calls this "the analogy of some kind of imitation" (*ST* I.44.3). In his *Quaestiones quodlibetales* VII, 1.1, ad 1 he explains that any generality ascribed to God is due to his causal action in all things: "the divine essence is not something general in being, since it is distinct from all other things, but only in causing" (translated by Aertsen in, *Medieval Philosophy and the Transcendentals*, 389).

74. Wippel notes that Thomas spells out three differences between God's relation to *esse commune* and the creature's relation to it: (1) creatures depend on *esse commune* while the *esse commune* itself depends on God; (2) non-divine existents are contained under *esse commune* while *esse commune* falls under the power of God, which is more extended than is created *esse* (i.e., God can create many things by his power to which *esse commune* does not actually extend); and (3) all non-divine existents participate in *esse*, but God does not. Wippel writes, "On the contrary, created *esse* is a kind of participation in God and a likeness of God" (*Metaphysical Thought*, 115). Maritain similarly concludes that, "the Act of Existing, subsistent by itself, is above the whole order of beings, perfections, [and] existences which are its created participations" (*Existence and the Existent*, 44).

general (*ens commune*) that encompasses every being in the world and even marks the world as a whole. Some have objected that the notion of God as the first cause of being suggests that he stands as the first among others. Is he not, after all, the highest instance of existence on the great chain of being, the first being to which all other beings take second place? Louis De Raeymaeker explains why such a conception of God is misguided: "The infinite cause does not include any limitation, or any extrinsic relativity. It cannot form part of an order or enter into a series. It is not accurate to say that it 'differs' from another cause as this being differs from that which is in the same line or on the same plane. In this respect, it is preferable to state that the infinite is not opposed to the finite, since they are not of the same order; they are diverse."[75]

God is not ontologically identified by relation to anything outside himself. The acknowledgment of God as first cause denotes a creative priority rather than a numeric one. Raeymaeker declares, "It seems certain to us that St. Thomas does not seek the 'first' Cause by passing through a series of causes, of which this cause would be the first term."[76] Rather, God is prior to the whole order or chain of creaturely being as its ontological efficient cause. The source of this chain of being is complete and perfect subsistent being in itself and so cannot be a participated being located somewhere upon the chain of being, not even as its top link, so to speak. The explanation for the chain of being cannot be a part of that chain unless one were to hold, in monistic fashion, that being in general is itself an undiversified self-subsistent being.

Distinct Orders of Being

Consider, furthermore, that God's existence and the existence of the world really constitute two entirely different *orders* of being. Given the radical nature of creation *ex nihilo* and the uniqueness of God as *ipsum esse subsistence* it follows that he cannot be categorized as yet another thing in the world.[77] This conclusion represents a fundamental distinc-

---

75. Raeymaeker, *Philosophy of Being*, 288–89.

76. Ibid., 297.

77. Jan Aertsen summarizes Aquinas's teaching that God transcends being in general as its efficient cause: "*Esse commune* signifies the formal principle which is required for any concrete entity to be in act. God is not included in this notion. He is the extrinsic cause of the proper subject of metaphysics, the universal cause of being as such. Thomas's conception is completely in accordance with his interpretation of God's com-

tion between the ontological outlooks of Thomistic and Reformed adherents to the DDS on the one hand, and the host of modern critics of
the doctrine on the other.

It should be observed that the univocal concept of being in which
God and creatures are simply different beings within one great ontological order is at the heart of recent "possible worlds" semantics (which
predominates among the analytic critics of the DDS) in which a possible
world is understood as any maximally consistent state of affairs.[78] One
adherent to this "possible worlds" ontology, Jay Richards, notes that, "An
approximate synonym of a state of affairs that obtains is the usual notion
of a *fact*."[79]

The danger, of course, is in making "fact," or the maximal "state
of affairs," something that stands over both God and creatures. What
binds God to creation (and even to the rules of modal logic) for many
Christian analytic philosophers is that he stands *with* man under the
unifying umbrella of "the maximal state of affairs." Placing God and
creatures together as so many facts within the actual world inevitably
tends toward ontological univocism. Gone is the ancient concern to
sharply differentiate between God and creatures at the level of existence;
rather, all existence has been brought under a single notion of "being"
redubbed "reality," "fact," "the actual world," or "the maximal state of
affairs." In this scheme God and man are now simply two facts within
the *one* domain of being.[80]

---

monness as a commonness by causality. God transcends being in general" (*Medieval
Philosophy and the Transcendentals*, 394).

78. It is in this connection that Lawrence Dewan charges Alvin Plantinga with univocism: "What characterizes Plantinga's discussion is a conception of such notions as
'being' and 'goodness' as fundamentally homogenized or univocal. Moreover, their uniform meaning binds them irrevocably to the *limited mode* they have in primary human
experience. This I would call 'metaphysical anthropomorphism.' It seems to blend with
a 'possible worlds' approach to problems. Plantinga envisages God as part of a universal scenario or possible world. Necessary truths, which apply in every possible world,
would apply to God. Certain intelligibilities would be beyond God's 'control' (146). As
he says: 'There is no possible world in which God does not exist' (140)" ("Saint Thomas,
Alvin Plantinga, and the Divine Simplicity," 150–51; the parenthetical page numbers refer to Plantinga's *Does God Have a Nature?*). In contrast to Plantinga, Dewan notes that
Thomas's doctrine of God aims "to take the mind *beyond* any and every possible world
to its source" (ibid., 151). At bottom, Plantinga's disagreement with Thomas is tied to
his alternative notion of God's existence as something *within* a given possible world.

79. Richards, *Untamed God*, 55.

80. It is clear that Richards understands God to be *within* whatever possible world
he chooses to actuate when he remarks that even if God were only free to create this

But the DDS does not insist upon distinguishing the absolute existence of God from the contingent existence of the world itself by suggesting that God's absoluteness and the creature's contingency are two ends or terms upon a single ontological continuum. Instead, the entire range of being that we call the "world" is a spectrum of caused and participated being that is related to God both by its likeness to him and by its ontological dependence upon him. It is existentially ordered to him, but he is not existentially ordered to it.[81] As caused, non-divine existence is not a mere extension of God's being and does not add additional being to him.[82] In a penetrating passage, Etienne Gilson explains why the existence of the world in no way adds to or determines the existence of God:

> It may be asked how creatures can be derived from God without
> either being confused with Him or added to Him. The solution
> of this problem brings us again to the problem of analogy . . .
> The creature is not what he possesses. God is what He possesses.
> He is His act-of-being, His goodness, His perfection. This is why

particular world, he would still have the option of not creating and thus there would be at least two possible worlds: "the world in which God does create this particular universe and the one in which he does not" (*Untamed God*, 84). This is helpful for understanding Richards's univocism inasmuch as he understands God to be *in* a world whether he creates or not. Since the "world" is simply whatever is factual then God must eternally be in a world. If he freely chooses to create then he must pass from that world in which he doesn't create into another world. In any case God is not apart from the world in the traditional sense of belonging to a different order of reality. There can only be, in Richards's ontology, *one* reality, or, we may say, one truth about how things *are*. Thus, God and creatures must stand together in a single existential order of being. They can only be distinguished by degrees and necessarily the world must add something (accidentally) to God.

81. Thomas writes, "Now the creature by its very name is referred to the Creator: and depends on the Creator who does not depend on it. Wherefore the relation whereby the creature is referred to the Creator must be a real relation, while in God it is only a logical relation" (*DP* 3.3). On real and logical relations see Gilles Emery's illuminating remarks in *The Trinitarian Theology of St Thomas Aquinas*, 86–88.

82. Henri Renard observes that in the act of causation the efficient cause does not change. First, the agent loses nothing of itself, no part or piece, in its act of moving a patient from potency to act. Second, it gains nothing by this action. Nothing is lost in production: "The truth is that the agent as agent loses nothing, else God, the angels, and the soul of man would be growing weaker and would soon vanish in thin air. A thing can change only inasmuch as it is in potency; but cause as cause is in act and not in potency; and consequently, cause as cause undergoes no change." In action the agent is entirely unchanged while the patient receives a new form related to the agent. The patient receives act and new form while the agent *receives* nothing (*Philosophy of Being*, 139).

creatures, even though they derive their act-of-being from that of God Himself, since He is *Esse* in its absolute sense, possess it nevertheless in a deficient manner which keeps them infinitely distant from the Creator. A mere *analogue* of the divine being, created being can neither constitute an integral part of the divine being, nor be added to it, nor subtracted from it. *Between two magnitudes not of the same order, there is no common measure.*[83]

God's absolute simplicity is central to Gilson's argument and he is certainly correct to stress not the duality of being within a *single* order but the duality of entire orders of being. This "duality" ensures the Creator-creature distinction at the existential level and helpfully qualifies the nature of creaturely participation in God's existence.[84]

Analogia Entis *and God's Likeness in Things*

The absolute distinction between the divine and creaturely orders of being brings us in the final consideration to the notion of the analogy of being (*analogia entis*) as a means for articulating the relationship between these two distinct "magnitudes" of being. Though the *analogia entis* has long been debated by philosophers and theologians, it seems that, with proper qualification, it is serviceable for the Christian concep-

83. Gilson, *The Christian Philosophy of St. Thomas Aquinas*, 126–27 (emphasis added). K. Scott Oliphint concurs with Gilson's distinction between God's being and the world's order of being: "If everything is created except God, then God must be of an entirely different order than anything else" (*Reasons for Faith*, 85). In *SCG* I.72 [9] Aquinas plainly denies that God and creatures are within a single order of being: "nothing is co-ordered with God, as within the same order, except Himself."

84. It may be helpful to go even further and deny that God's existence is really an *order* at all. Insofar as the notion of an "order" suggests "ordered to" or indicates a certain "orderliness" of constituent parts it cannot be rightly predicated of God. We speak of his existence as an order of being for the purpose of indicating that he is not ordered to any creature or series of participated existence. But speaking precisely, God is not an "order" of anything. In his case, though, the opposite of order is not disorder, but absolute simplicity. For a similar conclusion see Goris, *Free Creatures of an Eternal God*, 82. Additionally, it should be pointed out that the "duality" between divine being and being in general is not a duality *within* some unified ontological order such as a "maximal state of affairs." Indeed, this ontological distinction is not properly a form of numeric duality at all insofar as numeric addition and subtraction presuppose multiplicity within a single series. David Burrell warns, "[W]e must . . . be wary of picturing that distinction in a fashion which assimilates the creator to another item within the universe" ("Act of Creation with Its Theological Consequences," 40). If we are to speak of duality between God's being and the world's being it must be in an improper sense inasmuch as we cannot adequately comprehend this distinction intellectually.

tion of God's absolute being and the similarity or likeness of that being found in the multitude of contingent things.

It should be immediately pointed out that when we speak of the *analogia entis* we typically apply this one label to what are, in effect, various different analogies of being. These analogies can be broadly distinguished by observing whether they apply "at the horizontal or predicamental (categorical) level" or "at the vertical or transcendental level."[85] The categorical level, of course, comprises all the various analogies of being that can be applied to everything falling within Aristotle's ten categories of being, that is, to the created world. Inasmuch as God is not distinguished by the Aristotelian categories the analogy of being between him and the world is on a transcendental level.

Thomistic philosophers traditionally distinguish between the intrinsic analogies of proper proportion and of proper proportionality. Thomas expresses this distinction in his *Questiones disputatae de veritate*:

> Since an agreement according to proportion can happen in two ways, two kinds of community can be noted in analogy. There is a certain agreement between things having a proportion to each other from the fact that they have a determinate distance between each other or some other relation to each other, like the proportion which the number two has to unity in as far as it is the double of unity. Again, the agreement is occasionally noted not between two things which have a proportion between them, but rather between two related proportions—for example, six has something in common with four because six is two times three, just as four is two times two. The first type of agreement is one of proportion; the second, of proportionality.[86]

Aquinas initially rejects the analogy of proper proportion as an analogy between God and creatures inasmuch there is no "determinate distance" between them and thus no real proportion common to both. On the other hand, he is willing to apply the notion of the analogy of proper proportionality to explain the similarity between God and creatures:

> In those terms predicated according to the first type of analogy, there must be some definite relation between the things having something in common analogously. Consequently, nothing can

---

85. Wippel, "Metaphysics," 90. For a fine summary of Thomas's *analogia entis* see Aertsen, *Medieval Philosophy and the Transcendentals*, 383–87.

86. *Questiones disputatae de veritate* 2.11. This is cited hereafter as *DV*.

be predicated analogously of God and creature according to this type of analogy; for no creature has such a relation to God that it could determine the divine perfection. But in the other type of analogy, no definite relation is involved between the things which have something in common analogously, so there is no reason why some name cannot be predicated analogously of God and creature in this manner.[87]

In his later writings Thomas appears to have revised his earlier conclusion that the analogy of proper proportion (or analogy of intrinsic attribution) cannot be applied to the relation between God and the creature by accepting that "proper proportion" may also be understood as a two-term analogy and thereby not require a "definite relation" as conceived in a three-term analogy.[88] He concludes, instead, that one

87. Ibid. See the discussion in Stein, *Finite and Eternal Being*, 337. It is notable that Thomas does not appear to have taught the analogy of proper proportionality in any text other than this one in *De veritate*. Peter Weigel observes that in Thomas's use of the analogy of proper proportionality he is reluctant to say what God and creatures have in common (*Aquinas on Simplicity*, 216). Weigel also points out that in Thomas's analogical predication a good bit is already known about the predicates prior to any explanation of the analogical relation: "Analogical predication itself does not underwrite God as being a certain way or as having such and such positive names. Instead, we are dealing with patterns describing how the predication of certain positive names might occur, in which the predicates themselves have already been decided upon for other reasons" (ibid., 214). Certainly we would want to insist that one of the things *already* decided about God and creatures before we predicate any analogy of being between them is that God is absolutely simple and creatures are contingent composites that depend upon God for their existence. This should ensure that any analogy between them is not dependent upon some abstract notion of *esse* as a common denominator or prime analogate.

88. Weigel, *Aquinas on Simplicity*, 220. The explanation for Thomas's later endorsement of an analogy of proper proportion between God and creatures is not that he begins to drift toward univocism, but, rather, that he begins to appreciate the usefulness of "participation" as a means for explaining the creature's similarity to God as its Creator. Thomas also comes to recognize two distinct ways in which the analogy of proper proportion can be explained. First, it can indicate the similarity between two things by their shared likeness to some third thing or idea (i.e., many analogous to one; a three-term analogy). If this were used to explain God's *esse* and the world's *esse* then some generic or abstract notion of *esse* would stand over God and the world as their common prime analogate. Second, there is yet another kind of proper proportion in which one thing is an analogue of another (i.e., one analogous to one; a two-term analogy). In this relation there is no generic third term. This second way of understanding proper proportion is what enables us to say that there is an analogy between God's *esse* and the world's *esse* in such a way that God is not an analogue of the world even though the world is an analogue of him. The world, as effect, participates God's *esse*,

term, such as *esse*, can be predicated of both God and creatures accord-ing to the same *res significata* on account of the relation creatures have to God as their ultimate cause. The *esse* of the creature is a distinct likeness of the divine *esse* and even derives its name and intelligibility from God's *esse*. Even so, this is not an agreement of proportion in which God and creatures are simply modally distinct instantiations of some abstract or general concept of being. Rather, the meaning of the common term is identical with God's own Godhead and only applies analogously to the creature as God's effects bearing some likeness to their proper cause.

Highlighting God's ontological priority, Thomas writes, "as regards the assigning of the names, such names are primarily predicated of creatures, inasmuch as the intellect that assigns the names ascends from creatures to God. But as regards the thing signified by the name, they are primarily predicated of God, from whom the perfections descend to other beings."[89] Though we may, in some instances, name God from the creature, we understand that the creature first derives its name from God and not God from it. Weigel explains why a common name may be said truly, yet analogically, of both God and creatures: "As the cause virtually precontaining all perfections, the divine essence must be something to which the created instances of the absolute perfections bear enough of an ontological resemblance such that our concepts taken from these cre-ated instances legitimately correspond to the divine essence."[90]

---

but God does not mutually participate the world's *esse* since the analogy flows in only one direction and God is the prime analogate. We must sharply distinguish between these two versions of the analogy of proper proportion (many to one and one to one) inasmuch as the first version would imply some ontological commonality between God and creatures while the second precludes such. See the useful discussion in Klubertanz, *St. Thomas Aquinas on Analogy*, 86–100, 132–35.

89. *Compendium theologiae* 27. Even if we argue, as the Reformed often do, that the human knower may just as well descend from knowledge of God to knowledge of the creature (on account of an implanted knowledge of God) Thomas's point respecting God's *ontological* primacy stands.

90. Weigel, *Aquinas on Simplicity*, 221–22. With this creational context in view the (vertical) *analogia entis* between God and creatures is not rooted in an abstract no-tion of being. The Reformed theologian Cornelius Van Til has sounded an appropriate warning: "When one . . . begins with the abstract notion of the analogy of being, God and man are bound to come out of this vague sort of being as correlatives to one anoth-er. The various modes of being become, in that case, mutually analogical" (*Introduction to Systematic Theology*, 333). In *ST* I.13.5 Thomas writes, "[W]hatever is said of God and creatures, is said according to the relation of a creature to God as its principle and cause." Though we speak of God analogically, he not the analogue of creatures, but

The crucial element, then, in any analogy of being that pays due respect to divine simplicity and creaturely composition is that it be articulated according to the biblical teaching of creation *ex nihilo*.[91] To the extent that this creational context is not conspicuously prefixed to one's use of the analogy of being in explaining God's and his creatures' relationship, it appears to undermine the absoluteness of God as *ipsum esse subsistens* and as entirely above any ontological series of *ens commune*. Still, as a framework for explaining the likeness of God's existence and perfections in his creatures, it enables us to conceive of how one simple in himself could reproduce his image in composite existents.

CONCLUSION

Throughout this chapter it has been observed that God's absolute existence stands over against that of the creature's contingent existence on account of the fact that God's existence is uncaused, unreceived, and non-contracted. The real distinction between *essentia* and *esse* in creatures both signifies their finite existence and their dependence upon some cause of being whose being is not itself dependent upon a prior cause. As *ipsum esse subsistens*, God is shown to be the ontological sufficient reason for himself and the only possible agent who could produce the universal phenomenon of being in general, that is, of both *esse commune* and *ens commune*.

Again, it is God's simplicity that enables us to maintain that God is identical with *that by which* he exists. In a slight variation from the Westminster Confession, the Second London Confession of Faith (2.1) states that God is the one "whose subsistence is in himself." We have seen through the course of this chapter that such a confession is entirely

---

rather creatures of him. As for the *analogia entis* that is rooted in an abstract notion of being *qua* being, it is not hereby destroyed, but rather is regarded as an analogy that occurs solely on a horizontal level between creatures. Accordingly, Jan Aertsen writes, "Thomas emphasizes that there remains a fundamental difference between the application of the analogy of being to the categories and its application in theology" (*Medieval Philosophy and the Transcendentals*, 386).

91. On divine causality and creaturely likeness to God, see Klubertanz, *St. Thomas Aquinas on Analogy*, 46–55. Klubertanz helpfully renames the second version of the analogy of proper proportion as "analogy of imitation" and "analogy of causal participation" (ibid., 107, 135). Aertsen reinforces the same point when he observes, "The ontological structure of participation excludes for Thomas the possibility of predicating 'being' univocally of God and creatures" (*Medieval Philosophy and the Transcendentals*, 384). See also, Weed, "Creation as a Foundation of Analogy in Aquinas," 129–47.

dependent upon the real identity between God's essence and his act of existence. To the extent that this identity account of God's simplicity is upheld, his absolute existence is preserved and his ultimate sufficiency for the production of contingent existents is ensured.

5

Simplicity and God's Absolute Attributes

IN ADDITION TO MAINTAINING the real identity between God's essence and existence, the traditional DDS also holds that all of God's attributes are really identical in him. If God were a complex of really distinct attributes or properties then those various attributes would be more basic than the Godhead itself in explaining or accounting for what God is. To be considered most absolute with respect to all the various perfections predicated of him it is necessary that one regard those perfections as identical with God himself. *Identity* is the watchword of the strong account of divine simplicity and is crucial to the orthodox articulation of divine absoluteness. Often this identity is expressed in the claim that *all that is in God is God.*

Given their denial of any composition and diversity in God's essence and attributes, DDS supporters face the challenge of exactly how to understand the relation between the multifarious perfections attributed to God. Even if some of those perfections are acknowledged as improper or as Cambridge properties of God, certainly there remain many attributes that are *properly* predicated of him. But, the question is asked: How can an absolutely simple God have more than one attribute? The customary response of adherents to the strong version of the DDS has historically been to insist that even though the senses of the various attributes are really distinct, the referent, God, does not possess them as really distinct properties. The mode of human signification does not match the mode of God's subsistence. Indeed, in God each perfection is really identical with all the others inasmuch as each is identical with the Godhead and God cannot be really distinct from himself.[1]

1. Historically, not every adherent to the DDS adopted such a strong identity thesis. Andrew Radde-Gallwitz has recently shown, for instance, that this identity thesis

Ingenious as this Identity Account (IA) may at first appear, it is by no means obvious to many modern philosophers and theologians that it makes any sense. In fact, the lion's share of modern opposition to the DDS tends to take the line that the IA just doesn't square with what we know about properties and how they function. In chapter 1 it was noted that Richard Gale, Christopher Hughes, Thomas Morris, and Alvin Plantinga all level formidable "property" challenges against the DDS. In response, many recent defenders of the DDS have not questioned whether a Property Account (PA) is the appropriate way of construing the IA. Rather, they aim at undermining the narrower conception of properties presented by the various critics.[2] In this way they propose to defend the IA by constructing an explanation of divine properties suitable to its claims.

Other defenders of the DDS, feeling the pressure of the property challenge, have chosen instead to abandon the IA altogether rather than engage in the elaborate and seemingly ill-fated project of developing an adequate property explanation for it.[3] These DDS proponents prefer to explain the doctrine as teaching a harmonious unity among the divine attributes rather than a real identity. The point of divine simplicity, they maintain, is to show that there is no internal contradiction or disagreeableness among the intrinsic divine attributes. The more modest claims of this Harmony Account (HA) appear to rescue the DDS from the apparent unintelligibility of saying that each of God's perfections are identical with him and with each other.

But are the only options for defending the DDS to either develop a workable PA or abandon the IA in favor of the HA? This chapter proposes to take a third way of explaining the IA of the DDS. As will be shown below, the DDS does not demand that one think of God's perfec-

---

was clearly rejected by Gregory of Nyssa (*Basil of Caesarea, Gregory of Nyssa, and the Transformation of Divine Simplicity*, 182–212, 221). Of course, Gregory was not presented with the Identity Account as it came to be uniquely fashioned by Augustine and even more carefully by Aquinas; moreover, it does not seem that he would have endorsed it even if it had been available to him. Joseph O'Leary critiques Gregory's position from the vantage point of the later medieval theology in his, "Divine Simplicity and the Plurality of Attributes," 307–37.

2. Among these DDS defenders who utilize a version of the PA are Eleonore Stump, Norman Kretzmann, William Mann, and William Vallicella.

3. Included in this group are Richard Swinburne, Robert Burns, Gerrit Immink, and John Frame.

tions as "properties" at all. All that the DDS is concerned to establish is that God is the ultimate sufficient explanation for anything that is truly predicated of him. *There is no unit of intelligibility or explanation more basic than himself in virtue of which he is what he is.* One modern way of construing such a claim without resorting to a property explanation is to say that God is the "truthmaker" of anything truly ascribed to him. The Truthmaker Account (TA) is a proposal by which the IA of the DDS can be responsibly upheld without compromising divine absoluteness.[4]

This chapter proceeds through four sections. First, four traditional models for explaining the distinctions between God's attributes are introduced: real distinction; purely conceptual distinction; formal distinction; and virtual distinction. Second, the harmonist criticism of the IA is considered and evaluated. Third, various arguments of the property objection to the IA are summarized and answered. Finally, the Truthmaker Account is set forth as a useful and orthodox solution to the property challenge with some obvious advantages over the currently popular Property Accounts of the DDS. Also, it is observed that the TA appears more amenable than the various property explanations to the Thomistic and Reformed commitment to analogical predication about God and to the claim that God is "that by which" he is exists and possesses his perfections.

FOUR MODELS FOR EXPLAINING
DIVINE ATTRIBUTE DISTINCTIONS

Expressing the relation between the various divine attributes seems to be a particular problem for adherents to the DDS inasmuch as the fact of attribute multiplicity appears to undermine the very concept of divine simplicity. Those theists who deny the DDS altogether tend to advocate a strong *real* distinction between God's perfections. DDS subscribers, on the other hand, seem to have at least three different options available to them for differentiating the divine attributes: purely conceptual distinctions; formal distinctions; and virtual distinctions. Strong conceptualism (or nominalism) denies the real distinction by insisting that all divine attribute distinctions are grounded in the mind of the knower.

---

4. Recent DDS defenders who employ the TA are Michael Bergmann, Jeffrey Brower, and Alexander Pruss. Also, Brian Leftow presents a view that is striking similar to that of the TA proponents and so he can be classified with them for the purposes of this chapter.

Between these two extremes of the strong real distinction and the purely conceptual distinction are the formal distinction of Duns Scotus (closer to the real distinction) and the virtual or eminent distinction of Thomas Aquinas (closer to conceptualism). Richard Muller provides useful summary descriptions of these four models for distinguishing between God's attributes:

> (1) *Distinctio realis*, a real distinction, such as exists between two independent things; (2) *Distinctio formalis*, a formal distinction, such as exists between two (or more) formal aspects of the essence of a thing; as, e.g., between intellect and will, which are not separate things but which are also distinguishable within the thing, in this case, the soul or spirit of which they are predicated . . . (3) *Distinctio rationis ratiocinatae*, a distinction by reason of analysis, sometimes qualified or explicated as *distinctio rationis ratiocinatae quae habet fundamentum in re* ("a distinction by reason of analysis that has its basis or foundation in the thing"). Since this distinction is neither between things nor in a thing, it is purely rational; yet it is argued as a distinction expressive of extramental reality since it is grounded in the thing and therefore preserved from being merely a product of the mind. In other words, the *distinctio rationis ratiocinatae* represents no distinction in the thing but a truth of reason concerning the thing. (4) *Distinctio rationis rationans*, a distinction by reason reasoning; i.e., a merely rational distinction resting only on the operation of the reason and not on the thing.[5]

The real distinction (*distinctio realis*) position maintains that the same real distinctions observed among creaturely properties also apply to God.[6] Just as wisdom, goodness, power, and the like are not identical concepts, neither can they be identical properties. Nicholas Wolterstorff captures the underlying sentiment of the real distinction position over

---

5. Muller, *Dictionary of Latin and Greek Theological Terms*, 93–94. Muller's ordering of these descriptions moves from the strong realist position to the strong conceptualist position, indicating that the formal and virtual distinctions represent different ways of mixing realism and conceptualism.

6. Muller notes three different ways of understanding a real distinction: (1) between different things of different essences; (2) between two things of the same essence; or (3) between the separable parts of a composite thing (*PRRD*, III: 286). It is only (3) that is applied to the divine attributes. It would be wrong to think of the real distinction position as suggesting that God's various attributes are each complete essences or beings in themselves. They are considered, rather, as metaphysical parts in a single spiritual being.

against identity accounts: "We say of God that God is wise, and that God is good, and that God is powerful. In speaking thus, we are not simply repeating ourselves."[7] He reasons that unless all those attributes ascribed to God are merely synonyms there must be a *real* difference between them in God. The only other option appears to be pure conceptualism, which seems to result in agnosticism. Needless to say, those who hold to this real distinction between the divine attributes have no affinity for the DDS.

On the other end of the spectrum the conceptual distinction (*distinctio rationis rationans*) attempts to uphold the DDS by denying both the real distinction and any other attribute distinction that is based upon an extramental reality in God. Two of the most famous proponents of the conceptual distinction are the Jewish philosopher Moses Maimonides and the Christian nominalist William of Ockham. Maimonides affirms equivocal predication as the only way to adequately distinguish God from the creature: "[T]here is, in no way or sense, anything common to the attributes predicated of God, and those used in reference to ourselves; they have only the same names, and nothing else is common to them."[8] Any names that are ascribed to God, Maimonides contends, are purely negative and tell us nothing positive about him.[9] Furthermore, whatever diversity of names we do ascribe to God can only be on account of our perception of his diverse effects. But the foundation of these distinctions is not so much in God as in our conceptualizations of his effects. The relations that we discover between God and his works "exist only in the thoughts of men." Maimonides quickly adds that distinction based upon a purely conceptual foundation "is what we must believe

---

7. Wolterstorff, "Divine Simplicity," 549–50.

8. Maimonides, *The Guide for the Perplexed*, I: 56.

9. Ibid., I: 58. Aquinas, though sympathetic to Maimonides's desire to preserve God's incomprehensibility and transcendence, does not concur with the rabbi's extreme apophaticism. In *DP* 7.5 Thomas writes: "[T]he idea of negation is always based on an affirmation: as evinced by the fact that every negative proposition is proved by an affirmative: wherefore unless the human mind knew something positively about God, it would be unable to deny anything about him. And it would know nothing if nothing that it affirmed about God were positively verified about him. Hence following Dionysius (*Div. Nom.* xiii) we must hold that these terms signify the divine essence, albeit defectively and imperfectly." Thomas emphasizes the likeness of any effect to its cause as the reason that creation allows us to know, even if imperfectly, something positively about God. On the dissimilarity between the negative theologies of Maimonides and Thomas see Rocca, *Speaking the Incomprehensible God*, 297–313.

concerning the attributes [of God]."[10] On the whole, Maimonides's op-position to the "Attributist's" tendency to predicate properties of God as inherent qualities is agreeable to the DDS's denial of substance-accident composition; but he seems to go too far in holding that the attributes we do ascribe to God do not correspond *in any sense* to God as he is in himself.

William of Ockham sponsors a purely conceptual distinction be-tween the divine attributes based on the argument that an attribute (or "simple supposition") "does not stand for anything, except the concept itself, which is indeed a thing in the soul, but, if taken precisely *qua* thing, does not signify any other thing."[11] The foundations for attribute distinctions in this outlook are the *concepts* of the attributes themselves. Also, inasmuch as Ockham understands all attributes to be really dis-tinct singulars they cannot have a simple God as their foundation. Every single attribute, being founded on a conception, requires that its par-ticular foundation be distinct from the foundation of every other at-tribute. It follows for Ockham that if God is undivided in his essence he cannot be the foundation for the multiplicity of perfections attributed to him. Ockham's concern, like Thomas's before him, is to preserve God's transcendent incomprehensibility and absolute simplicity. But he does not allow for any mediating position between the extreme realist notion of immediate apprehension of the divine essence, which he rejects, and the extreme nominalist view in which the theologian's analysis of the divine attributes is really an analysis of his own concepts, and not of God himself.[12]

John Duns Scotus maintains that a formal distinction (*distinctio formalis*) between the divine attributes avoids the tendency of conceptu-alism to destroy all meaningful distinction between God's attributes and the tendency of the strong real distinction to undermine the unity and

10. Maimonides, *The Guide for the Perplexed*, I: 53.

11. Gilson, *History of Christian Philosophy in the Middle Ages*, 493. See Ockham's *Summa Logicae*, I: 64.

12. See Copleston, *Ockham to Suarez*, 84–88. Richard Muller notes Ockham's rejec-tion of both Thomist and Scotist modifications of the real distinction: "Ockham views the Thomist and Scotist discussions of predication as violations of the divine simplicity because they make the distinction of attributes more than a mere distinction between our concepts. Ockham will allow neither the formal distinction nor the (Thomist) ra-tional distinction founded in the thing by reason of analysis" (*PRRD*, III: 75). See also, Maurer, *Medieval Philosophy*, 271–75.

simplicity of God. The formal distinction holds that though God's attributes may be really identical in him they must be formally distinct from each other since the form of any attribute cannot be identical with the form of any other attribute. Scotus states, "There is therefore there [viz., among the divine attributes] a distinction that is in every way prior to the [operation of] the intellect, and it is this: that wisdom actually exists naturally, and goodness actually exists naturally, and actual wisdom is formally not actual goodness."[13] This formal distinction (or formal non-identity) is not merely in the mind, but is in objects themselves, including God. Underlying this formal distinction is Scotus's commitment to univocism in which attributes are said univocally of God and creatures with the difference being located in God's infinite mode of being and the creature's finite mode. Richard Cross describes how this univocism bears upon Scotus's formal distinction:

> According to this theory, the basic lexical definitions of some of the terms applied to God are exactly the same as the lexical definition of those terms when applied to creatures. Now, the lexical definitions of many such terms, when applied to creatures, are different from each other. And Scotus's main criterion for a formal distinction between different attributes is, roughly, that the attributes admit of different lexical definitions. So different divine attributes will be formally distinct from each other. Scotus makes the point by arguing that, if these different attributes were not distinct in God, then (given his univocity theory) they would not be distinct in creatures either.[14]

It is true that this formal distinction weakens the DDS, but it purports not to go so far as to conclude that God is composed of parts. The distinction is between formalities (*formalitates*), not separable things (*res*). Cross explains:

13. Duns Scotus, *Ordinatio*, I.8.1.4 n. 192, cited in Cross, *Duns Scotus*, 43 (brackets supplied by Cross).

14. Cross, *Duns Scotus*, 43. For Scotus, "every inquiry regarding God is based upon the supposition that the intellect has the same univocal concept which it obtains from creatures" (ibid., 38). Elsewhere Cross writes, "Scotus's position is that, if nominalism about properties is false, then it must be so globally. Thus, if there are extramental distinctions between relevant creaturely properties, then there must be such distinctions between corresponding divine properties too" (*Duns Scotus on God*, 104). See also, Dumont, "Scotus's Doctrine of Univocity and the Medieval Tradition of Metaphysics," 193–212.

So univocity, as understood by Scotus, entails a weak account of divine simplicity, according to which the divine attributes are distinct from each other. On Scotus's account, divine simplicity is consistent with God's having several formally distinct transcendental attributes. As Scotus puts it, "This formal non-identity is compatible with God's simplicity." Simplicity, for Scotus, entails no more than that a simple being cannot have *really* distinct parts . . . He suggests that his account just shows that a formal distinction does not entail any kind of limitation (i.e., that a formal distinction does not entail having parts).[15]

Though Scotus's formal distinction allows for the inseparability of the divine attributes and even permits one to espouse their real identity at some level,[16] it does suggest that the most basic explanation for the various attributes is not the divine essence as such, but the multiple distinct forms in virtue of which the attributes are what they are. It is precisely here that Scotus weakens the Thomistic DDS inasmuch as Thomas is concerned to say that God *alone* is that by which he is any of those attributes rightly ascribed to him. If the "forms" of God's attributes are neither identical with the Godhead, nor with each other, as Scotus insists, then that by which God is wise is not identical with that by which he is powerful or that by which he is any of those various perfections as-

15. Cross, *Duns Scotus*, 43. The Scotus citation is from *Ordinatio*, I.8.1.4 n. 209. One of the reasons that Scotus can continue to confess that God is not composed of "parts" is because he tends to think of parts as "things" (*res*) possessing distinct essences. This extreme essentialism runs into numerous metaphysical challenges when attempting to explain the unity of being in a composite creature that is supposedly composed of numerous parts, each of which differs essentially from the others. This tends to reduce Scotus's position to the absurd claim that every composite being is really a community of numerous essences or substantial forms. On Scotus's unique brand of essentialism see Maurer, "Scotism and Ockhamism," 214–15. Elevating "parts" to the level of distinct essences indicates that Scotus has a much different understanding of parts than is found in Thomas and the Reformed scholastics. See chapter 2 above on the denial that parts are complete essences or things (*res*). Gilson observes, "The formal distinction is weaker than the real distinction, because it entails no distinction in actual existence; but it is stronger than the modal distinction, because it entails a distinction between two formally distinct essences, or quiddities" (*History of Christian Philosophy in the Middle Ages*, 765). See also, Muller, *PRRD*, III: 71–73.

16. It is because of the actual infinitude of every attribute that Scotus is able to say that God's attributes are *really* identical. All actual infinites, though formally distinct, must converge in reality. If they did not so converge into a single reality their infinity would be diminished by their actual difference from each other. But actual identity, for Scotus, does not suggest formal identity; each attribute still retains a distinct and irreducible quiddity of its own in God. See Maurer, *Medieval Philosophy*, 230.

cribed to him. Since the "forms" are not "things," though, Scotus can still say that God is not composite; but this is a weakened non-composition in which the Godhead itself is not the most basic sufficient explanation of the divine attributes.[17] The distinct forms in God, though not properly things or parts, comprise a multitude of *that by whiches*, as it were, which are thought to ensure some meaningful distinction among the divine attributes. Again, though, Scotus measures what counts as a *meaningful* distinction in terms of his univocal notion of attributes in which those distinctions that are meaningful among creatures must hold in God as well.[18] In this scheme God and creatures are both measured by a modally-neutral transcendental lexicon of formal definitions. The distinctions between the formal definitions must be maintained in those things, infinite or finite, that instantiate those forms in reality.

Thomas Aquinas explains the distinction between God's attributes as a virtual distinction (*distinctio virtualis*), which is a distinction of reason with an extramental foundation in its object (*distinctio rationis ratiocinatae quae habet fundamentum in re*).[19] As close as this may appear to Ockham's later nominalism, it is a decidedly different position inasmuch as the foundation of each attribute is not a distinct concept underlying it, but is, rather, the divine essence itself.[20]

Prompting Thomas's virtual distinction is his insistence that God is named by us through our perception of his likeness as it is found in his various effects. In his effects the perfection of God's undivided essence is imaged forth in a vast diversity of creaturely perfections. What is a simple unity in God is presented to the human knower under the form of creaturely multiplicity. As the efficient cause of all things God possesses the perfections of all creatures in an eminent manner. Again, this

---

17. Some critics find Scotus's weaker version of the DDS to be no real DDS at all. For instance, Herman Bavinck notes, "Duns Scotus, who for that matter expressly taught the doctrine of God's simplicity, came into conflict with it insofar as he assumed that the attributes are formally distinct from each other as well as from the divine essence" (*RD*, II: 174).

18. Cross remarks that, for Scotus, "every inquiry regarding God is based upon the supposition that the intellect has the same univocal concept which it obtains from creatures" (*Duns Scotus*, 38).

19. See *SCG* I.32 and *ST* I.13.5 for clear evidence that Thomas rejects the univocism later endorsed by Scotus.

20. See the discussions in Muller, *PRRD*, III: 284–98; Copleston, *Augustine to Scotus*, 360–61; and Holloway, *Natural Theology*, 248–58.

accords with Thomas's maxim that all effects preexist *eminenter* in their
cause. From this he concludes that *many* perfections may be attributed
to God without entailing that they are distinguished in God as they are
in his effects:

> We have said that all the perfections found in other things are
> attributed to God in the same way as effects are found in their
> equivocal causes. These effects are in their causes virtually . . .
> [T]he perfections of all things, which belong to the rest of things
> through diverse forms, must be attributed to God through one
> and the same power in Him. This power is nothing other than
> His essence, since, as we have proved, there can be no accident in
> God. Thus, therefore, God is called wise not only in so far as He
> produces wisdom, but also because, in so far as we are wise, we
> imitate to some extent the power by which He makes us wise.[21]

The "one and the same power" Thomas mentions is not to be understood as a reference to God's omnipotence but, rather, to *that by
which* (denominated below as "truthmaker") God is what he is. In the
passage Thomas explicitly identifies this power as the divine essence itself. Thus, that by which God is wise, powerful, good, and the like is the
singular and simple divine essence, while that which makes creatures
wise, powerful, and good are the diverse forms of those properties as
they are discovered in any creature. Thomas states, "Through His one
simple being God possesses every kind of perfection that all other things
come to possess, but in a much more diminished way, through diverse
principles."[22] He further argues that even those attributes that cannot
be properly ascribed to God (such as all those that require extension
or corporeity) can still be understood as imitations of something in his
essence insofar as he is their efficient cause: "God is not called a stone,
even though He has made stones, because in the name stone there is
understood a determinate mode of being according to which a stone

---

21. *SCG* I.31 [2].

22. Ibid., I.31 [3]. These "principles" are what Scotus calls "forms" or "formalities."
Recall that Thomas denies that God is the *principle* of his own existence. Likewise, he is
not the principle of his various attributes because no principle is identical with that of
which it is the principle. Though we maintain that God is the sufficient reason of each
attribute we ascribe to him, we should not think that he is thereby the *principle* of those
attributes. To say that God is the foundation for our various predications about him is
not the same as saying that he is the principle of his perfections. We maintain instead
that God *just is*, in an undivided manner, all those things we attribute to him.

is distinguished from God. But the stone imitates God as its cause in being and goodness, and other such characteristics, as do also the rest of creatures."[23]

The diversity in our ascription of attributes to God does not arise from a corresponding diversity *in him* even though those diverse attributes are all named from his simple essence. Thomas writes: "From this we see the necessity of giving to God many names. For, since we cannot know Him naturally except by arriving at Him from His effects, the names by which we signify His perfection must be diverse, just as the perfections belonging to things are found to be diverse. Were we able to understand the divine essence itself as it is and give to it the name that belongs to it, we would express it by only one name."[24] This does not mean, though, that the numerous names we attribute to him are all synonymous. The *sense* of each name still differs meaningfully from every other, though the referent, God, does not bear some corresponding internal complex of principles or formalities. Thomas explains:

> But our intellect, since it knows God from creatures, in order to understand God, forms conceptions proportional to the perfections flowing from God to creatures, which perfections pre-exist in God unitedly and simply, whereas in creatures they are received and divided and multiplied. As therefore, to the different perfections of creatures, there corresponds one simple principle represented by different perfections of creatures in a various and manifold manner, so also to the various and multiplied conceptions of our intellect, there corresponds one altogether simple principle, according to these conceptions, imperfectly understood. Therefore although the names applied to God signify one thing, still because they signify that under many and different aspects, they are not synonymous.[25]

The virtual or eminent distinction between the divine attributes is a realist position insofar as it finds the ground for each of these attributes in the divine essence itself and not merely in the theologian's own concepts; but it is a conceptualist distinction to the extent that it grounds the *diversity* of attribute predications upon the diversity of creaturely likenesses to the divine essence. In keeping with this virtual distinction,

23. Ibid., I.31 [2].
24. Ibid., I.31 [4].
25. *ST* I.13.4.

Thomas and the Reformed argue that the divine attributes are really identical in God. This Identity Account (IA) of the DDS is fashioned to explain how it is that God is most absolute in each of his attributes.

HARMONIST CHALLENGE
TO THE IDENTITY ACCOUNT

The identity of each divine attribute with every other in God follows from the prior commitment of the real identity of God with his *esse* and of his *esse* with his essence (see chapter 4). If God is identical with his own "to be" then there cannot be any determination of being, such as an attribute or property, that is added to him. Accordingly, he does not possess attributes as so many *determinations* of being. It is a mainstay of the Thomistic and Reformed DDS that God does not *possess* attributes at all, but, rather, he just *is* all those perfections that are attributed to him. Of course, his identity with those attributes does not mirror, in a modal sense, the way in which he reveals those attributes in Scripture or the way humans know them through their likeness in the assortment of created things. As Thomas states, "ll perfections existing in creatures divided and multiplied, pre-exist in God unitedly."[26] Recently this account of the unity of God's attributes as a unity of real identity has been challenged by some critics who seek to uphold a modified version of the DDS that teaches a perfect harmony and sublime agreement among God's attributes rather than a real identity.

Before we consider the Harmony Account (HA) of the DDS, the claims of the Identity Account (IA) should be briefly set forth.[27] Reformed theologian John Owen expresses it this way: "*The attributes of God*, which alone seem to be distinct things in the essence of God, *are all of them essentially the same with one another*, and every one the same

---

26. *ST* I.13.5.

27. Brian Leftow notes the historical pedigree of the identity version of the DDS: "The dominant view prior to 1300 was that God's relation to his necessary intrinsic attributes is *identity*—that God is identical with omnipotence, identical with omniscience and so on. This surprising claim was a component of doctrines of divine simplicity held by Augustine, Boethius, Anselm, Aquinas, and hosts of lesser lights. For the claim that God is 'simple,' in these writers, is shorthand for the claim that He exemplifies no metaphysical distinctions whatsoever, including that between subject and essential attribute. Though abstruse, the claim that God is simple is at the heart of these thinkers' concepts of God" ("Is God an Abstract Object?" 581).

with the essence of God itself."[28] Thomas Aquinas's reason for holding the real identity of God with his attributes and his attributes with each other flows from his prior conclusion that God is *ipsum esse subsistens*: "[I]n a simple being, being and that which is are the same. For, if one is not the other, the simplicity is then removed. But . . . God is absolutely simple. Therefore, for God to be good is identical with God. He is, therefore, His goodness."[29] This argument for identity between God and his goodness holds for his other attributes as well. The perfections attributed to God are just so many ways of *being*. In creatures these attributes function as actualization principles by which a creature is determined to *actually be* this or that. But if God is *ipsum esse subsistens* he cannot be said "to be" this or that by anything other than himself. If he were not identical with every one of those attributes rightly attributed to him he would be determined "to be" by something other than himself and thus neither simple nor "most absolute." For Thomas, existential simplicity requires that the Identity Account be applied to the divine attributes as well as the divine *esse*. Indeed, he seems unwilling to grant that any other account is rightly deserving of the name "simplicity."

Contrary to Thomas and his heirs, many recent defenders of the DDS are of the opinion that the IA strains the limits of intelligibility. Could not the benefits of the DDS be preserved by simply insisting that there is no internal conflict between God's essential attributes and that he possesses each of his intrinsic attributes necessarily? Gerrit Immink is one such DDS adherent who believes that the doctrine can still be used to establish divine aseity and immutability without entangling itself in the untoward implications of the IA. Consider, for example, his emphasis upon essential properties and property equivalence rather than attribute identity:

> When Aquinas says that there are not accidents in God, he most likely means to say that *God's perfecting properties, unlike qualities in created reality, are not accidental to him*. Accidental properties are the properties one may lose. How could God lose one of his perfections, say his justice or goodness? Then God would not be God. So it is very likely that God has all his *perfecting* properties essentially. He is equivalent with his perfecting properties. That

---

28. Owen, *Vindicae Evangelicae*, XII: 72 (emphasis his). The emphasis upon *essential* sameness between the attributes rules out the Scotist formal distinction.

29. *SCG* I.38 [6].

does not mean that *all* his properties—or what Plantinga does consider as properties—are essential to him. But the point is that God, who obviously has perfecting properties, has these properties essentially.[30]

This passage attempts to rescue Thomas from his IA based on a metaphysical scheme that Thomas himself rejects. For Thomas, *all* properties are qualities that inhere in an essence and thus are "removable" (at least conceptually) without causing any deficiency in the essence *qua* essence. Immink, on the other hand, thinks of essences as bundles of non-contingent properties. This is why he can say that God is "equivalent" with his perfecting properties. *But this is not the equivalence of identity.* In fact, Immink suggests that Thomas might possibly be read as claiming something less than a real identity between God's attributes: "It could be . . . that Aquinas didn't really mean to affirm *identity* . . . but only some substantial equivalence. Perhaps a weaker claim suffices, namely, that God's perfecting properties are equivalent."[31] Elsewhere, though, he seems to recognize that Thomas *does* intend to uphold a real identity between God and his attributes and between the attributes themselves. But Immink disapproves of this identity inasmuch as it seems to preclude any meaningful talk about God: "Aquinas's logical account of God's otherness and transcendence ends in a complete identity. Since no distinctions can be made in God, God is identical with each of his properties and each of his properties is identical with each of his properties. I believe this conclusion ought to be rejected; God's otherness does not render him utterly indescribable."[32]

Such criticism of the IA raises the question of what sort of description of God Immink thinks counts as an acceptable description. Does the creaturely *manner* or *mode* of imitating the divine perfections, for instance, mean that the divine perfections must subsist in a manner or mode isomorphic to that of the creature? In his criticism of the IA Immink makes no distinction between the creaturely mode of predication or knowledge and divine mode of subsistence. In fact, he concludes that Thomas's IA "is a consequence of [his] overaccentuation of God's otherness."[33] Immink prefers instead to construe the DDS as teaching

30. Immink, *Divine Simplicity*, 92.

31. Ibid., 95.

32. Ibid., 173.

33. Ibid., 176.

a special unity among the divine attributes rather than a strict identity: "God has more than one perfection, and although God's perfections are *united* in a special way, they are not one and the same thing . . . [C]onsidered from a theological point of view, this strict identity is not required, and, considered from a logical point of view, this identity is either a remnant of Platonic philosophy or follows from a mistaken idea of God's transcendence."[34] Immink wants to say nothing more than that "God has his divine and perfecting properties *essentially*."[35]

Richard Swinburne is another proponent of the DDS who disapproves of the strong Identity Account of the doctrine. He remarks that the DDS "recently got a bad name for itself by being equated with the very paradoxical way in which it was expounded in late patristic and subsequent medieval philosophy."[36] For Swinburne, that "paradoxical way" is that in which "all the divine properties are identical with each other and with God." Swinburne asks, "But how can God, who is a substance, an entity who possesses properties, be the same as those properties? And how can they be identical with each other? How can omnipotence be the same property as omniscience?"[37] These are not unreasonable questions.

Swinburne proposes that the intention of ensuring divine unity, which he understands to be the motivation for Aquinas's IA, can be preserved by omitting the "residual Platonism" that led Thomas to "hypostatize" abstract properties and to insist that "unless they were part of God, they would be entities independent of God."[38] Abstract entities are not, according to Swinburne, constituents of the universe, but "mere convenient fictions."[39] That is to say that the properties found in things are not really so many "things" joined together to form the wholes in which they are found: "Wisdom and suchlike are properties and not substances; they have no existence apart from their existence in sub-

---

34. Ibid., 176–77 (emphasis his).

35. Ibid., 176. For all his vigorous assertions against the IA, Immink does not engage Thomas's teaching on the analogy of being and analogy of predication, his virtual distinction argument, or his understanding of God's infinity. Absent interaction with these other Thomistic commitments a denial of Thomas's IA seems precipitate.

36. Swinburne, *The Christian God*, 160.

37. Ibid., 161.

38. Ibid., 162.

39. Ibid.

stances; and when they exist in substances, they are not parts of those substances."[40]

It is difficult to see how Swinburne's Aristotelian-like explanation of properties (and universals) differs in any appreciable way from Thomas's except that Swinburne seems to think that only complete substances can function as "parts." His logic is as follows: parts are always substances; but properties are not substances (i.e., they don't subsist *per se*); therefore the properties that cause a subject to be in this or that way are not "parts" of that subject. Thomists simply disagree with Swinburne's major premise. *A "part" is anything in a subject that is less than the whole and without which the subject would be different than it is.* Some parts are necessary to the very existence of the subject, such as *esse* and *essentia*, and others merely accidental modifications of the subject, such as the necessary and contingent properties that inhere in the subject.[41] Swinburne avoids the IA by denying that properties are parts. And since they are not parts there is no danger in maintaining their real or formal distinction; whatever the nature is of the distinction between the divine properties it is not such as would undermine the unity of God's attributes. Thus, God can still be described as "a very simple being."[42] Again, though, this is the "simplicity" of harmony among the divine attributes, not identity.

With Immink and Swinburne, Robert Burns and John Frame also affirm a version of the DDS that conceives of a harmony rather than a real identity among the divine attributes. Burns rejects Thomas's assumption that every non-simple thing is composed of parts: "[T]he direct opposite of 'simple' is 'complex,' not 'composed,' and it is by no means self-evident that every complex must literally be a composite. Unquestionably, a single first cause would have to possess unassailable integrity but it does not follow that it might not be characterized by an internal set of factors which might be distinguishable from one another, given their equally

40. Ibid.

41. It appears that Swinburne rejects Thomas's ontological outlook on account of his own over-hypostatization of parts. What's more, his charge that Thomas takes a Platonic position on properties seems misplaced. In terms of metaphysics, Thomas seems to have mixed a Platonic/Neoplatonic participation scheme with an Aristotelian conception of universals in which properties are only actual in existing substances, that is, *per aliud*. Nowhere does Thomas claim that properties subsist outside of subjects as Swinburne suggests he does.

42. Swinburne, *The Christian God*, 160. Swinburne does not think of God as *absolutely* simple since God supposedly possesses an intrinsic diversity of properties.

secure harmony."[43] Like Immink, Burns assumes that the human mode of knowledge and predication about God must correspond to God's internal ontological structure. From our various and genuinely distinct predications of divine attributes he concludes that God is characterized by an "internal set of factors" more or less structured in the same way as the human set of predications about him. These internal "factors" are what make it the case that God is good, wise, powerful, and the like. By insisting that these factors are really distinct from each other Burns concludes that that by which God is what he is must be distinct for each and every attribute. It follows, then, that God is intrinsically and ultimately characterized by numerous "factors" not strictly identical with his divine nature. Burns assures us that these factors are adequately harmonious as to guarantee God's unity, while complex enough to preserve the intelligible distinctions made in our God-talk.

Frame follows a similar argument in which he assumes our mode of predication must correspond univocally to God's mode of being. He states, "The multiple attributes refer to genuine complexities in his essence."[44] Furthermore, Frame thinks that Thomas's IA involves a purely conceptual distinction among God's attributes. "On this view," he remarks, "it is not enough to say that God's attributes, for example, are necessary to his being; rather, the multiplicity of attributes is only apparent. In reality, God is a being without any multiplicity at all, a simple being for whom any language suggesting complexity, distinctions, or multiplicity, is entirely unsuited."[45]

But as was shown above, Thomas does not believe that human language about multiple attributes is "entirely unsuited" to God. In fact, inasmuch as humans, as creatures, can only know God through created things (including the language and words by which God speaks in the Bible) it follows that *only* the language of attribute multiplicity is suitable for human predication about God. This complex God-talk, though marked by the creaturely mode of predication and modeled on the creaturely mode of imitating or reflecting the divine nature, conveys a real knowledge of God's essence. But by no means does this entail a

---

43. Burns, "The Divine Simplicity in St. Thomas," 273.

44. Frame, *Doctrine of God*, 229.

45. Ibid., 227. Apparently Frame believes that necessity itself is adequate to account for God's existence and attributes.

direct comprehension of that essence or its simple mode of subsistence.[46] Frame is incorrect to suggest that Thomas holds God to be "utterly beyond the descriptive power of human language."[47] Rather, God conveys a true description of himself through his creatures inasmuch as every creature bears some likeness to the divine nature. By insisting upon this creational bond in which creatures bear the image of the Creator (as their non-univocal cause of being), Thomas ensures that we have a description of God that is true, even if conveyed analogically under the creaturely form of being and knowing.[48]

46. George Joyce writes, "Our minds can form no single concept to express that all-embracing unity of [God's] being: our only resource is to form partial concepts, each of which exhibits some aspect of Divine fullness . . . The attributes . . . are not distinct determinations in God, as are justice and mercy in man: the distinction is the work of the mind. But it is grounded on the reality, because the fullness of the Divine being contains all that is involved in these terms" (*Natural Theology*, 260–61).

47. Frame, *Doctrine of God*, 227. Frame's resistance to Thomas's IA of the DDS stems from his rejection of Thomas's doctrine of analogy. He writes, "God is as clearly revealed to us, and as clearly known to us, as any created thing" (ibid., 208). Accordingly, "We need not be afraid of saying that some of our language about God is univocal or literal. God has given us language that literally applies to him" (ibid., 209). Frame apparently does not think that anything predicated "properly" of God (such as goodness, wisdom, and power) can be regarded as an analogous predication. By "literal" language he appears to mean language that is adequate to univocally convey the very intrinsic form of God's nature to the mind of the human knower. Frame has a Reformed precedent for this univocism in the position of Charles Hodge who writes, "To say, as the schoolmen, and so many even of Protestant theologians, ancient and modern, were accustomed to say, that the divine attributes differ only in name, or in our conceptions, or in their effects, is to destroy all true knowledge of God." Hodge avers, "Knowledge is no more identical with power in God than it is in us. Thought in him is no more creative than thought in us" (*Systematic Theology*, I: 371–72). Herman Bavinck faults Hodge for assuming "an objective difference in God at the expense of his simplicity and immutability" (*RD*, II: 119).

48. Bavinck concurs with Aquinas on the creaturely character of our knowledge of God: "[I]t must not be overlooked that we have no knowledge of God other than from his revelation in the creaturely world . . . Of God we have no direct but only an indirect kind of knowledge, a concept derived from the creaturely world. Though not exhaustive, it is not untrue, since all creatures are God's creatures and therefore display something of his perfections . . . Scripture, which is theological through and through and derives all things from God, over and over in its method of knowing nevertheless—or rather because of this—ascends to God from a position in the world (Isa 40:26; Rom 1:20). Precisely because everything comes from God, everything points back to God. All who think about him or want to speak about him derive—whether by way of affirmation or negation—the forms and images needed for that purpose from the world around them" (*RD*, II: 130).

Two objections to these Harmony Accounts of the DDS should be noted. First, Immink, Swinburne, and Burns each seem to think that the DDS is a doctrine primarily about God's *unity*. If some model other then the IA can secure an "unassailable integrity" among God's attributes then the IA would seem to be unnecessary. But the emphasis upon God's simple unity by proponents of the classical DDS is really an entailment of their more basic concern to account for the nature and existence of God as the *absolute self-sufficient first cause of being*. As was shown in our consideration of unity in chapter 3, many things that are not absolutely simple can express a high degree of unity by which it may even be said that they are relatively immutable and stable. But the motivation for the DDS is not merely to establish divine unity *qua* unity, but to achieve a conception of unity that needs nothing more basic or primitive than itself to account for itself. An absolutely simple unity alone would be ontologically sufficient to explain itself and to cause the being of anything else. But insisting, as they do, upon the non-identity of the divine attributes in God by which he is said to be this or that, the harmonists forfeit precisely the sort of unity needed to adequately account for the existence and essence of God as well as of other things. Barry Miller rightly faults Swinburne on this account: "[Swinburne] quite misrepresents the rationale of the identity thesis, which has nothing to do with unity in the wider sense, and everything to do with the special unity which is identity. The point is that only a being that is identical with its existence (and hence with its other real properties) can be the *creator* of the Universe."[49]

Second, the harmonist constructions of the divine attributes tend to maintain that the *necessity* of God's intrinsic attributes is sufficient to account for their unity and stability (or irremovability). But saying that all of God's intrinsic attributes are essential or necessary does not accomplish the intention of the DDS, which is to establish that God himself is the sufficient reason for the attributes ascribed to him. Merely arguing that the attributes are *necessary* or *essential* to God does not in itself reveal whether God is the reason for those attributes or whether those attributes are the reason for God.[50] By further insisting that those

---

49. Miller, *A Most Unlikely God*, 94.

50. The problem with trying to preserve God's immutability or other such orthodox convictions by insisting upon his *necessity* is that it decouples modality (e.g., divine necessity) from its requisite ontological foundation (e.g., divine simplicity). Modalities

attributes are really distinct in God, the harmonists seem to hold the latter. It is only by upholding the real identity of God with his attributes (and thus, his attributes with each other) that one can maintain that God himself is the most absolute reason for his attributes rather than vice versa. Indeed, in the IA of the DDS the problem of whether God is prior or subsequent to his attributes does not even arise.

PROPERTY CHALLENGE TO THE IDENTITY ACCOUNT

In chapter 1 many modern property objections to the DDS were set forth. It is fitting at this juncture to briefly summarize those challenges and to offer a response to each.[51] This is by way of preparation for the more complete answer in the next section to how it is that the Identity Account of the DDS is able to establish the absoluteness of God's attributes.

The property challenge to the IA can be generally classified into three distinct arguments: (1) properties are abstract but God is supposedly concrete and personal; (2) God shares some properties with creatures, but not all of them and thus they cannot be identical with God or with each other; and (3) the sense of a property is just what that property is and so those different in sense cannot possibly be identical *qua* properties. Each of these arguments warrants a direct response.

Abstract Properties

First, it appears that if God were identical with each of his attributes then God would be neither concrete nor personal since properties are necessarily abstract. A property (or a form) has no power, awareness, love, or life and cannot possibly be a causal factor. But each of these is ascribed to God. If the IA of the DDS is true then God isn't a person, "but a mere abstract object."[52] Brian Leftow distills the reasoning of this "abstract property" challenge: "To Plantinga, that God is a person is non-negotiable for theists, it is obvious . . . that a property cannot be a person, the Identity Thesis identifies God with a property, so this thesis

---

are always grounded in the ontological reality of some existing entity. Thus, things account for modalities, not modalities for things.

51. For a fuller exposition of the property challenges consult the sections in chapter 1 on Gale, Hughes, Morris, and Plantinga.

52. Plantinga, *Does God Have a Nature?* 47. See also, Gale, *Nature and Existence of God*, 24, and Morris, *Our Idea of God*, 117.

does entail that God is not a person, and so the Identity Thesis must go." "But," Leftow adds, "Plantinga's move from God's identity with a property to God's not being a person is a bit fast."[53]

Many Christians who would agree with Plantinga that the IA makes God too abstract to be a person still admit numerous other typically abstract things are predicated of him without diminishing the genuineness of his personhood. By way of example, Leftow observes, "Many theists claim that God exists necessarily and is present in space without precluding the presence in the same place of material things; some also assert that God is timeless and immutable. Many philosophers would say that only abstract entities (and not all of *them*) have these features. So far from demonstrating an incoherence in the concept of God, the Identity Thesis could help to explain why God has features which no other apparently concrete thing seems to have."[54] Leftow's point is that Christians often ascribe abstract concepts to God without assuming that God must therefore be partly abstract.

This answer to the abstract property challenge is even more forcibly developed by Lawrence Dewan. He does not disagree with Plantinga that "property" denotes something non-subsistent and abstract. Where Plantinga goes wrong, though, is in thinking that the IA intends to identify God with *properties* at all: "Thomas himself would say: a god is a person, and a person is not a property (that is, an inherent); a god is goodness itself; hence, in a god, goodness *is not*, as it is *in us*, a property."[55] This is to say that God's perfections are not in him as inhering properties. What Plantinga cannot accept is that any perfection or attribute could possibly be conceived as anything other than some sort of abstraction, either a property or a state of affairs. But, as Dewan indicates, this is precisely the assumption Thomists make when insisting upon the IA of the DDS:

> Now, I would say that Thomas Aquinas would not accept "God is a property." He would not accept reasoning such as: knowledge is a property; God is knowledge itself; hence, God is a property. He would say that while knowledge, as found in creatures, is

53. Leftow, "Is God an Abstract Object?" 593.

54. Ibid., 593–94.

55. Dewan, "Saint Thomas, Alvin Plantinga, and the Divine Simplicity," 143. It is not necessary to adopt Dewan's use of the weaker designation "a god" in place of "God" in order to appreciate the insight of his argument.

(and cannot but be) a property, we reason from creatures to the existence of a being which is knowing itself *subsisting*, and this being we call "a god." And he would continue: moreover, the term "knowledge" is appropriately said of God, since the precise focus of its signification is the *perfection* found in the reality it speaks of, whereas the *secondary mode of being* which is involved, that is, its being an *inherent*, (a "property") rather than a *subsistent* or concrete thing, is relegated to the *abstract mode of signifying* which the term "knowledge" has. Thus, we say that *what the word signifies* is truly verified (that is, is to be found) in the very being or substance of God (though in a more perfect mode), whereas *the way the word says it* is inapplicable—insofar as it (that is, "knowledge") indicates inherence rather than subsistence.[56]

The basic point here is that it is not of the nature of perfections *qua* perfections to be properties. Of course, in anything that is not identical with its perfections the perfections it exhibits will *inhere* in it and thus constitute so many *properties* of that subject. But the fact of inherence is occasioned by the creaturely subject's non-simple mode of being. To assume that those perfections predicated both of creatures and God must always bear a uniform relation to their subject is to preclude divine simplicity at the outset. This is exactly what the argument from the abstract nature of properties does. It presupposes that if properties are abstract then perfections are necessarily abstract as well. This would be true if we predicated perfections of God and creatures univocally. But IA proponents are committed to analogical predication as the only way by which creatures can speak of God. Dewan explains the implications for divine perfections:

A word like "property," insofar as it includes *inherence* in its signification, and not merely in its mode of signifying, could never be properly said of God. The doctrine of analogy depends on our ability to isolate for consideration a *perfection*, and to relegate to the zone of "mode of signifying" the *imperfect mode of being* which the observed perfection has in the things we primarily know. Words like "goodness" and "the good" are the result of such an ability. Words like "property" and "accident" are designed to signify the *imperfect modes themselves*. Hence, in the analogy between creatures and God, they represent precisely what is *left aside* when the word is said of God. For example, "goodness," in our experience, names what is in fact an inhering perfection.

56. Ibid., 144.

We attribute to God the perfections but not the inherence. To attempt, as Plantinga does, to apply "property" (which to Plantinga himself clearly conveys *inherence*: otherwise it would cause no difficulty) to creatures and to God suggests that he has failed to grasp the doctrine of analogy between creatures and God.[57]

In fine, though every property is an attribute or perfection, not every perfection or attribute is a property. Those who criticize the IA do not generally acknowledge this important distinction between God's mode of simple subsistence and the creature's mode of composite and dependent subsistence. Accordingly, they speak of God as though he were a property-bearing substance because of their instinctive commitment to ontological univocism.

Shared Properties

A second argument of the property challenge contends that if God were identical with his attributes, and his attributes with each other, then he could not share some of his attributes (such as goodness, wisdom, and the like) with creatures without sharing all of them. Put differently, he could not possess "insular" or incommunicable attributes (such as the "omni" attributes) while also sharing some of his other attributes with creatures. If he could then it would appear that his attributes are not really identical with each other in him. But IA proponents do believe that God and creatures share some common attributes.[58]

57. Ibid., 144–45. This is not to say that we cannot speak of divine "properties" in any sense whatsoever, but that we recognize that we say "property" improperly. Aquinas explains: "The mode of signification of the names we give things is consequent upon our mode of understanding: for names signify the concepts of our intellect (*Peri Herm.* i). Now our intellect understands being according to the mode in which it finds it in things here below from which it gathers its knowledge, and wherein being is not subsistent but inherent. Now our reason tells us that there is a self-subsistent being: wherefore although the term being has a signification by way of concretion, yet our intellect in ascribing being to God soars above the mode of its signification, and ascribes to God the thing signified, but not the mode of signification" (*DP* 7.2, ad 7). The notion of properties as inhering perfections is removed when those same attributes are said of God. Of course, univocists do not have the ontological motivation to make such a removal.

58. See Hughes, *On a Complex Theory*, 40, 66–70; Morris, "God and Mann," 313–14. Another variation of the shared property challenge holds that if the IA were true God could not share any property in common with creatures since each creaturely instantiation of a shared property would be an instantiation of God himself (see Gale, *Nature and Existence of God*, 24). It seems that Lawrence Dewan's denial that the IA entails that God is identical with an abstract property or universal (see above) would sufficiently answer this version of the shared property challenge.

The assumption triggering this argument is that God's attributes are just so many concrete instances of the same abstract universal properties instantiated and concretized in creatures. God and creatures, then, both participate in the same general properties. The only difference is that God possesses a far greater number of great-making properties than any creature does. Thomas Morris represents this modern Perfect-being perspective on divine attributes when he states, "God is thought of as exemplifying necessarily a maximally perfect set of compossible great-making properties."[59] Now, many of these great-making properties may be held in common with creatures. What makes God distinct is his instantiation of a "maximally perfect set" of such properties. Morris goes so far as to suggest that the co-exemplification of this maximally perfect set of properties "might even be taken to be the clearly intelligible core of the doctrine of divine simplicity."[60] But the distinction between the divine attributes, in Morris's scheme, is still a real distinction inasmuch as the divine nature is composed of a "collection" of properties.[61] Furthermore, Morris conceives of God as a property-bearer, which suggests that he thinks that God has his attributes by participation in universals.[62]

59. Morris, *Anselmian Explorations*, 12. He explains that "a great-making property is understood to be a property that it is intrinsically better to have than to lack" (ibid.).

60. Ibid., 21. Modern Anselmians, it seems, are inclined to trade Anselm's own IA for the modern harmonist version of the DDS.

61. Ibid., 70. For Morris, the properties that make God great are "intrinsically" great in and of themselves; that is, their greatness is due to what they themselves are and thus seems to be an entirely self-explanatory greatness. It is important to note that for Morris it is the great-making properties that are the reason for God's greatness rather than God who is the reason for the greatness of these properties. This, in fact, contradicts the core intention of the DDS. Whatever absoluteness Morris ascribes to God, it is not the sort of absoluteness in which God is the most absolute sufficient reason for his own greatness.

62. Since Morris regards God as a subject who possesses his attributes by participation he is forced to explain how it is that God comes to be characterized by properties really distinct from himself. His answer is that God is the one who causes himself to possess the maximally perfect set of great-making properties. This position complies with Alvin Plantinga's notion that God is somehow sovereign over his own nature. For Morris's affirmation that God creates his own nature see Thomas Morris and Christopher Menzel, "Absolute Creation," 359–60. Brian Leftow offers three arguments against Morris's claim that God is self-caused: First, if ability to create is something essential to God's nature then he must have his nature prior to creation. Accordingly, God's nature cannot be among the things he creates. Second, if some person creates the divine nature, then the divine nature does not exist until that person creates it. If the divine nature presupposes the existence of that person then that person must preexist,

Given their assumption that God's attributes are property instances it is no wonder that Morris and Hughes, along with many modern Perfect-being theologians, find the challenge of shared properties so devastating to the IA. The problem with their criticism, though, is that the IA was never *intended* to make sense according to their univocist assumptions about the being of God and creatures. As with the abstract properties argument, the shared properties argument goes wrong in assuming that the *manner* in which perfections are true of creatures (i.e., as inhering properties) is identical to the manner in which they are true of God. The reasoning is that if creatures are good or wise by participation in goodness or wisdom, then God must be good or wise in the same way (and so on for all the attributes ascribed to God or creatures). But when the DDS proponent insists that God is identical with his attributes, so that he is goodness itself or wisdom itself, the claim is not that God is identical with goodness in general or wisdom in general and so forth. Just as it is denied that identifying God as *ipsum esse* identifies him with *esse commune* (see the relevant discussion in chapter 4), so also it is denied that God's identity with his attributes means that he is identical with those attributes in general. In sum, there is no shared property problem for the IA since the IA denies that there are univocally shared properties.

Of course, there are perfections attributed to both God and creatures according to the same sense. But the likeness discovered between a divine attribute and its creaturely counterpart does not necessarily indicate the presence of a shared property; that would suggest that God and creatures stand in a similar relation to some third term from which they derive their perfection. Thomas explains the attribute likeness between God and a creature in terms of the creature's partial imitation of the divine nature. In creating, God impresses a finite likeness of himself in every one of his effects. But the *manner* or *mode* of the divine perfec-

---

complete with his nature, in order that the divine nature may exist. Thus the creating person's nature cannot be equal to the divine nature because it must exist before it. Third, God cannot exist until the divine nature exists, "since being God = exemplifying the divine nature." If God is created then he cannot preexist his own creation and his existing must presuppose the existence of the causal conditions of his existing. God cannot be the causal condition of his own existing since it is impossible that God cause himself to exist (see "Is God an Abstract Object?" 588). Leftow concludes against Morris that, "If there is no way to maintain that God can create His own nature (or part of it), we have no way to avoid the Identity Thesis" (ibid., 591).

tions is not reproduced in the creature.[63] Accordingly, Thomas explains, "Likeness of creatures to God is not affirmed on account of agreement in form according to the formality of the same genus or species, but solely according to analogy, inasmuch as God is essential being, whereas other things are beings by participation."[64] Gregory Rocca distills the essence of Thomas's claim: "Since nothing participated is held as one's natural possession, creatures are not their own being but possess their being as something clinging to their substance."[65] The perfection participated is the principle of act by which the participator is made to *actually* exemplify the perfection: "[W]hatever participates in a thing is compared to the thing participated in as act to potentiality, since by that which is participated the participator is actualized in such and such a way. But . . . God alone is essentially a being, whereas all other things participate in being."[66]

Because each of the divine perfections is identical with God's existence and essence it follows that those perfections are not in him as so many shareable determinations of being in which he participates along with other existents.[67] The likeness of God's attributes in creatures is explained by the preexistence of all effects supereminently in their cause

63. This would be impossible inasmuch as it would require God to create a perfect duplicate of himself and thereby destroy his absolute simplicity and infinity by making him ontologically correlative to some other being.

64. *ST* I.4.3, ad 3. Barry Miller notes that without an *analogia entis* critics of the DDS inevitably resort to explaining God's perfections as property instances (see *A Most Unlikely God*, 77, 81).

65. Rocca, *Speaking the Incomprehensible God*, 285. See also, Aquinas, *DV* 15.1: "what is . . . shared is not held as a possession, that is, as something perfectly within the power of the one who has it."

66. *SCG* II.53 [4].

67. This has led some Reformed theologians to retreat from making a distinction between communicable and incommunicable attributes in God. John Wilson, in his editorial remarks on Thomas Ridgeley's commentary on the Westminster Larger Catechism, maintains: "The distinction between communicable and incommunicable perfections of Deity, ought not to be made. All the divine perfections are alike absolute, alike glorious, alike infinite, alike identical with the divinity. They are not to be considered . . . as apart from God, or as properties of the divine subsistence. God's perfections are God himself, and God himself is his perfections. To suppose some of them to be more and some of them less distinctive of Deity, or some to be communicable and some incommunicable, is to conceive of the divine subsistence abstractedly from itself, or to compare God with God. Mere 'resemblances' between the creature and the Creator do not lessen the distance between finitude and infinitude" (in Ridgeley, *Commentary on the Larger Catechism*, 123).

and not by the common participation of God and creatures in abstract universals.[68] In the final analysis the shared property challenge fails to confront the IA on the basis of the DDS's own ontological assumptions about the analogical relationship between God and creatures.[69] Also, it assumes that God depends upon the intrinsic perfection and stability of abstract properties in order to make use of them in constituting his own nature. The classical DDS, on the other hand, denies that God is self-constituted and is thereby required to uphold a strong IA. Identity with his attributes seems to be the only alternative to the position that God is dependent upon universals and self-caused in some sense.

Sense Distinction among Properties

A third argument of the property challenge holds that properties that differ in sense must also differ in reality since the sense of any property is just what that property is. This holds no matter what the *degree* of the property may be. Therefore, unless one is prepared to argue that the sense of each divine property is identical to the sense of every other divine property, the IA must be forfeited upon pain of absurdity (e.g., claiming that God has only one property) or total agnosticism about the divine essence.[70]

It is the belief of those who make this argument that the properties of a thing cause the perfections found in that subject; that is, the properties are that *in virtue of which* anything is this or that. On a strictly hori-

---

68. This does not mean that the similarity between creatures themselves may not be explained according to some scheme of participation in abstract universals. But the universals themselves are merely the mental conceptions of creaturely imitations of the divine nature and are not the sufficient reason for themselves (*pace* the Platonic assumptions of Morris and Plantinga).

69. It is not surprising that both Morris and Hughes say nothing about Thomas's explanation of creaturely likeness to God as rooted in the doctrine of creation. But without taking into account Thomas's analogy of similitude as informed by his doctrine of divine creation it is difficult to see how the classical Identity Account is threatened by the notion of shared properties. Diversity in the creature's imitation of the divine essence is already accounted for by Thomas's understanding of creatures as created analogues that imitate divine nature in a limited or partial manner.

70. See Gale, *Nature and Existence of God*, 24; Morris, "On God and Mann," 307–8; Plantinga, *Does God Have a Nature?* 46–47. Historically, Eunomius famously insisted that all the divine attributes are identical in sense and that God really possesses only one property, namely ingeneracy. See the lucid discussion in Radde-Gallwitz, *Basil of Caesarea, Gregory of Nyssa, and the Transformation of Divine Simplicity*, 96–112.

zontal level, IA adherents do not contest this metaphysical claim when properly qualified. What they do oppose is the idea that a multiplicity of properties is required in God in order to account for the multiplicity of attributes ascribed to him. Why cannot the simple divine essence be the lone foundation for the many different perfections (including all their distinct senses) attributed to God?

Peter Geach explains that "in 'the wisdom of God' and 'the power of God,' 'the wisdom of' and 'the power of' differ in reference from the word 'God' and from one another." He concludes that "this conflicts with Aquinas's teaching on divine simplicity."[71] Geach attempts to explain how numerous attributes may be attributed to a single referent without yielding the conclusion that all these attributes are identical to each other or to the subject: "Again—to get an analogy to the three designations 'God,' 'the wisdom of God,' 'the power of God'—the square and the cube are quite distinct functions, but '1' and 'the square of 1' and 'the cube of 1' all designate the same number, and there is no distinction even in thought between the 1 that is the square and the 1 that is the cube and the 1 that is squared and cubed."[72] Geach is suggesting that each predicate is an individual form, a distinct "that by which" or "truthmaker." So, that by which the number 1 is an ordinal singular is different from that by which 1 is the square root of 1, and both are different from that by which 1 is the cube of 1. Thus, Geach concludes, there are three distinct forms present by which the number 1 is variously characterized. While we may allow that a multitude of forms may explain the different qualities ascribed to certain numbers, it is not so easy to admit such formal distinctions with relation to God's own existence and attributes. That by which God is wise, powerful, and divine is not three distinct forms, but is simply the one undivided and indivisible divine nature.

Geach's formal distinctions are not entirely inadmissible, but the distinctions lie on the side of the human knower and not in God's own being. Our tendency to formally distinguish God's wisdom, power, and other such attributes corresponds to the fact that we conceive of such perfections through their likeness in creatures, and in creatures these perfections *are* formally distinguished. Predications about God that genuinely differ in sense are linguistic and mental forms that reflect the ontological and epistemological capacity and situation of humans. But,

71. Geach, "Form and Existence," 39.
72. Ibid., 40.

again, the IA insists that diversity in the forms of human knowledge and predication is not required to isomorphically correspond to ontological forms in the thing spoken of, and especially not in God, in order to meaningfully and truly convey knowledge.

The question that Geach and others do not answer is why it is that the distinctions between the unique senses of each divine attribute must signal the presence of a real diversity in God's own ontological structure. To insist that it is this way in creatures and so must hold for God seems to beg the question by assuming a univocist ontology when it is univocism itself that is in question. Leftow helpfully highlights this lacuna in the sense distinction argument against the IA:

> Plantinga . . . objects that if each of God's essential attributes = God, then God has but one essential attribute, and such apparently distinct attributes as omniscience and omnipotence turn out identical, both of which are counterintuitive results. This objection has no more force than the first [that the DDS makes God to be an abstract property]. Omniscience is or supervenes on that state which is God's knowing what He does. Omnipotence is or supervenes on that state which is God's having the abilities He has. The terms "omniscience" and "omnipotence" of course carry distinct senses, but what reason is there to find it odd that God satisfies them in virtue of the same inner state? Is this any more surprising than that some substance satisfies "water" (taken as having a sense involving directly perceptible attributes) and "H2O" in virtue of the same inner constitution?[73]

Again, the unproven supposition of the sense distinction argument is that that in virtue of which God is said to be this or that must correspond to a diversity of intrinsic divine properties that are making it so. This would be problematic for modern Perfect-being theologians who still endeavor to uphold some version of the DDS (inasmuch as they are committed to the univocity of being between God and creatures), but does not carry much weight against those DDS subscribers who insist that we only know God analogically. The sense distinction argument against the DDS can only succeed within a univocist ontology.

---

73. Leftow, "Is God an Abstract Object?" 598.

TRUTHMAKER ACCOUNT AS THE LOGIC
OF THE IDENTITY ACCOUNT

In the past three decades the challenges to the DDS by analytic philosophers and Perfect-being theologians have focused predominantly on the impropriety of identifying God with a property, set of properties, or property instance. Many DDS advocates have sought to avoid such impropriety by exploring models by which a divine personal being and a property might be identical. The consensus among these defenders—including Eleonore Stump, Norman Kretzmann, William Mann, and William Vallicella—has really not advanced beyond the Thomistic insistence that God's identity with his perfections does not mean that he is identical with universals or properties in general. What is perplexing, though, is that these defenders of the DDS continue to conceive of the divine perfections as properties at all.[74]

---

74. The positions of Stump, Kretzmann, and Mann are discussed in chapter 1 above (see the sections on Gale and Morris). Stump and Kretzmann seem to think that God is identical with his attributes and each of them with each other insofar as he is the intrinsic maxima, or perfect instance, of those perfections. At the point of perfection, they reason, all of God's attributes (perfect power, perfect wisdom, and the like) converge in a single indistinguishable perfection, much like the single summit where a mountain's diverse slopes converge into a unity at their uppermost point ("Absolute Simplicity," 356–57). The problem, though, is that this view still locates God upon a single ontological continuum with creatures and his perfections are still conceived as property instances, perfect and indistinguishable though they may be. By making "perfection" the distinguishing mark between God's attributes and the creature's exemplification of the same attributes, Stump and Kretzmann seem to regard the divine attributes as a special *kind* or *species* of participated properties. See Hughes, *On a Complex Theory*, 62, for a similar critique. Stump and Kretzmann are susceptible to Hughes's criticism to the extent that they share his univocal outlook on the being of God and creatures. In another version of the PA William Vallicella maintains that God is a self-exemplifying first-level property (see his, "Divine Simplicity," 508–25). Barry Miller is unconvinced: "To say that a first-level property is self-exemplifying is to say that it is a property of itself. But, since a property of a first-level property is a second-level property, this amounts to saying that a self-exemplifying first-level property is *both* a first- and a second-level property." He adds, "The doctrine of divine simplicity is indeed defensible, but not by denying the absolute difference between first- and second-level predicables, nor by affirming the possibility of property self-exemplification" ("On 'Divine Simplicity: A New Defense," 474, 476). Miller would agree with Christopher Hughes's sentiment that "the idea of a property that is its own and only its own property certainly looks incoherent" (*On a Complex Theory*, 63). Hughes resolves the dilemma by denying the DDS while Miller resolves it by denying that God instantiates properties or is a property instance.

For all their orthodox and Thomistic intuition, these recent defenses are still beset by the metaphysical infelicity of claiming that God is a property or a property instance. Inasmuch as it is the nature of a property *qua* property to exist by dependence upon a substance, it seems best to abandon the Property Account of the DDS altogether. Properties can only really exist in a substance that is in potency to them and receives them as so many determinations of actuality.[75] Denying that God is composed of act and potency requires that DDS proponents fashion a non-property explanation of God's identity with his attributes. Recently, some philosophers have begun to formulate such an alternative by explaining that God is the absolutely simple "truthmaker" of all his attributes. The notion of a "truthmaker" fulfills the function that properties play in the various Property Accounts of the DDS without importing any of the problems that properties pose for a simple God.

Brian Leftow, though not wholly in agreement, comes very near to the Truthmaker Account (TA) of the divine attributes in his expla-

---

75. This is why Francis Turretin declares: "Attributes are not ascribed to God properly as something superadded to his essence (something accidental to the subject), making it perfect and really distinct from himself; but improperly and transumptively inasmuch as they indicate perfections essential to the divine nature *conceived by us as properties*" (*IET*, 3.5.2; emphasis mine). James Thornwell concurs: "[God's] infinite perfections are veiled under finite symbols. It is only the shadow of them that falls upon the human understanding" (*Collected Writings*, I: 118). Talk of divine properties is an accommodation to the customary human way of speaking about a subject's attributes. We speak as though God possesses properties, but we are not saying that there are proper metaphysical properties in God as there are in composite creatures. David Oderberg provides a penetrating discussion of properties that explains why we cannot attribute them to God in any strict metaphysical sense. His basic contention is that properties are always really distinct from essences. He includes the following supporting arguments: (1) properties flow from and are explained by essences, not the reverse; (2) there is a difference between what is *constitutive* of a thing and what *constitutes* it; (3) properties are not a specific difference by which a species is marked out; and (4) while some predicables ascribed to a subject, such as genus, species, and difference are *constitutive* predicables, others, such as accidents and properties, are *characterizing* predicables. See *Real Essentialism*, 156–62 for a detailed development of each of these points. Inasmuch as God's essence is not characterized by something other than itself, it follows, upon Oderberg's explanation, that God possesses no properties. We may speak of God's perfections and attributes as *characteristics*, but in reality we are only naming the divine essence itself improperly, that is, through a mode of predication that is only proper to property-bearers and composite beings. Inasmuch as all creatures bear some likeness to God, though, this "improper" manner of predicating is sufficient to convey the true knowledge of the divine essence without conveying to us the very form of God's incomprehensible manner or mode of self-subsistence.

nation of Augustine's DDS in which the Bishop of Hippo identifies God with (Platonic) Forms. *Prima facie* it may appear that Augustine is subject to Plantinga's charge that the IA of the DDS makes God out to be an abstract object. Leftow argues, though, that Augustine's use of the Platonic language of Forms makes the notion of Forms undergo a radical and theological transformation: "[T]hat Augustine's DDS deals in Forms may seem not to help much against Plantinga if Forms are as abstract as properties. But Plantinga takes it without argument that if one identifies God and something abstract, the result is something abstract. It might instead be to eliminate the abstract entity, leaving God as He was. Augustine identifies God with Forms to eliminate the Forms and have God take over their role in the theory of attributes."[76] Augustine understands the role of any Form to be that of a standard.[77] To identify God with Forms, then, is simply to say that he is identical with the standard for each divine attribute; he simply *is* the measure of the attribute. Augustine affirms that God is the measure of all things though he himself is unmeasured. Leftow explains:

> [F]or Augustine, God, not God's wisdom, is the standard case of wisdom. To be wise is not to be like God's wisdom. It is to be like God, who is wise. Further, for Augustine, God has no accidents [*De Trinitate*, V, xvi, 17]. God's wisdom is just God. So for Augustine, it is not the case that one is wise like the wise God by having a case of wisdom like God's case of wisdom. One is wise by so "participating in" God that one counts as wise.[78]

Upon Augustine's understanding of the DDS God's nature eliminates Forms. Leftow helpfully elucidates this point:

> Augustine took God as the paradigm replacing all Forms God might have in common with creatures: his "what He has, He is" identifies with God Forms in which God might participate and thereby eliminates the Forms. Say that God is The Good—as Augustine did—and we can adapt the logic just sketched: God's

76. Leftow, "Divine Simplicity," 366–67.

77. Leftow notes, "Standards are precisely particular things which 'measure' other particular things for various attributes" (ibid., 368). When we speak of wisdom *itself*, power *itself*, goodness *itself*, and the like we are speaking of the *standards* of wisdom, power, and goodness. It is these standards that the DDS holds to be identical with God.

78. Ibid., 370. Remember that this is a participation of created similitude, not of ontological confluence. Leftow suggests that Plato's notion of participation, though not made clear by him, "is at least likeness plus some sort of real dependence" (ibid.).

being good is just His being Himself, as The Good's was. The same goes for the rest of the Forms whose place God takes. There is no need for a trope, universal or other abstract constituent to make it true that God is good (etc.): what serves as the standard for all these things does so just by being itself.[79]

The conclusion of Augustine's IA is that God is *that by which* he is what he is. Some recent philosophers have expressed this claim by saying that God is the "truthmaker" for each of the attributes ascribed to him. Jeffrey Brower, a leading proponent of the Truthmaker Account of the DDS, explains that "truthmaker" does not refer to *making* in the sense of efficient causality: "Despite the misleading connotations suggested by its name, the notion of a truthmaker is not to be understood in terms of (efficient) causality. On the contrary, it is to be understood in terms of broadly logical necessitation—as is evident from the fact that contemporary philosophers habitually speak of truthmakers as *entailing* the truth of certain statements or predications."[80] Brower suggests that truthmakers are rightly understood as simply "truth-explainers."[81] To

79. Ibid., 370–71. Leftow further explains the value of reading the DDS as a statement about absolute standards and not about abstract properties: "If we so read Augustine's DDS, 'God = Justice' does not claim that God is a property. It asserts rather that God is the standard for justice. On my account, a standard is any item with a particular role: the standard for justice, say, is a particular just thing, the just thing such that to be just is to be like *this* just thing (in a particular way), and therefore the just thing which determines what it is to be just. So one pre-requisite for being the standard for justice is being a just thing. Abstract entities cannot be just. Only persons can. On my account, then, *only* a person could be the standard for justice. I do not say: only a person's justice. On my account, standards are concrete" (ibid., 372). This is a helpful argument, though a caveat is in order: God is not a "particular thing" as though he stood at the head of a series of other particular things. Leftow tends to speak of God as if he were the prototype of a series (note that prototypes themselves are members of a series; exemplars and limit cases are not); to this extent he seems unable to break free of an underlying ontological univocity between God and creatures. But he is correct insofar as he means that the standard for any perfection is itself that perfection in some concrete actuality.

80. Brower, "Making Sense of Divine Simplicity," 17. Brower formulates the truth-maker entailment principle as follows: "If an entity E is a truthmaker for a predication P, then E is necessarily (or essentially) such that P" (ibid., 18). With this formula in mind we may speak of necessitation in God's nature along the lines of the statement, "If God, then _____ must necessarily be true." But according to truthmaker theory this necessitation of God's intrinsic attributes need not be explained as the supervenience of properties in God (*pace* Thomas Morris).

81. Brower, "Simplicity and Aseity," 125. This broad conception of truthmakers does not commit itself to any particular ontological category, such as properties or substanc-

say, then, that God is the truthmaker for all his attributes amounts to saying that there is no plurality of constituents in him that necessitates his being good, wise, powerful, and the like. Rather, his simple and perfect nature itself ultimately explains his intrinsic attributes.

The TA of the DDS can only begin to be appreciated if we acknowledge the inability of the various modern Property Accounts to explain the identity of God with each of his attributes. In this connection, Graham Oppy deduces that the modern propensity to count any true statement or fact as indicating the presence of a distinct property entails that nothing can possess only one property and perhaps that everything possesses an infinite number of properties. Oppy explains: "Suppose that a has the property F. Then it also has the property of having at least one property (where this second property is distinct from F). So, it also has the property of having at least two properties (where this third property is distinct from F, and from the property of having at least one property). And so on."[82] This critique demonstrates the recalcitrance of modern property theories to any version of the IA. It appears trivial at best, and nonsensical at worst, to say that God is identical with every one of his properties if everything truly said of God just is one of his properties.

But the TA raises the important question: Are *properties* the only sufficient explanation for true statements about a thing, especially about God? Oppy contends that they are not:

> Suppose that it is not the case that every predicate that features in true atomic sentences expresses a property. Suppose, more generally, that the nature of the reality that makes true sentences true does not have a structure that is reflected in the grammatical structure of the sentences that are made true. Then, holding that sentences of the form "God is F" are true does not require us to suppose that there is some property that corresponds to the predicate "F" that is possessed by God and that contributes to making the sentence in question true. So, we can say, on the one hand, that God is omnipotent, omniscient, and all the rest—and we can mean what we say in a straightforward literal sense; and, we can also say, on the other hand, that God has no parts and

---

es (see discussion below). Truthmakers, or truth-explainers, may appear differently in various ontological categories depending what it is to which a given predication refers. In other words, there is no uniform class of truthmakers for every true predication.

82. Oppy, "The Devilish Complexities of Divine Simplicity," 14–15.

that there are no categorical distinctions to be drawn in the case of God.[83]

These remarks are nothing less than a frontal attack on the modern analytic conception of properties.[84] The critics of the Identity Account of the DDS generally assume that the *manner* in which we speak of God (i.e., subject + predicate) is sufficient to disclose the underlying ontological structure that makes the statements true. But, according to Oppy, this betrays a gratuitous assumption about the relationship between language and ontology. "[W]e must not suppose," he writes, "that when we say something that is literally true of God, that we can read off the ontological structure of that which makes the sentence true from the surface syntactic form of the sentence in question."[85] The unfounded assumption is that every true statement about a subject's attributes must be made true in virtue of some property or state of affairs.

Michael Bergmann and Jeffrey Brower contend that both those who uphold a property challenge to the DDS as well as those who seek to fashion a PA in favor of the DDS have made a category error in assuming that perfections truly attributed to God must be true in virtue of properties God possesses. The notion of God exemplifying properties is, they argue, an unwarranted intrusion of Platonism into Christian theology that makes the IA of the DDS appear absurd. They write: "Now why does this identification of God with his properties seem so objectionable? Because one of the most *obvious* things about God is that he isn't

---

83. Ibid., 15–16. For a similar critique of "property-based metaphysics" see Nash-Marshall, "Properties, Conflation, and Attribution," 1–18. Nash-Marshall distinguishes between a "property," which always speaks of some part in a thing, and a "characteristic," which is used to predicate of the entire thing. Both may be regarded as a thing's attributes. Of course, this distinction alone does not prove the IA of the DDS, but it does call into question the reliability of the PA as employed both by defenders and deniers of divine simplicity.

84. Jay Richards is representative of this modern analytic outlook when he writes, "property as I mean it is at least some fact about an entity in the world, some truth about it" (*Untamed God*, 65). For Richards, God is one of the entities in the world and so he also has as many properties as there are true statements that can be made about him.

85. Oppy, "The Devilish Complexities of Divine Simplicity," 17. Radde-Gallwitz points out that in the early church Aetius and Eunomius held that "[t]he linguistic realm is a direct map of the ontological" (*Basil of Caesarea, Gregory of Nyssa, and the Transformation of Divine Simplicity*, 114). They were opposed by Basil of Caesarea and Gregory of Nyssa with their insistence upon the incomprehensibility of the divine essence.

an exemplifiable. Unlike universals, tropes, or property-instances, God is a person and persons aren't the sorts of things that can be exemplified. The doctrine of divine simplicity, therefore, seems to be guilty of making a category mistake: it places a non-exemplifiable thing, a person, into the category of exemplifiables."[86] Could it not be, though, that the critics of the DDS are the ones who have made the category mistake in presuming that the referents of such abstract-sounding terms as "God's goodness" and "God's wisdom" must be exemplifiables?

To what could God's attributes refer if not to divine properties?[87] The TA answers that these attributes refer to the divine substance itself. But substances and properties cannot be in a single ontological category. Therefore, when an attribute is ascribed to God its referent is the divine substance, while, when applied to a creature, the same attribute refers to a property in the creature. Both the divine nature and the creaturely properties function as truthmakers for their respective attributes. It follows, then, that not all predications are made true by the same underlying ontological structure. The same predication (e.g., "_____ is wise") applied to different ontological referents will not be made true according

---

86. Bergman and Brower, "A Theistic Argument against Platonism (and in Support of Truthmakers and Divine Simplicity)," 282. For the same reason that he denies God is an exemplifiable, Brower also denies that God could be a concrete universal. Since it is the nature of universals to be exemplified as a constituent part in those things that participate them, God, as ontologically other than his creation, cannot be a universal, that is, he cannot be a constituent in some non-divine thing. Furthermore, Brower insists, "no concrete particular is a universal" ("Making Sense of Divine Simplicity," 8).

87. Alvin Plantinga suggests the possibility that the divine attributes may refer to states of affairs (see chapter 1). After all, there is no obvious absurdity in saying that the state of affairs by which God is wise is identical with the state of affairs by which he is powerful. But Plantinga ultimately rejects this as an explanation for the DDS since a personal God cannot be identical with a state of affairs inasmuch as a state of affairs is just as abstract as a property. Brower readily acknowledges that states of affairs cannot serve as the referents of the divine attributes. Furthermore, as he sees it, Brian Leftow's attempt to rescue the states of affairs explanation by identifying states of affairs with concrete particular substances is equally problematic. The DDS requires that God exhibit no metaphysical parts, constituents, or complexity. "But concrete states of affairs," Brower explains, "as they are typically conceived, are structured complexes having constituents. Thus, an ordinary (thick) particular such as Socrates . . . is a structured complex whose constituents are a bare substratum (or 'thin particular') and various properties (namely, those that make up Socrates' nature). But, then, evidently, an absolutely simple God cannot be identified with a state of affairs of this sort" ("Making Sense of Divine Simplicity," 13). For Leftow's proposal see "Is God an Abstract Object?" 593–94.

to the same ontological conditions. Brower insists that since divine attributes refer to the divine substance[88] and creaturely attributes (almost always) refer to creaturely properties, "the doctrine of divine simplicity cannot be interpreted solely in terms of either properties or states of affairs—or indeed in terms of entities belonging to *any* single ontological category."[89] A more elastic understanding of attribute predication is needed.

Brower holds that in all predicating it is the notion of *truthmaking*, rather than of constituents, that does the important theoretical work. He formulates the TA of predication as follows: "If an intrinsic predication of the form 'a is F' is true, then *a's F-ness* exists, where this entity is to be understood as the truthmaker of 'a is F.'"[90] This formula simply drops the need for truthmakers to be "constituents" of the subject. Upon the TA, then, we may say that God is the absolutely simple truthmaker for every one of his intrinsic attributes "without intermediate reference to constituents." Brower thus concludes, "The fact that the truthmaker interpretation of simplicity can be adequately stated without any reference to constituents (but not vice versa), confirms that it is the notion of *truthmaking* (rather than *constituency*) that is crucial for interpreting the doctrine of simplicity."[91]

Once it is acknowledged that the primary referents of predications are truthmakers and not constituents or properties (though they may

88. See Thomas's affirmation that all proper names of God signify the divine substance in *ST* I.13.2.

89. Brower, "Making Sense of Divine Simplicity," 13. As a qualification of Brower's thesis it should be observed that the ontological distinction between the categories of property and substance may still be conceived as a distinction among categories *within* the created order of being. Though substance is properly ascribed to God, he is not properly in the *category* of substance (see the treatment of substance in chapter 2 above as well as Aquinas, *DP* 7.3, ad 4). Thus, the ontological distinction between substances and properties is not the most basic and fundamental distinction we need to recognize. That most basic distinction is generated by the difference between God as *ipsum esse subsistens* and creatures as composite and dependent existents which possess *esse* via participation. Even so, Brower's point is sound inasmuch as he means that when we attribute perfections to God we refer to *him* and not to properties inhering in him.

90. Ibid., 17.

91. Ibid. Brower believes that the TA is the most faithful representation of "the actual views of medievals such as Augustine, Anselm, and Aquinas on predication and abstract reference" (ibid.). John Fox also concludes that the modified Aristotelianism of the medievals is best understood as subscribing to a truthmaker account of predication ("Truthmaker," 199–201).

function as truthmakers in composite beings) one is free to hold the IA of the DDS without pain of absurdity or contradiction. Moreover, Brower's description of the TA seems to capture very nicely the central concern of the DDS to maintain that God is "that by which" he exists and "that by which" he is what he is:

> According to the truthmaker interpretation, God is identical with the truthmakers for each of the true (intrinsic) predications that can be made about him. Thus, if God is divine, he is identical with that which makes him divine; if he is good, he is identical with that which makes him good; and so on in every other such case. Now, since nothing can be regarded as identical with anything other than itself, this interpretation just amounts to the claim that God *is* the truthmaker for each of the predications in question.[92]

Finally, an important qualification of the TA that enables the DDS to overcome the charges that God must possess really distinct attributes *in se* is that God is the *minimal* truthmaker for each intrinsic predication about him. Again, Brower is instructive as he writes:

> God is the *minimal* truthmaker for each of his true intrinsic predications—where an entity E is a minimal truthmaker for a predication P just in case E is such that no proper part of it also makes P true . . . [T]his qualification is needed since on some theories of truthmaking, if E is a truthmaker for P, then so is anything of which E is a part. Once the qualification is added, however, the absolute simplicity of God follows immediately. For if God had any proper parts, there would be true intrinsic divine predications (namely, about these parts) whose minimal truthmakers would not be God (but the parts).[93]

---

92. Brower, "Making Sense of Divine Simplicity," 19.

93. Brower, "Simplicity and Aseity," 125. Alexander Pruss concurs with Brower: "The claim that God's being merciful and God's being just are identical is, I take it, the claim that the ontological basis for predicating mercy of God is identical with the ontological basis for predicating justice of God. Or . . . it is simply the claim that God's justice is identical with God's mercy, i.e., that the same thing is the minimal truthmaker of the claim that God is just and the claim that God is merciful." Pruss offers the following formulation: "All non-tautological truths solely about God or his parts have God as their minimal truthmaker . . . It follows immediately from [this formula] that God has no proper parts, since if A were a proper part of God, then A rather than God would be the minimal truthmaker of the claim that A exists" ("On Two Problems of Divine Simplicity," 153).

Some will undoubtedly detect circularity in the claim that God is the minimal truthmaker for himself. But inasmuch as we are talking about the absolute final reason for God's existence and essence, and given God's creation of the world *ex nihilo*, the sufficient reason for all created being, this is exactly what one should expect. Brower acknowledges that "truthmaking is a primitive or *sui generis* form of necessitation, one that does not admit of (non-circular) analysis or definition."[94]

The TA of the DDS means that God himself is the ultimate stopping place for explaining the divine existence and attributes. For the purposes of this present study we may say that on account of the strong IA version of the DDS God is the most absolute reason and explanation for himself. He is most absolute in every one of his intrinsic attributes because every one of those attributes is identical with the divine nature, which is *ipsum esse subsistens*. God's attributes are not intrinsic determinations of his being, but rather they are just so many truths about the one indivisible and infinite existence and essence of God. Accordingly, the perfect model or exemplar for all the creaturely properties that imitate the divine nature, is not some greater property or property instance, but is simply God himself.

CONCLUSION

The only way to hold that God is most absolute with respect to his intrinsic perfections is if we understand God himself as the minimal truthmaker for each one. If God possesses his attributes as properties in the strict metaphysical sense then he will only be, at best, a *relative* absolute inasmuch as he will depend upon the stability and integrity of the properties themselves. In this scheme the divine attributes account for God rather than the other way around. To make this assumption, as so many modern Christian philosophers and theologians are wont to do, is to diminish God's absoluteness and to allow a soft Platonism to lodge within the Christian doctrine of God.

94. Brower, "Simplicity and Aseity," 111.

6

Simplicity and God's Absolute Knowledge and Will

WIDE RANGING DEBATE OVER God's intellective and volitional attributes of knowledge and will has persisted throughout the history of the church even down to the present time. One aspect of this debate is determining whether or not God's omniscience and will are compatible with the DDS. Really, these are two different, though related, questions. The first question is: How can a simple God have a proper knowledge of many *different* things without thereby possessing a complex intellect *composed* of many different ideas? The second is: How can a simple God exercise volition inasmuch as all willing seems to add some sort of actuality to the one willing? This chapter deals with each of these challenges in turn and argues that, rather than undermine God's omniscience and will, the DDS actually serves to establish the absoluteness of both the intellective and volitional aspects of the divine mind.

As in the foregoing chapters, the thesis that God is that by which he exists and by which he has the quiddity he does continues to function as a key argument in discussing the DDS's relation to God's intellective and volitional activity. With respect to his knowledge he is that by which he knows all things. This stands in stark contrast to the creaturely way of knowing inasmuch human knowledge is wholly derived, either by acquisition or implantation. This suggests a real distinction between the knower and his or her act of knowing. In humans the act of knowledge runs interference, as it were, between the knowing subject and the thing known, enabling the knower to receive the knowledge. The classical DDS claims that in God no such real distinction exists; knower, knowing, and known are all identical. But if we hold that in his omniscience God knows *many* things other than himself, how are we not to conclude that his knowledge is actually complex? Moreover, if the Identity

Account of the DDS is true, how are we not to conclude that God *himself* is intrinsically complex at the level of his essence and existence? The traditional Thomist and Reformed scholastic response to these challenges has been to claim that God does not possess his knowledge of diverse things through the reception of multiple intelligible species or forms in his intellect, but, rather, has this vast knowledge of things in knowing his own essence as imitable. Additionally, the claim that God is pure act seems to proscribe the possibility that he ever receives knowledge or *comes* to know things.

It is also argued that God is that by which he wills all things. This somewhat curious assertion means that God's act of will, in both its free and necessary aspects, is identical with God himself. Similar to his knowledge, in God willer, willing, and willed are really identical. The final end or goal of all God's willing, that which supplies the reason for his will, is nothing other than himself. In all his willing he is his own ultimate object of desire, as it were. Furthermore, the act by which God wills himself is identical with the act by which he exists. His act of volition is not something in him in addition to his very essence. The will of God is simply God willing. In this regard, the divine will is not to be regarded as a divine *faculty* in any proper sense.

The question naturally arises of how it is that a simple God wills non-divine things. Would not his will for other things be really distinct both from his essence and from his will for himself? Thomists and many Reformed theologians answer that the act of God's will is explained by its final goal or end, and inasmuch as God is the end even in his willing of creatures, the act by which he wills those creatures cannot be really distinct from the act by which he wills himself. Though his will for himself is naturally necessary and his will for other things is only suppositionally necessary, God nevertheless wills all in a single volitional act. The particular difficulty of God's free will respecting creatures is addressed in the next chapter. The goal of this chapter is to highlight the unique function of the DDS in fixing the absoluteness of God's knowledge and will.

KNOWLEDGE OF MANY THROUGH KNOWLEDGE OF ONE

Real Identity in God of Knower, Knowing, and Known

In order to understand how the DDS secures the absoluteness of God's knowledge it is first crucial that we explicate the impact of the *actus purus* conception of God (see the relevant discussion in chapter 4 above) upon any explanation of his understanding.[1] Thomas Aquinas argues that if God and his object of knowledge are not identical then God cannot be pure act since his knowledge would be informed by something other than himself. This would logically require some intellectual movement in God from the state of "could know" (a state of passive potency) to that of "does know" (a state of actuality). This would hold whether we refer to God's knowledge of himself or his knowledge of non-divine things. But if God is pure act then there can be no real distinction in him between knower (subject), knowing (act), and known (object). Thomas writes:

> Since therefore God has nothing in Him of potentiality, but is pure act, His intellect and its object are altogether the same; so that He neither is without the intelligible species, as is the case with our intellect when it understands potentially; nor does the intelligible species differ from the substance of the divine intellect, as it differs in our intellect when it understands actually; but the intelligible species itself is the divine intellect itself, and thus God understands Himself through Himself.[2]

The key element in Thomas's argument is the denial of real distinction between God's intellect and the "intelligible species" by which he knows himself and all things. Without digressing into an extended discussion of Thomas's philosophy of mind,[3] his distinction between the human subject's intellect, act of knowing, and object of knowledge should be noted. When Socrates, for instance, knows himself to be a human there is a real distinction between Socrates as the subject and that intelligible species, "humanity," by which he knows himself to be human. Socrates is not identical with humanity (i.e., there is a real distinction in

1. Aquinas remarks in *ST* I.14.1, ad 1: "[K]nowledge is not a quality of God, nor a habit; but substance and pure act." With a similar emphasis upon pure actuality, Barry Miller denies that God's knowledge is an ability that he exercises: "His omniscience is not even a fully exercised ability or fully actualized potentiality. Rather, it is his actually knowing whatever is to be known without, however, having any ability to be exercised or potentiality to be actualized" (*A Most Unlikely God*, 97). God does not know by the actualization of some potency or capacity in him. Likewise, Stephen Charnock states, "God is all act in the knowledge of himself and his knowledge of other things" (*Existence and Attributes of God*, I: 416).

2. *ST* I.14.2. See also, Davies, *Thought of Thomas Aquinas*, 128–32.

3. For that discussion see Kenny, *Aquinas on Mind*; Feser, *Aquinas*, 142–51; Brennan, *Thomistic Psychology*, 169–209; and Pasnau, *Thomas Aquinas on Human Nature*, 267–329.

him between supposit and nature). As a concrete human Socrates stands outside of that humanity by which he knows himself to be human. His self-knowledge is accordingly discursive and derived from the form of humanity that impresses itself upon his intellect. In short, his intellect is *in*-formed because the form by which it knows comes to him from without. This holds, according to Thomas, for everything that the human knows, both for self-knowledge and the knowledge of other things. Accordingly, no human intellect can be described as pure act since it is always moved from potency to act by the informing power of some intelligible species with which it is not identical.[4]

Inasmuch as there is no real distinction in God between supposit and nature there is no reason to suppose that his self-knowledge is possessed by way of *in*-formation or discursive reasoning. God is the divinity by which he is divine and thus knows himself *by* himself. This self-knowledge, furthermore, is not an act of self-impressed knowledge by way of self-representation. That is, God does not *cause* himself to know himself. Rather, he just is that act of knowledge by which he knows himself. Consider Thomas's explanation:

> It must be said that the act of God's intellect is His substance. For if His act of understanding were other than His substance, then something else . . . would be the act and perfection of the divine substance, to which the divine substance would be related, as potentiality is to act, which is altogether impossible; because the act of understanding is the perfection and act of the one [who is] understanding. Let us now consider how this is . . . [T]o understand is not an act passing to anything extrinsic; for it remains in the operator as his own act and perfection; as existence is the perfection of the one existing: just as existence follows on the form, so in like manner to understand follows on the intelligible species. Now in God there is no form which is something other than His existence, as shown above [*ST* I.3.4]. Hence as His essence itself is also His intelligible species, it necessarily follows that His act of understanding must be His essence and His existence.[5]

---

4. See *ST* I.84.3 for Thomas's discussion of the movement from potency to act in the human intellect: "Now we observe that man sometimes is only a potential knower, both as to sense and as to intellect. And he is reduced from such potentiality to act—through the action of sensible objects on his senses, to the act of sensation—by instruction or discovery, to the act of understanding. Wherefore we must say that the cognitive soul is in potentiality both to the images which are the principles of sensing, and to those which are the principles of understanding."

5. *ST* I.14.4.

This is a challenging yet significant passage. Thomas's point depends upon his understanding of the proportionality between the intellectual and existential orders. As God's essence cannot be further perfected by the reception of accidental forms, so his intellect cannot be further perfected or enriched by the reception of intelligible species or forms with which he is not identical. Garrigou-Lagrange points out, "This means that, just as God's essence does not differ from His existence, so His intelligible essence does not differ from His act of understanding."[6] Just as God is wholly undetermined and independent in his existence, so his knowledge is wholly undetermined and unreceptive of any intelligible species by which it may be enriched (i.e., perfected) and informed.[7] Whereas humans know themselves by way of information, God does not. He is wholly identical both with his intelligible nature and the intellectual act by which he knows his nature.

While many may acknowledge that the identity between knower and known in God is useful for explaining the superiority of his *self*-knowledge over the human's discursive mode of self-knowledge, it is less clear how there can be a real identity between God and the object of his knowledge when that object is anything non-divine. How can God be *that by which* he knows creatures? Surely, the divine essence cannot be the intelligible species by which God knows non-divine things. Yet this is precisely what must be affirmed if God's knowledge is to be regarded as simple, most absolute, and independent of the creature. God does not stand in the same relation to known objects outside himself as humans do.[8] While human knowledge is always informed by some intelligible species really distinct from the individual, God's knowledge moves, as it were, in exactly the opposite direction. His knowledge *in*forms creatures rather than being informed by them. In this sense created beings are never the *primary* object of God's knowledge if by "object" we mean

6. Garrigou-Lagrange, *The One God*, 425.

7. John Wippel explains that this contrasts with the human intellect which "bears a determined relationship to forms it abstracts from sense experience" (*Metaphysical Thought*, 508). Joseph Owens observes that the acquisition of knowledge in man results in an accidental enrichment of his being. It adds accidental form to his substantial existence thus causing him to undergo an accidental change (see *An Elementary Christian Metaphysics*, 230). See also, Renard, *The Philosophy of God*, 116–18.

8. Eleonore Stump observes, "Aquinas has a clear view of how epistemic contact is established when a human being cognizes an external object: the thing being cognized has an effect on the cognizer's senses, and that causal connection constitutes the epistemic contact. But, of course, this kind of explanation cannot be what accounts for God's epistemic contact with creatures" (*Aquinas*, 184).

"the specifying term of knowledge."[9] Rather than his knowledge being specified by creatures, creatures are themselves specified by his knowledge.[10] God knows these non-divine things in knowing himself and inasmuch as he is identical with his act of self-knowledge he is identical with that act by which he knows all creatures, both actual and possible. This knowledge of creatures through himself has been explained as God knowing the imitability, or participability, of his essence.

Imitability and God's Knowledge of Creatures

Two questions must be answered in seeking to reconcile God's simple act of knowledge with his knowledge of multiple creatures. First, how can he possess a perfect knowledge of them if they are not the primary objects of his knowledge? Second, how can he know them properly as individuals, genuinely distinct from each other, if he knows each of them through the same "form," namely, his own essence?

One source of the multiplicity in human knowledge is the host of intelligible species by which that knowledge is actuated. The principle of act for one bit of our knowledge is really distinct from the principle of act for the many other bits of our knowledge insofar as the intelligible "forms" of things that actuate our knowledge are really distinct from each other. The multiplicity of intelligible species known produces a corresponding multiplicity and complexity in the human mind. But God's knowledge of things is entirely undetermined by the things themselves and, hence, is not comprised of many distinct acts of cognition. Of course, this still leaves the question of how it is possible that God knows non-divine things at all. The notion of wholly undetermined knowledge, which, strictly speaking, is knowledge without information or educa-

9. Maritain, *Existence and the Existent*, 105. This seems to be the point of WCF 2.2 when it affirms that God's knowledge is "independent upon the creature." God's knowledge of creatures is only rightly construed as "independent" of them if they do not function as the primary determinative objects of that knowledge, that is, as the intelligible species by which God knows them. God knows creatures primarily in knowing himself as their exemplar nature and cause. See Renard, *The Philosophy of God*, 120–22, and Doolan, "Is Thomas's Doctrine of Divine Ideas Thomistic?" 157–59.

10. Thomas remarks, "[T]he divine intellect through its knowledge is the cause of things . . . The divine intellect, therefore, is related to things as things are related to the human intellect" (*SCG* I.61 [7]). Thomas means that just as things cause human knowledge by an informing power, so divine knowledge causes things by an informing power. The informing power in divine and human acts of knowledge moves in exactly opposite directions relative to external objects known.

tion, strikes many as, *prima facie*, an indication of total ignorance. If God does not possess creatures as the primary objects of his knowledge (recall that the DDS identifies knower and known in God) how can he know them at all?

In answer to this challenge one must first consider that God is infinite in his being. As infinite act he cannot receive additional intellectual data inasmuch as that would constitute an enrichment of his knowledge and no purely actual infinite can be made more actual than it already is. Furthermore, this infinite actuality requires that there cannot be any finite existent or quality whose perfections of being are not already present in God in an eminently superior fashion. Accordingly, his knowledge of any actuality cannot properly derive from some being outside himself, but must originate in his own self-knowledge. God knows creatures properly, then, not by directly perceiving them in their essences or properties but in comprehending his own essence as imitable or participable, that is, able to be imaged forth in finite things. Thomas explains this "indirect" divine knowledge of creatures:

> Now in order to know how God knows things other than Himself, we must consider that a thing is known in two ways: in itself, and in another. A thing is known in itself when it is known by the proper species adequate to the knowable object; as when the eye sees a man through the image of a man. A thing is seen in another through the image of that which contains it; as when a part is seen in the whole by the image of the whole; or when a man is seen in a mirror by the image in the mirror, or by any other mode by which one thing is seen in another.[11]

The first way of knowing seems to require no medium whereas the second does. It is a common assumption that the more perfect of these two ways of knowing is that which requires no medium.[12] It may appear somewhat surprising, then, that Thomas denies that God knows creatures directly in themselves. He argues, instead, that God knows creatures through the medium of his own essence. Consider his conclusion:

11. *ST* I.14.5.

12. There is a sense in which even our direct knowledge of things in themselves is mediated to us through the actions and properties of those things so that we never perceive their naked essences, so to speak. In this way all human knowledge is mediated. Thomas makes a distinction between knowledge mediated by its image (seen in its actions and properties) and knowledge of a thing mediated through the image of something else altogether. See the useful discussion in Clarke, *Explorations in Metaphysics*, 45–64.

"So we say that God sees Himself in Himself, because He sees Himself through His essence; and He sees other things not in themselves, but in Himself; inasmuch as His essence contains the similitude of things other than Himself."[13]

It is important to notice that Thomas *does* affirm that God knows non-divine things as something genuinely *other* than his essence. But his knowledge of them first passes through his essence as one's vision of an image in a mirror first sees the mirror and then, within that medium, sees the image reflected in it.[14] Of course, the mirror illustration breaks down inasmuch as the essence of the mirror itself is not the exemplar nature after which the natures it reflects are patterned and produced. It is probably for this reason that we tend to think of indirect knowledge through media as somehow less perfect than direct apprehension of things in themselves. The medium, being essentially unlike the thing it reflects, seems to obscure or diminish our knowledge of the object we perceive in it. But in this sense, God's knowledge of things through the medium of his own essence is radically unlike human knowledge through media; the non-divine objects God knows are modeled after and caused to exist by the medium itself, namely, his essence. And just as effects exist more perfectly and eminently in their exemplars and efficient causes, so God's knowledge of creatures through his own essence as their exemplar and efficient cause yields a more perfect knowledge of them than if he just knew them by having their proper intelligible species impressed upon his mind.

So what is it about the divine essence that God knows that enables him to consider something other than simply the essence itself? How does he come to know things non-identical with himself in the act of

13. *ST* I.14.5. Thomas regards Augustine's doctrine as substantially in agreement with his own: "The passage of Augustine in which it is said that God 'sees nothing outside Himself' [*Book of 83 Questions*, q.46] is not to be taken in such a way, as if God saw nothing outside Himself, but in the sense that what is outside Himself He does not see except in Himself, as above explained" (*ST* I.15.5, ad 1). Similarly, Francis Turretin argues that God's knowledge of all things is perfect "because he knows all things by himself or by his essence [and] . . . not by forms abstracted from things—as is the case with creatures" (*IET*, 3.12.2).

14. This description displays the limitation of human concepts and language in describing the intellectual activity of an eternal and purely actual God. Obviously, if God's life and intellect are not measured by sequential moments this notion of what he knows primarily and what he knows secondarily cannot correspond to an actual intrinsic order of first followed by second.

knowing himself? An initial answer to this question that Aquinas and many Reformed theologians offer is that God's perfect self-knowledge entails knowledge of his power and no power is perfectly known without knowing to what it extends.[15] Thus, God knows all things in knowing the full extent of his power to produce them. But this is not the whole answer. Thomas also turns his attention upon the *imitability*, or image-ability, of the divine essence. He insists that God does not only know being in general by knowing himself as the principle of being, but he also knows particular beings with all their perfections in knowing the ways his essence can be imitated and participated. Thus he writes,

> As therefore the essence of God contains in itself all the perfection contained in the essence of any other being, and far more, God can know in Himself all of them with proper knowledge. For the nature proper to each thing consists in some degree of participation in the divine perfection. Now God could not be said to know Himself perfectly unless He knew all the ways in which His own perfection can be shared by others. Neither could He know the very nature of being perfectly, unless He knew all modes of being. Hence it is manifest that God knows all things with proper knowledge, in their distinction from each other.[16]

In knowing his essence as imitable, or shareable, Thomas means that God's essence supplies the "intelligible character" of every creaturely participant: "God knows all things by one principle, for that principle has the intelligible character of many. This principle is His essence, which is the likeness of all things; and since His essence is the proper intelligible character of each and every thing, He has proper knowledge of all things."[17] In one respect, this explanation enables us to explain how

---

15. See *ST* I.14.5. See also, *DV* 2.4; Gilson, *Elements of Christian Philosophy*, 166–67.

16. *ST* I.14.6. See also, Wippel, *Metaphysical Thought*, 592, and Renard, *Philosophy of Being*, 112. Stephen Charnock concurs with Thomas when he writes, "Since he [God] contains in himself all things possible, past, present, and to come, he cannot know himself without knowing them" (*Existence and Attributes of God*, I: 404). On the participability of the divine nature, Herman Bavinck remarks, "Every creature is a revelation of God and participates in God's being. The nature of this participation is not such that creatures are modifications of the divine being or that they have in some realistic sense received this divine being into themselves" (*RD*, II: 206).

17. *DV* 2.4, ad 2. In similar fashion Louis De Raeymaeker writes, "God does not discover reality as a fact to be explained; He possesses it clearly in its absolute foundation; for He possesses Himself completely . . . What does God know? He knows Himself perfectly, hence He grasps all things in the measure in which He is their principle, that is, absolutely" (*Philosophy of Being*, 314).

God's knowledge is "most absolute" by showing how we might preserve his independence from creatures while recognizing his true and proper knowledge of them. By identifying knower and known in God via the DDS there is no reason to think of God's knowledge as a real complex of distinctly actuated bits of information that are dependent upon an external multitude of intelligible species.

But, even if the "imitability" explanation seems to solve the problem of how a simple God can remain independent in his knowledge of things outside himself, there is still the matter of how God can properly know *many* particular creatures through the *one* divine essence. It would seem much easier to conclude that he knows only "being in general" (*ens commune*) through his essence, and not particular beings.[18] But no Christian can accept a merely *general* divine knowledge. In answer to this challenge Thomas does not concoct a whole new explanation, but simply points out that in perfectly knowing his essence as imitable God knows every finite mode in which that imitation might consist:[19]

> The divine essence is the intelligible character of a thing inasmuch as that thing imitates the divine essence. No created thing, however, fully imitates the divine essence. For, if so, there would be only one such imitation, and the divine essence considered in that way would be the proper intelligible character of only one being . . . However, since a created thing imperfectly imitates the divine essence, it happens that different things imitate it in different ways; yet every one of them has been produced according to a likeness of the divine essence. Thus, whatever is proper to each finds in the divine essence that which it imitates. In this respect, the divine essence is the likeness of a thing, even in regard to what is proper to it. Similarly, it is the proper intelligible character of that thing, and, for the same reason, the proper character of another thing, and also of all other things. Therefore, it is the common character of all things in so far as it is the one thing which all things imitate; but it is the proper character of this or that thing inasmuch as things imitate it in different ways. In this

18. Thomas rejects this proposal in *SCG* I.54 [1].

19. Thomas denies that God's infinite nature could be imitated by another actually infinite thing inasmuch as the existence of second *actual* infinite is impossible. In order to be genuinely *other* this second infinite nature must exhibit at least one difference from its exemplar. But this difference itself would necessarily be less than infinite since the only way to differ from an infinite is by some finitude. Thus, two actual infinites is an impossibility.

way the divine essence causes proper knowledge of each and every thing, for it is the proper intelligible character of all.[20]

God does not merely know *that* his essence is imitable, but he knows every way in which the possible imitations may fall short of his absolute and infinite perfection. Yet, inasmuch as his knowledge of these diverse and finite modes does not derive from the diverse things themselves, it is not a composite knowledge. Thomas does not hesitate to affirm that God's knowledge of diverse participables signals a multiplicity of ideas in him. But, as Henri Renard points out, these many ideas do not signify a collection of really distinct intellectual acts in God and thus do not conflict with ascribing simple knowledge to him: "This multiplicity [of divine ideas] is not opposed to the divine simplicity, for the intelligible species by which God understands these various creatable essences is one: it is the divine essence. Certainly, it is not contrary to the simplicity of the divine intellect to know many things. But it would indeed be the denial of divine simplicity, and in truth the denial of God, if the divine intellect were informed by a multitude of distinct intelligible species."[21] Renard's final remark assumes that if God's knowledge were informed, as human knowledge is, God would be dependent upon the creature for some (accidental) aspect of his being, namely, his intellectual actuality.

Recent Thomist scholarship is not uniformly agreed on what to make of Thomas's affirmation of multiple ideas in God.[22] Though a thorough investigation of that inter-Thomist debate is beyond the scope of the present consideration, a few observations should be noted concerning how God can have multiple ideas without necessarily being intellectually complex or composite. According to Thomas, as an exemplar

20. *DV* 2.4, ad 2. See also, *DP* 3.16, ad 24.

21. Renard, *The Philosophy of God*, 140.

22. Some assume that, as with the divine attributes, the diversity of the divine ideas is only from the side of our creaturely conceptions of God's knowledge. For example, see Gilson, *Christian Philosophy*, 106–8. Others hold that the diversity of the divine ideas is an intrinsic diversity in God, even if only a logical one. This view assumes that there are good reasons for holding a logical distinction between the divine ideas but not between the divine attributes. In particular, the divine ideas signify God's knowledge of his essence as it is imitable by creatures and thus according to some proportion to creatures. The divine attributes as such do not exhibit any such proportionality and therefore do not need to be logically distinguished in God. For this position see Wippel, *Thomas Aquinas on the Divine Ideas*, and Doolan, *Aquinas on the Divine Ideas as Exemplar Causes*. It seems to me that Wippel and Doolan are more faithful to Thomas's teaching on this matter.

an idea bears a distinct relationship to something other than the one possessing the idea. It is an exemplar after which something is produced. Inasmuch as God is identical with his intellect and knows everything that can be produced in the likeness of his essence, his essence serves as the "idea" for those things.[23] It follows, Thomas explains, that God's ideas may be "multiplied by their relations to things."[24] The obvious question is: How does this not introduce multiplicity into the divine essence if, indeed, the essence is identical with the *multiple* ideas? One sees the attraction of saying that God has simply one idea of many things. But, if he had only one exemplar idea it would seem that he could only ever produce one creaturely likeness of himself. The multiplicity of ideas corresponds to the fact that the one divine essence "can be shared diversely by different things."[25]

John Wippel explains that the divine essence is not an idea with reference to itself, "but insofar as it is the likeness or reason for this or that thing."[26] Simply put, the divine essence is not a *likeness* or *exemplar* of itself; it just is itself. There is no proportion between God's knowledge of his essence and the essence itself (assuming that God's essence is wholly uncaused and not possessed via participation), and thus there is no need for an exemplar idea of his essence. But there *is* a proportion between his knowledge of his essence as imitable and the things that imitate his essence. Thomas writes, "Although God knows Himself and all else by His own essence, yet His essence is the operative principle of all things, except of Himself. It has therefore the nature of an idea *with respect to other things*; though not with respect to Himself."[27] Likewise, he adds, "The divine essence is not called an idea in so far as it is that essence, but only in so far as it is the likeness or type of this or that thing. Hence ideas are said to be many, inasmuch as many types are understood through

---

23. In *ST* I.15.1, ad 3 Thomas writes, "God is the similitude of all things according to His essence; therefore an idea in God is identical with His essence." Cornelius Van Til agrees: "In him, ideas and being are one" (*An Introduction to Systematic Theology*, 377). See also, Bavinck, *RD*, II: 211.

24. *ST* I.44.3. In the Thomistic and Reformed view the relation between God and creatures is not strictly symbiotic.

25. Ibid.

26. Wippel, *Thomas Aquinas on the Divine Ideas*, 35.

27. *ST* I.15.1, ad 2 (emphasis added). Clearly, he uses "idea" here in the specialized sense of an exemplar for some producible thing.

the self-same essence."[28] Thomas concludes that the essence *qua* essence is the one idea for many things, while the essence *qua* imitable is many ideas: "If we consider the essence alone . . . there is but one idea for all things; but if we consider the different proportions of creatures to the divine essence, then there can be said to be a plurality of ideas."[29]

The *manner* in which God possesses his plurality of ideas is such that it does not conflict with his simplicity. Gregory Doolan offers useful insight in this regard:

> [T]he crux of Thomas's argument defending the plurality of divine ideas lies in the distinction that he makes between a form taken as the first principle of an act of understanding (an intelligible species) and form taken as the terminus of such an act (an idea). Since God is pure act, nothing other than his own essence actualizes his intellect as the first principle of understanding. Thus, there can be only one such principle. Since that essence is imitable in a variety of ways, however, God can have many ideas as the termini of his act of understanding. In this way, his unity is not compromised, for even though these ideas constitute a multiplicity of things *that* he understands, the medium *by which* he understands them is the one divine essence. In short, the multiplicity of the divine ideas is a logical multiplicity, not a real one.[30]

The ideas would be *really* distinct if they were determined by a multiplicity of intelligible species. This concurs with the point made above that, rather than being specified by creatures, God's knowledge is what specifies *them*. It is this feature of God's knowledge that enables us to deny that it is dependent or really composite. Herman Bavinck highlights the transcendence of God's omniscience, declaring, "His knowledge of all

---

28. Ibid., I.15.2, ad 1.

29. *DV* 3.2.

30. Doolan, "Is Thomas's Doctrine of Divine Ideas Thomistic?" 159. Consider Thomas's argument in *DV* 3.2, ad 3: "A plurality of concepts is sometimes reduced to a diversity in the thing. For example, there is a rational distinction between Socrates and Socrates sitting, and this is reduced to the difference that there is between substance and accident. Similarly, man and animal differ rationally; and this difference is reduced to the difference between form and matter, because genus is taken from matter but the specific difference from form. Consequently, such a conceptual difference is repugnant to the highest unity or simplicity. On the other hand, a conceptual difference sometimes is reduced not to any diversity in the thing, but to its truth, which can be understood in different ways. It is in this sense that we say that there is a plurality of intelligible characters in God. Hence, this plurality is not repugnant to His highest unity or simplicity."

things is not based on things after they came into existence, for then they would have emerged . . . from the unconscious. Rather he knows all things in and of and by himself. For that reason his knowledge is undivided, simple, unchangeable, eternal."[31] Only insofar as God is *that by which* he knows himself and all things can we say that his knowledge is most absolute. In fine, God's knowledge is most absolute on account of his simplicity.

GOD'S WILLING OF HIMSELF AND OTHER THINGS

Before engaging the challenge of divine volitional freedom in chapter 7, it is first necessary that some general considerations be set down regarding the relation between God's essence, his act of will, and the object of his will. Here, as with God's knowledge, divine simplicity plays a crucial role in establishing the absoluteness of the divine will. In short, the DDS claims that God's essence, his willing, and the ultimate object of his will are really identical in him and that the act by which God wills himself is the very same act by which he wills all non-divine things. God's final object or end in all his willing is himself, and inasmuch as he is eternally pure act there can be no uncertainty or contingency in his will any more than there is in his existence or essence. Unlike human volition, God's will is never passive, indifferent, or liable to frustration. He eternally wills and possesses his end perfectly. Aquinas articulates his uncommonly strong account of God's volitional perfection by appealing to the DDS in *De veritate* 23.1: "Wherever more perfect conditions for willing are found, will exists in a more perfect way. But in God the conditions for willing are found most perfectly. In Him there is no separation of the will from its subject, because His essence is His will. There is no separation of the will from its act, because His action also is His essence. There is no separation of the will from the end, its object, because His will is His goodness. Therefore will is found most perfectly in God." Furthermore, the identity of the divine will with its final object is precisely what establishes the superiority and absoluteness of God's volitional freedom. Thomas thus adds: "Will is the root of freedom. But freedom belongs especially to God. In the words of the Philosopher, 'a free person is one who is for his own sake,' and this is most true of

---

31. Bavinck, *RD*, II: 196.

God."[32] We shall consider two features of the Thomistic and Reformed[33] doctrine of divine will that highlight the role of the DDS in establishing God's volitional absoluteness: (1) the real identity in God of willer, willing, and willed; and (2) God's willing of creatures in willing himself.

Real Identity in God of Willer, Willing, and Willed

The Identity Account of the DDS entails that God is identical both with his volitional action as well as the object of that action. The reason he must be identical with his act of will is that if he were not he would not be pure act and his will would be in him as an accidental act causing him to be in some sense. In other words, something other than God's own Godhead, namely, his will, would determine the volitional aspect of his actuality. Moreover, the reason God must be identical with the end or final object of his will is that the object is the reason for the act. It accounts for the will's action. But it is a leading claim of the DDS that God has no reason for being (even volitional being) back of or alongside himself. Thus, there can be no final object of God's will with which he is not identical or which furnishes an extrinsic reason for his willing. God alone is the sufficient reason and explanation for all that is in him, including his act of will.

Aquinas develops these arguments in *Summa theologiae* I.19.1 and *Summa contra gentiles* I.73–74. In *ST* I.19.1 he considers three arguments against God possessing a will: (1) the object of the will is the end and the good, but we cannot assign an end to God (because he is pure act) and so cannot acknowledge a divine will; (2) inasmuch as will is a kind of appetite directed at things not possessed, to say God has a will seems to admit some imperfection or incompleteness in him; and (3) the will moves and is moved, but as the unmoved mover God cannot exhibit such volitional change.[34]

---

32. *DV* 23.1, sed contra 3 and 4. Thomas makes the same argument with respect to God's freedom in *SCG* I.72 [8] and I.88 [6].

33. It should be noted that the Reformed, just as with their Catholic counterparts, are not universally committed to Thomas's intellectualist emphasis. Some, such as William Twisse, manifest a predilection for Scotistic voluntarism. Even so, a plurality, including Turretin, Charnock, Owen, and later Bavinck, are plainly partial to Thomistic intellectualism.

34. *ST* I.19.1, obj. 1–3.

The lynchpin in Thomas's response to these objections is his DDS. Against (1) he insists that God himself is the end for which he wills all things.[35] God's own essence is that goodness that supplies the reason for any act of his will. The will is always directed toward the goodness of some intelligible form.[36] But the goodness of all intelligible creaturely forms is known by God through the form of his own goodness, which is identical with his essence (see the foregoing discussion of God's knowledge of creatures). Garrigou-Lagrange points out that in one respect the objection is correct in denying that God has an "end" since an end always functions as an extrinsic cause for the human will. As things are distinct from their causes, so non-divine volitional agents are distinct from the ends by which their wills are caused or moved. Obviously, such a conception of the end as a final cause cannot be applied to God who is wholly uncaused. Even so, it is possible to remove the element of final causality from the concept of the end and still preserve its function as the *reason* for the will.[37] In fact, the function of the end as the will's *raison d'être* seems to be more properly basic than its function as a final *cause* for human wills. Final causality only characterizes the end on account of the creature's finite and contingent mode of being and so cannot be ascribed God as infinite and absolute. Moreover, if the end of God's will is not a *cause* of his will there is no reason to suppose that it is necessarily extrinsic to him as it is with humans. Hence, the good end by which God is said to will is nothing other than himself, and not being self-caused, there is no obvious conflict in saying that God has a will.

In response to (2) Aquinas explains that the activity of the will is twofold: first, the will may seek what is does not possess; and second, it may love and delight in what it does possess.[38] The first sort of volitional activity cannot apply to God, while the second is entirely appropriate. Thomas remarks that God always has the good that he wills since

---

35. Ibid., I.19.1, ad 1.

36. In *SCG* I.72 [2] Thomas elaborates on the inseparable relation between knowing and willing: "From the fact that God is endowed with intellect it follows that He is endowed with will. For, since the understood good is the proper object of the will, the understood good is, as such, willed. Now that which is understood is by reference to one who understands. Hence, he who grasps the good by his intellect is, as such, endowed with will."

37. Garrigou-Lagrange, *The One God*, 495.

38. *ST* I.19.1, ad 2. See also, *SCG* I.72 [4].

"it is not distinct from his essence."[39] Finally, in response to objection (3) Thomas observes that it is only the will of that agent whose principal object is extrinsic to him that is properly said to move and be moved. But the principal object of God's will is his own goodness, which, again, is nothing other than his essence. "Hence," Thomas concludes, "since the will of God is His essence, it is not moved by another than itself, but by itself alone, in the same sense as understanding and willing are said to be in movement."[40]

Aquinas is even more forthcoming about God's real identity with the act and object of his will in *SCG* I.73–74. The real identity between God and his will is inextricably bound up with the teaching that God is really identical with his intellect. Every act of will is explained by some good end that is either sought after (in the case of creatures) or is presently enjoyed (as is always true of God's will and sometimes true of the human will). It is the intellect that presents this end to the will. Inasmuch as God is identical with the intellectual act by which he knows all things, Thomas reasons, so he must likewise be identical with the volitional act by which he wills all things.[41] This is because, properly speaking, "the will is in the intellect."[42]

Another argument for God's identity with his volitional act is rooted in the perfection of his being. God is perfect and therefore cannot receive any additional determination to being. Thomas explains: "[A]s to understand is the perfection of the one understanding, so to will is the perfection of the one willing . . . But the understanding of God is His being, as was proved above [*SCG* I.45]. For, since the divine being is in itself most perfect, it admits of no superadded perfection, as was proved above [*SCG* I.23 and 28]. The divine willing also is, therefore, His being; and hence the will of God is His essence."[43] The human will is constantly in movement toward some extrinsic end and thus perpetually being perfected while never fully arriving at absolute perfection. Indeed, absolute perfection is impossible for finite beings. But God's will is ab-

---

39. Ibid. George Joyce points out that there can be no question of self-seeking in God's willing of himself (*Principles of Natural Theology*, 378).

40. Ibid., I.19.1, ad 3. Apparently, by "movement" he means nothing more than "activity" and is not suggesting that God's will is moved from passive potency to actuality.

41. *SCG* I.73 [2].

42. Ibid., I.72 [3].

43. Ibid., I.73 [3].

solutely perfect because it is perfect through his own Godhead and not through the addition of further actuality.

It is further argued that as essentially pure act, all of God's operations, including his volitional activity, must be through his essence. His will, then, is not something added to his essence, but is identical with it.[44] Thomas accordingly argues: "[I]f will were something added to the divine substance, since the divine substance is something complete in being it would follow that will would be added to it as an accident to a subject, that the divine substance would be related to it as potency to act, and that there would be composition in God . . . Hence, it is not possible that the divine will be something added to the divine substance."[45] If God's will were an accident in him then neither his substance nor his volition could be characterized as "most absolute." Indeed, both would be relative in some sense.

Finally, in addition to identifying God with his act of will, Thomas also identifies him with the principal object of his will.[46] First, it is the *understood* good that is the object of the will, and inasmuch as God principally understands the goodness of his divine essence the divine essence is naturally what God principally wills. Second, the wills of those agents who are not identical with their primary objects are said to be moved by those objects. "If, then, the principal object of the divine will be other than the divine essence," Thomas explains, "it will follow that there is something higher than the divine will moving it."[47] Third, as the principal object willed is the ultimate cause of the agent's willing, God can have no principal object other than himself. Thomas argues, "If . . . God should principally will something other than Himself, it will follow that something other is the cause of His willing. But His willing is His being . . . Hence, something other will be the cause if His being—which is contrary to the nature of the first being."[48] Fourth, as the highest good God is also the ultimate end and so must principally will himself. Fifth, every power is proportioned equally, or adequately, to its principal object "for the power of a thing is measured according to its objects."[49] Thomas

44. Ibid., I.73 [4]. See also the discussion in Holloway, *Introduction*, 319–20.

45. Ibid., I.73 [5].

46. Ibid., I.74.

47. Ibid., I.74 [3].

48. Ibid., I.74 [4].

49. Ibid., I.74 [6].

proceeds: "Now, nothing is proportioned with equality to the divine will save only God's essence. Therefore, the principal object of the divine will is the divine essence."[50] All told, if God principally willed something other than himself, he would no longer be the ultimate sufficient reason for his own will or his being. John Wippel nicely summarizes Thomas's argument: "[J]ust as only God's essence can be the adequate object of his knowledge, so too, his essence is the only adequate and proportionate object of his will."[51]

Willing Creatures in Willing Himself

Even if it is granted that God is identical with the act and principal object of his will, there is still a question of how it is that he wills things other than himself without thereby adding accidental volitional actuality to himself. Aquinas's answer to this challenge follows closely his answer to the challenge of God's knowledge of creatures. Just as God knows all non-divine things in knowing his own essence, so he wills all non-divine things in willing the goodness of his essence.[52] The primary object of God's knowledge and will is himself, while creatures are always second-ary objects. And just as primary and secondary objects are known in a single intellectual act, so the primary and secondary objects of God's volition are willed in a single act. Thomas explains, "As the divine intel-lect is one, as seeing the many only in the one, in the same way the divine will is one and simple, as willing the many only through the one, that is, through its own goodness."[53] We shall consider the Angelic Doctor's elaboration of this position as he develops it in *Summa contra gentiles* I.75–77.

In *SCG* I.75 Thomas stipulates that God wills all other things in willing himself. A few points relevant to the DDS can be drawn from Thomas's defense of this thesis. First, all things that are ordered to an end are willed for the sake of the end. Inasmuch as all non-divine things are ordered to God's goodness and glory, God wills them in willing him-self.[54] Also, since God wills creatures *for* himself and not *for* themselves,

50. Ibid.
51. Wippel, *Metaphysical Themes II*, 229.
52. See *ST* I.19.2.
53. *ST* I.19.2, ad 4.
54. See Joyce, *Principles of Natural Theology*, 379.

no creature functions as a final object of God's will. Hence, if he wills creatures at all he must do so by virtue of willing himself. If any creature were an end or final object of God's will then that creature would be the reason for God's will and God would not be the sufficient reason for his volitional actuality. Second, God loves and wills things other than himself inasmuch as those things bear the image of his own goodness, which he chiefly loves and wills. Thus, it is not the creature *per se* that explains why God loves and wills it, but, rather, the divine goodness that is imaged forth in the creature via its participation in God's own goodness. God loves and wills other things in loving and willing himself. It should be borne in mind that Thomas's point in this argument is not that God's goodness is the efficient reason for his willing of creatures, but only to highlight his essence as the final reason for willing non-divine things. Third, inasmuch as all created things preexist in God, his nature being the exemplar for all non-divine things (see the discussion above on the participability of his essence), he must chiefly will the perfection of those things in willing himself. Put differently, there is no creaturely perfection that God does not principally will in willing himself.

In *SCG* I.76 Aquinas proceeds to explain that God wills himself and other things in a *single* act of will. First, an act of will is marked off, as it were, by the final object at which it aims. Inasmuch as God only aims at one final object, himself, it follows that whatever else he wills is willed inasmuch as it is directed toward that end and is thereby willed in the very act by which the end is willed. Thomas writes: "Since, then, God wills other things for His own sake as for the sake of the end . . . He wills Himself and other things by one act of will.[55] *So long as the end or final reason for willing is one, the act of will is one.* Humans have numerous ends by which our wills are caused to act, and thus we exhibit numerous volitional acts. But God's end is always the same since only one object is worthy and proportionate to the perfection of his will, namely, his own glory and goodness. Second, since God wills himself perfectly and all other things for himself, he must will himself and all things by a single act of will. If he possessed a second volitional act his will would not be absolutely perfect or complete. This is because each act of will would lack the actuality that belonged properly to the other, and thus not be a perfect act of will proportionate to the perfect and infinite act of God's being. Third, just as God's knowledge is non-discursive, so also is his

55. *SCG* I.76 [2].

will. Thomas explains, "If, then, someone wills separately the end and the things ordered to the end, there will be a certain discursiveness in His will. But this cannot be in God, since He is outside all motion."[56] Fourth, God's simplicity proscribes the possibility of his possessing two simultaneous operations: "since God wills Himself always, if He wills Himself and other things by different acts it will follow that there are at once two acts of will in Him. This is impossible, since one simple power does not have at once two operations."[57] Fifth, if God had multiple acts of will, then something other than himself must move his will in all those acts not moved by himself as the end. But God cannot be moved by another. Sixth, since all that is in God is God, his will is his being. Thomas remarks, "But in God there is only one being. Therefore, there is in Him only one willing."[58] Seventh, and finally, Thomas argues for the singularity of God's volitional act from the singularity of his intellectual act: "Again, willing belongs to God according as He is intelligent. Therefore, just as by one act He understands Himself and other things, in so far as His essence is the exemplar of all things, so by one act He wills Himself and other things, in so far as His goodness is the likeness of all goodness."[59]

In *SCG* I.77 Aquinas makes the case that God's simplicity is not compromised by his willing of many non-divine things. It is the multiple objects of a human's will that account for the multiplicity of his or her volitional acts. But God has only one final object of his will and all other objects are comprehended in and directed to this object, which is his own goodness and glory. The multitude of secondary objects, accordingly, does not multiply volitional actuality in God and thus presents no dilemma for his simplicity. Indeed, just as knowing many non-divine things produces no multiplicity in God's knowledge, so willing many non-divine things causes no multiplicity in his will. Of course, this also means that God does not directly will creatures just as he does not directly know them. As with his knowledge, though, this indirectness does not betray a weakness in God's will. His willing of creatures through the willing of himself is actually a more perfect and immutable manner of

56. Ibid., I.76 [4].

57. Ibid., I.76 [5].

58. Ibid., I.76 [7]. Thomas is simply making that point that God is not actuated by accidents. In him there is no composition of substance and accident.

59. Ibid., I.76 [8].

willing than is found in the direct volition by which creatures will things other than themselves. Because God is identical with the end for which he wills creatures, and already possesses that end perfectly, his will for those things ordered to himself as the end is absolute and unshakeable. That is, there is no mutability in God's willing of creatures because there is no real distinction between God, his volitional act, and the end at which his will is directed. It is according to this understanding that the DDS secures the absoluteness of God's will, even his will of creatures.

It might appear from all that has been said to this point that God must will creatures by an absolute necessity. But Aquinas and the Reformed deny that this follows. God wills himself, they argue, with an absolute necessity, but he wills non-divine things only according to a suppositional necessity.[60] We will briefly consider this explanation before evaluating and responding to some recent challenges to compatibility of God's free will and the DDS in the following chapter.

Aquinas sets out his position succinctly in *Summa theologiae* I.19.3. He answers the question of whether whatever God wills he wills necessarily. His response is worthy of full citation:

> There are two ways in which a thing is said to be necessary, namely, absolutely, and by supposition. We judge a thing to be absolutely necessary from the relation of the terms, as when the predicate forms part of the definition of the subject: thus it is absolutely necessary that man is an animal. It is the same when the subject forms part of the notion of the predicate; thus it is absolutely necessary that a number must be odd or even. In this way it is not necessary that Socrates sits: wherefore it is not necessary absolutely, though it may be so by supposition; for, granted that he is sitting, he must necessarily sit, as long as he is sitting. Accordingly as to things willed by God, we must observe that He wills something of absolute necessity: but this is not true of all that He wills. For the divine will has a necessary relation to the divine goodness, since that is its proper object. Hence God wills His own goodness necessarily, even as we will our own happiness necessarily, and as any other faculty has necessary relation to its proper and principal object . . . But God wills things apart from Himself in so far as they are ordered to His own goodness as their end. Now in willing an end we do not necessarily will things that conduce to it, unless they are such that the end cannot be at-

60. See, for example, *ST* I.19.3; *SCG* I.80–83; *DP* 3.15; *DV* 23.4; Turretin, *IET*, 3.14.5; Bavinck, *RD*, II: 233–40; and Muller, *PRRD*, III: 453–55.

tained without them; as, we will to take food to preserve life, or to take ship in order to cross the sea. But we do not necessarily will things without which the end is attainable, such as a horse for a journey which we can take on foot, for we can make the journey without one. The same applies to other means. Hence, since the goodness of God is perfect, and can exist without other things inasmuch as no perfection can accrue to Him from them, it follows that His willing things apart from Himself is not absolutely necessary. Yet it can be necessary by supposition, for supposing that He wills a thing, then He is unable not to will it, as His will cannot change.[61]

A few observations are in order. Because God is identical with the end of all his willing none of those non-divine things he wills can function as *means* to his end. God requires nothing beyond himself for the perfect enjoyment of himself. Consequently, non-divine things are not willed with the absoluteness by which he wills his own goodness. Also, no creature is necessary to God's being or understanding of himself and thus is not willed with the same strength of absoluteness by which he wills himself. Only if God derived his identity by correlation to something outside himself would anything non-divine be entailed in his will with absolute necessity. But, as pure act, this cannot be true of God. Finally, the non-absoluteness of creatures does not mean that God's will is mutable with respect to them. Upon the supposition that he eternally and actually wills them, they are willed necessarily since God is pure act and cannot change. Of course, this leaves the question of whether God could have willed otherwise with respect to creatures. We will turn our focus upon that challenge in the final chapter.

CONCLUSION

God is most absolute in his intellective activities of knowing and willing. The fact that he knows and wills many different things does not diminish his absoluteness or undermine the simplicity in which it is rooted. Indeed, it is the simplicity of his act of knowledge and volition that ensures that these divine realities are infinitely superior to their created likenesses in creatures. Affirming that God is *that by which* he knows and wills all things establishes the aseity and independence of God with respect to his intellect and volition. It enables one to confess that his

61. *ST* I.19.3.

knowledge is "independent upon the creature" and that his will is not "contingent or uncertain" (WCF 2.2). Inasmuch as *human* knowledge and *human* will always signal dependency and change in the creature, it is critical that we have a way for explaining the independence and absoluteness of God's intellect and volition. Divine simplicity supplies this explanation by enabling us to maintain that God is really identical with both the act and object of his knowledge and his will and thus that it is in virtue of his own Godhead that he knows and wills.

7

Simplicity and the Difficulty of Divine Freedom

IT IS A PECULIAR difficulty for the DDS to account for the relationship between God's simplicity and his freedom to create or not create the world, or even to create a different possible world altogether. If he is pure act and *ipsum esse subsistens*, how can one continue to confess that he is "most free" (WCF 2.1)? For many critics of the DDS this is the Achilles heel of the doctrine. In this chapter some of the recent challenges to both divine freedom and the DDS are considered. Many scholars find it impossible to maintain both. Also, Eleonore Stump's attempt to reconcile divine contra-causal freedom with divine simplicity is examined and critiqued. Next, the argument is put forth that, given the DDS, God's freedom cannot be characterized as passive counterfactual openness. Finally, I aim to highlight the importance of maintaining both divine freedom and the DDS while acknowledging their ultimate incomprehensibility.

CHALLENGES TO DIVINE FREEDOM AND SIMPLICITY

The Christian tradition insists that the existence of all non-divine things is the result of God's *freely* willing them to be. But if God is pure act it is difficult to conceive how he could have freely chosen this contingent world instead of some other possible world. Does pure actuality leave any space for choosing between alternative courses of action? To complicate matters, the Identity Account of the DDS requires one to say that God is essentially and existentially identical with his act of free will. Yet, if the world could have been other than it is, it seems that God's very nature and existence could have been different as well. But then God would be mutable, even if only accidentally, and most certainly would be composed of act and potency. Eleonore Stump does not exaggerate when she observes, "The most recalcitrant difficulties generated by the doctrine of simplicity are those that result from combining the doctrine with the traditional ascription to God of free will."[1] Many scholars feel compelled to resolve the dilemma by either denying or severely minimizing one side or other. The remainder of this section aims to elucidate the precise nature of this challenge and to consider the opposing solutions put forward by Norman Kretzmann (minimizing divine freedom) and Jay Richards (minimizing divine simplicity).

Thomas Aquinas, as with the Christian tradition generally, breaks with Neoplatonism and Avicenna in affirming that God wills the world freely and not by absolute or natural necessity:

> That there is free choice in God is apparent from the fact that He has for His will an end which He naturally wills, His own goodness; and all other things He wills as ordained to this end. These latter, absolutely speaking, He does not will necessarily . . . because His goodness has no need of the things which are ordained to it, and the manifestation of that goodness can suitably take place in a number of different ways. There remains for Him, then, a judgment free to will this or that, just as there is in us. On this account it must be said that free choice is found in God.[2]

Likewise, Thomas states in *SCG* II.23 [1], "God acts, in the realm of created things, not by necessity of His nature, but by the free choice of His will." Similarly, in *ST* I.19.10 he writes, "Since then God necessarily wills His own goodness, but other things not necessarily . . . He has free will with respect to what He does not necessarily will." While these statements themselves are broadly agreeable with Christian conviction, they do seem to pose a dilemma for the DDS inasmuch as they seem to suggest a real distinction in God between the necessary willing of himself and the contingent willing of other things.[3]

Indeed, without this real distinction in God's will and between God and his will generally, there seems to be no way to account for how God could freely have chosen any other possible world. Stump distills the essence of this difficulty: "Since no one whose will is bound to just one

---

1. Stump, "Simplicity," 252.

2. *DV* 24.3. Elsewhere Thomas states, "without any doubt we must hold that God by the decree of his will and by no natural necessity brought creatures into being" (*DP* 3.15).

3. Stump asks, "How is this not a real distinction in God?" (*Aquinas*, 101).

set of acts of will makes real choices among alternative acts, it looks as if accepting God's absolute simplicity as a datum leads to the conclusion that God has no alternative to doing what he does."[4] *Prima facie*, the DDS appears to undermine divine contra-causal freedom.

Though primarily criticizing the strong account of divine immutability, Richard Cross asks a pertinent question that also applies, by extension, to the DDS: "How can the notion of contra-causal freedom have any purchase in the context of complete immutability?"[5] His point is that without some change in God from a state of "could will *A* or *B*" to a state of "wills *A* or *B*" the notion that God could have done otherwise with respect to creation seems nonsensical. Brian Leftow highlights this difficulty by noting how it is bound up with yet another feature of God's simplicity, namely, atemporal eternity:

> If *P* is only conditionally necessary, ¬*P* could have been true: ¬*P* was possible, though it is no longer. From God's timeless standpoint, when "was" it possible that He not create? If God timelessly limits the possible to worlds in which He creates, "when" were non-creation worlds possible? At God's timeless standpoint, God has already—timelessly—eliminated non-creative worlds from possibility. It is not possible that He do other than create; the best Thomas can do, it seems, is claim that non-creation worlds are only contingently impossible, and are so due to God's choice. More worrying, the same applies to worlds in which God creates any other than what were actually the initial creatures. On Thomas's account, it was never possible that God do other than create what He initially did; it merely could have been possible. Those who've thought God free to do other than create what he has have usually meant that other alternatives are open to Him in a thicker sense than this.[6]

---

4. Stump, *Aquinas*, 100. As will be noted below, there is a difficulty in how Stump understands "real choices" for God. Does she think God stands passively before a range of options?

5. Cross, *Duns Scotus on God*, 120.

6. Leftow, "Aquinas, Divine Simplicity and Divine Freedom," 28. Leftow's remarks show that the question of counter-causal freedom is not merely a problem for divine simplicity, but also for divine atemporality. In fact, it is a challenge for any of those traditional divine attributes entailed in the DDS, especially immutability and eternality. Leftow proposes various solutions to this difficulty of contra-causal freedom but concludes that none of them finally succeeds without introducing some variety of intrinsic real distinction into God (see ibid., 28–36).

This is a powerful observation and one that has prompted some modern philosophers and theologians to either diminish the claims of divine freedom (in order to preserve simplicity) or, as is more often the case, abandon the traditional DDS (in order to preserve freedom). In this connection we shall consider a representative of each position.

Norman Kretzmann, who endorses Aquinas's DDS, is unconvinced that God's single act of will can be both necessary (with respect to himself) and free (with respect to other things). If God is simple and is the end of all his willing, his will to create seems to be naturally necessary. Accordingly, Kretzmann declares, "I see no way of avoiding the inconsistency (or, at least, ambivalence) in Aquinas's account as it stands."[7] In particular, Kretzmann finds Thomas's insistence that God creates non-divine things because of the self-diffusive nature of his goodness to flatly contradict his view that God could freely have chosen not to create anything at all.[8] If goodness is necessarily diffusive of itself it would seem that creation is *naturally* necessary for a God who is identical with his goodness (which is entailed in the DDS). God could not have willed otherwise without *being* otherwise in himself. But Thomas insists that he could have willed otherwise.[9] This tension between necessitarianism and voluntarism, Kretzmann explains, is not due to Thomas's synthesis of Hebrew theology and Greek philosophy, as many have supposed, but rather stems from his synthesis of Platonic self-diffusiveness and

---

7. Kretzmann, "A General Problem of Creation," 215. Gerard Hughes expresses similar concerns with direct reference to the challenge simplicity poses for libertarian freedom: "Aquinas clearly admits that God could have chosen otherwise than he (eternally) does and that therefore some things which can truly be said of God are contingent truths *about God*, and not merely about other things which are related to God." He adds, "What remains puzzling is how Aquinas believes this can be true without God having any intrinsic accidental properties" (*The Nature of God*, 40). Hughes concludes that there is a genuine conflict between Thomas's teaching on simplicity in *ST* I.3.6 and his position on God's free will in *ST* I.19.3. Hughes resolves the tension by emphasizing the latter and softening the former. Interestingly, Kretzmann resolves the tension in exactly the opposite direction.

8. Texts arguing for divine self-diffusive goodness include: *SCG* I.37 [5] (in which Thomas ties self-diffusive goodness to being in act); *SCG* I.75 [6]; *ST* I.19.2. Those arguing for God's free choice not to create at all include: *DP* 3.15, ad 12; *SCG* I.81 [1]; *SCG* II.28 [9].

9. The difficulty of Thomas's two-fold affirmation on this account is especially apparent in his words in *DP* 3.15, ad 15: "As in God there is naught but good, so is there naught but what is necessary. But it does not follow that whatsoever proceeds from him does so of necessity."

Aristotelian self-sufficiency in his characterizations of God.[10] Thomas employs both of these perspectives to advance seemingly contradictory claims: (1) God's goodness moves him, as it were, to share his divine life with others (and these could only be creatures), while (2) his self-sufficiency requires that he stand in no necessary relation to those creatures.

Kretzmann proposes to rescue Thomas from this quandary by taking diffusive goodness as the principle most consistent with Thomas's overall theology and lessening the scope of God's contra-causal freedom.[11] As naturally self-diffusive God does not have the freedom to refrain from creating. Rather, as Kretzmann has it, God's power of contrary choice is simply for choosing the particular things with which to share his goodness. In this way Kretzmann devises a scheme in which classical Christian theists can still affirm that God can cause things freely and that no particular thing or possible world is absolutely necessary to him. In sum, it is naturally necessary that God create, but not naturally necessary that he create any *particular* thing or possible world; he is not free to choose *whether* to create, but only *what* to create.[12]

Throughout his "diffusive goodness" argument Kretzmann only indirectly engages the challenge that contra-causal freedom poses to the

10. Kretzmann, "A General Problem of Creation," 222. On the one hand, there is the challenge to explain why God creates anything at all. Merely answering that created things exist because God wills them suggests that God might will without a purpose or reason. But saying that he wills creatures in order to manifest his goodness in them is much more satisfying and even seems to comport nicely with the biblical record. On the other hand, saying that God's goodness is the reason for creatures seems to suggest that God could not refrain from willing creatures any more than he could deny his own goodness. Hence, in order to maintain God's absolute self-sufficiency and independence of the creature it seems incumbent upon the Christian theologian to uphold God's freedom not to create at all. Herein lies the "problem" as Kretzmann perceives it: If God is free not to create anything at all it would appear that the "shared goodness" explanation for *why* God creates is sapped of its explanatory power and the Christian is again forced to admit that the final reason for God's will to create is unknown.

11. Lest it be thought that the Reformed escape the difficulty facing the Thomistic predicament of self-diffusive goodness, it should be noted that many of the strongest Reformed proponents of the DDS hold a similar view of God's goodness. For instance, Turretin writes: "The goodness of God is that by which he is conceived not only absolutely and in himself as supremely good and perfect (as it were) and the only good . . . because he is such originally, perfectly and immutably; but also relatively and extrinsically as beneficent toward creatures . . . *because it is of the reason of good to be communicative of itself*" (*IET* 3.20.2; emphasis added). See also, Muller, *PRRD*, III: 503–10.

12. Kretzmann, "A General Problem of Creation," 223. See also, Kretzmann, "A Particular Problem of Creation," 229–30.

DDS inasmuch as he regards God's perfect goodness as an entailment of his pure actuality.[13] But in his volume *The Metaphysics of Theism* he confronts the challenge more directly. In Thomas's account of God's willing things other than himself two problems emerge: "First, since God's willing of other things is presented as occurring *in* his necessary, choiceless willing of himself, there's still no sign of divine choice even in God's willing of other things . . . And, second, attributing to God the willing of all the uncountably many things there are certainly seems to threaten absolute simplicity."[14] Kretzmann notes that the way Thomas deals with the simplicity problem, by holding forth that God wills all things in the very same act by which he wills himself (see *SCG* I.76), "only makes the first problem harder."[15]

As with the challenge of divine diffusive goodness, Kretzmann accommodates Thomas's strong DDS by endorsing the view that God's willing to create is absolutely necessary inasmuch as he wills on account of his goodness and, per simplicity, God's goodness and will are identical in him.[16] When it comes to God's will about whether or not to create, God seems to be devoid of all contra-causal freedom on account of his simplicity and goodness.[17] Undoubtedly, most orthodox Christians, as with Aquinas himself, will not recognize this necessitarian explanation as leaving God sufficiently free in his choice of the world. The question,

13. If goodness is a transcendental of being (along with oneness and truth) there is a strong convertibility between God's existence and his goodness. In this sense, what holds for his goodness holds for his being and if God's goodness is naturally self-diffusive then so also is his being. On this understanding the creation of being *ad extra* would appear unavoidable for God. Thomas writes, "[I]t is said that the good is diffusive of itself *and of being*. But this diffusion befits God because . . . being through Himself the necessary being, God is the cause of being for other things" (*SCG* I.37 [5]; emphasis added).

14. Kretzmann, *Metaphysics of Theism*, 219.

15. Ibid.

16. Ibid., 223. See also, *SCG* I.87 [2].

17. Kretzmann does allow a certain sense of freedom even in God's necessary will insofar as that will exhibits a natural and *uncoerced* necessity. His simple premise is that not all necessity entails coercion or force. For example, man naturally and necessarily wills his happiness, though we would not say that his will is coerced or constrained by this happiness. Dispositional necessity that does not violently compel the will is consistent with the will's freedom. The power of contrary choice, then, is not the only meaningful sense in which we can ascribe freedom to one's will. See *Metaphysics of Theism*, 223–25.

though, is whether the classical DDS allows its adherents to affirm God's freedom to choose not to create; Kretzmann contends that it does not.[18]

Jay Richards identifies the same apparent tension between God's free will and simplicity as Kretzmann does, though he tacks in the opposite direction. For him, it is the demands of classical simplicity that must be lessened, not divine libertarian free will. Departing from the DDS's long-standing claim that God possesses no accidents, Richards appeals to divine free will as one indicator that God possesses accidental properties:

> If saying that God is free has any real sense, then choice among alternatives—in the sense that God could have done otherwise—must be one of its necessary elements, even if it is not a sufficient one. This implies that God will have contingent or accidental properties, that is, properties that could change. These contingent properties concerning God's relation to a contingent creation are the expression of his freedom, as are all his contingent properties; so they do not imply any significant ontological dependence of God on the world.[19]

Richards's final comment is true enough insofar as he is concerned to maintain that God could not be changed *by others*. But at the same time he wants to affirm that God changes himself in his exercise of free will and is, in a softened sense, accidentally (i.e., non-essentially) mutable. For Richards, nothing that God freely wills, including his relation as Creator to the world, counts as a necessary or immutable attribute of his. Of divine knowledge, for instance, he writes, "[E]ven if in the actual world God's knowledge is unchanging, it does not follow that it is impossible that God's knowledge change."[20] But the classical DDS, with its

---

18. For a rejoinder to Kretzmann see Wippel, "Norman Kretzmann on Aquinas's Attribution of Will and Freedom to Create to God," 287–98. See also his discussion in *Metaphysical Themes II*, 218–37. Wippel's argument, in short, is that Kretzmann fails to see that in teaching God's self-diffusive goodness as the reason for creatures, Aquinas is not speaking of the efficient reason of their being, but simply the final reason. This is why one can say that God creates because of his self-diffusive goodness, while not implying that God's goodness is the *efficient* reason for his willing of creatures. When we ascribe free will to God we mean that he is free in respect to efficient causation, not that he is free in regard to final causation. If he wills anything at all, he *must* will himself as the end. If God efficiently wills (freely) to create he *must* diffuse his goodness into that creation. Kretzmann simply fails to perceive the crucial distinction between efficient and final causality in Thomas's texts.

19. Richards, *Untamed God*, 202.

20. Ibid., 207.

concomitant doctrine of divine immutability, argues that God's knowledge is not only unchanging in the actual world, but from all eternity. Intellectual changeability in God necessarily precludes the strong sense of divine simplicity. Of course, Richards would reply that the strong DDS undermines the "real sense" of divine freedom and the meaningful affirmation that God could have created other possible worlds.

In a challenging passage, Richards further argues for a real distinction between act and potency in God in order to accommodate his contra-causal freedom:

> We need to make these distinctions [between act and potency], not because of requirements extrinsic to the doctrine of God or from penchant for novelty in theology, but simply because Christians speak of the gratuity and freedom of God's creating, and a fortiori of the contingency of creation itself. For instance, if God is free in creating the actual world (wa), then he could have refrained from doing so or could have created a world different from the one he has created. But in such a case, God exists with countless possibilities, that is, unactualized possibilities, which are just those things he could choose to do but does not, and those things precluded because of the choices he does take. So if God could have created a world wd different from and incompossible with the world he actually created (wa) then he has a potentiality to create wd which can never be realized, since it is precluded by his actually creating wa.[21]

On the face of it Richards makes a compelling argument and we might wonder how any orthodox Christian could fail to find it persuasive. The one troubling feature, though, is that he does not make any attempt to characterize the modal sense of "could have" with respect to God. He treats the notion of "possibility" as if it meant the same thing for God as it does for creatures. But surely classical Christian theists disallow such univocity when they qualify God's free will as eternal and immutable. For Richards's argument to succeed he would also need to dispense with immutability and eternity as well, and not merely with the act-potency denial of the DDS. But if he refuses to banish those commitments, then it seems that he does not have a solid reason to banish divine *actus purus* either.

In a final salvo against the classical DDS, Richards argues that denial of act-potency composition in God yields a truncated notion

21. Ibid., 234.

of his freedom: "So what exactly is the problem with God exercising choices and making decisions? Quite clearly, the problem is that they are inconsistent with a type of simplicity that denies the distinctions of essence and accident and actual and potential in God. So the person enamored by strong simplicity must settle for a truncated definition of divine freedom."[22] We may say, alternatively, that the person enamored by strong libertarian freedom must settle, as Richards seems willing to do, for a truncated definition of divine simplicity.[23] True, this does not remove the challenge of his remarks. But it does call into question why Richards grants hegemony to his notion of libertarian freedom over that of divine simplicity. Apparently he does so to protect the divine power of contrary choice. But he does not attempt to explain the nature of such a choice in light of other equally orthodox and biblical doctrines, most importantly, God's eternality and immutability. Rather, he is content to map onto God a human psychology of libertarian freedom and insist that God's freedom is only significant and plausible if it measures up to that creaturely conception: "Mere freedom of choice may not be sufficient to express divine freedom, but certainly it is necessary. *Surely God is at least as free as we are when we exercise freedom* (assuming, as I do, that we sometimes exercise libertarian freedom)."[24]

22. Ibid., 239.

23. Calvinist theologian John Cooper shares Richards's misgivings about the strong classical account of divine simplicity: "The strong version [of divine immutability], which follows from logical simplicity, completely identifies God's essence and existence and thus makes everything that God is and does absolutely necessary and unalterable. There is no freedom or contingency in God. Absolutely nothing could have been otherwise." Cooper wants to affirm the immutability of God's nature while denying the real identity of God's existence and essence and the unchangeableness of his life: "God's freedom to create also entails a distinction between his essence/nature and existence. If God had chosen not to create the world or not to become incarnate in Jesus Christ, then the full actuality of God's existence, including the life of the Trinity, would be different than it is. Thus classical Christian theism must affirm an element of contingency in God's life quite apart from the issue of his involvement in temporal change" (*Panentheism, the Other God of the Philosophers*, 327). It is not surprising that Cooper readily affirms movement in God from potency to act: "His creation of the world alters the mode of [divine] immanence from possible to actual existence" (ibid., 329). Given these sentiments it is quite perplexing that Cooper continues to represent his position as upholding a classical version of the DDS. He probably does so because he conceives simplicity according to the harmonist explanation considered above in chapter 5. Anyhow, Cooper appears to be substantially in agreement with Richards in lessening the austerity of the traditional DDS.

24. Richards, *Untamed God*, 239 (emphasis added). Again, it bears pointing out that Richards presupposes ontological univocity in his understanding of God's relation to

Both Kretzmann and Richards identify a difficulty in affirming both divine simplicity and contra-causal freedom, but they are at odds on how to resolve the tension. Kretzmann rejects the strong account of God's freedom while Richards discards the strong account of God's simplicity.

ELEONORE STUMP'S (PROBLEMATIC) RESOLUTION

The great challenge for DDS adherents, as well as for all who hold to the immutability and atemporality of God's knowledge and will, is to explain the status of the modal operator "could have" when it is used to express God's freedom with respect to creation. What does it mean to say "God could have _____" in the context of also confessing him as eternal, immutable, and pure act? To be sure, DDS proponents historically have not devoted extensive attention to this question. Yet the tendency among modern DDS opponents to grant controlling status to the counterfactual expression, "God could have done otherwise," calls for a response. Does such an expression make sense in a classical Christian doctrine of God and, furthermore, does it accurately represent what Christians have historically meant in affirming that God exercises free will in his creation of the world? There seem to be two directions in which the DDS subscriber may go in answer to this question. First, some answer by formulating a scheme in which God could conceivably be really different than he is by having created a world different from this one. Such difference, it is argued, does not fall in the category of either accidental or substantial change and so does not threaten the DDS. Second, others answer by denying that openness to alternatives (or counterfactual possibility) is an adequate explanation of divine free will.

Eleonore Stump aims to meet the challenge of divine free will according to first approach, by proposing a scheme in which God is intrinsically different in different possible worlds without necessarily acquiring accidental properties.[25] Her basic premise is that when Thomas

---

creatures. God's volitional freedom, by his lights, can never be anything but a grander instance of the exact same sort of freedom discovered in humans. The strong version of the DDS was never intended to make sense within this univocist conception of reality. Indeed, if the strong classical account of simplicity is correct, then Richards's ontological univocism must be abandoned.

25. See Stump, *Aquinas*, 111–13. See also, Stump and Kretzmann, "Absolute Simplicity," 369.

denies that God possesses accidents he means God cannot change *over time*. But, Stump explains, this does not mean that God could not be otherwise given the existence of a different possible world. Thomas, she observes, frames his denial of divine accidents within a discussion of God's immutability, chiefly emphasizing the impossibility that any of his attributes be corrupted. This emphasis upon incorruptibility suggests that Thomas is thinking of accidents according to temporal modality and not according to possible world modalities. Stump clarifies her central claim: "Aquinas assumes the description of an accident given by Peter of Spain, as something that can come to or be absent from a subject without the corruption of that subject . . . He does *not* characterize an accident as any property a thing has in some but not all possible worlds in which it exists, so that every feature a thing fails to have in all the worlds in which it exists has to count as an accident."[26] In effect, Stump declares Thomas's denial of accidents in God irrelevant when discussing difference across possible worlds. The only denial she perceives Thomas to make is that God could be *first* one way and *then* another over time and within the same world. Her goal is to preserve some place for an affirmation of divine contra-causal freedom with respect to possible worlds.

The critical element enabling Stump to claim that God's intrinsic difference across different possible worlds is within Thomistic bounds is her explanation of how Thomas views accidents. According to Stump, Thomas denies accidents in God because of the incomplete nature of any accident.[27] Recall from the discussion above in chapter 2 that no accident is sufficient for its own *esse*; it only *is* by inherence in some substance and thereby acquires *inesse*, and not *esse* properly speaking. Stump insists that if we can avoid saying that God is incomplete in any of those possible worlds in which he may exist, then we will have satisfied all of Thomas's concerns about accidents. We need not suppose that the denial of accidents was ever intended to proscribe all possibility that God be intrinsically other than he is. "If this is right," Stump remarks, "then this is the sense that we should understand that God has no accidents—not that God is exactly the same in all possible worlds in which he exists but that there is nothing at all that is incomplete or insubstantial about God in any respect, even though God is not the same in all possible worlds."[28]

26. Ibid., 112.
27. Ibid., 113.
28. Ibid.

Stump's concern to retain some meaningful sense of the DDS is apparent when she further writes:

> [Thomas] does not take any property anything has in some but not all possible worlds in which it exists as an accident of that thing; and, on his view, a thing can be its own nature [i.e., simple] without that thing having only properties necessary to it. However exactly Aquinas does understand the notions of having an accident and being one's own nature, it is clear, then, that for him the denial that God has accidents does not entail that God is the same in all possible worlds in which he exists, and the claim that God is his own nature does not entail that God is necessarily whatever he is.[29]

But Stump's account is fraught with difficulties. The question immediately comes to mind: What is it about God that is "not the same" in different possible worlds? Furthermore, if this divine difference is intrinsic yet not accidental, is it not then substantial or essential? Simply saying that God is not "insubstantial" in any possible world in which he exists is not the same as saying that he is substantially or essentially the same in every possible world. God might be one complete substance or essence in world *A* and a different complete substance or essence in world *B*. Either way there is nothing "insubstantial" about him. If this is what Stump's explanation amounts to then it is hard to square with Thomas's *actus purus* conception of God's simplicity. Surely Aquinas did not simply mean to say that God is pure act in whatever world he happens to create but that he could have been a different pure act if he had chosen to create a different possible world. Pure act simply will not allow one to introduce *differentia* into the divine essence and existence.

Stump ignores the connection between the denial of accidents in God and the strong existential account of the *actus purus* doctrine. The reason God cannot possess accidents is not merely because there is nothing "insubstantial" in him, but because all accidents are determinations to being and God is *ispsum esse subsistens*. It is this commitment that makes Thomas's account radically incompatible with Stump's proposal. Her God who is "not the same" in all possible worlds seems to require some additional determination of being (via his free will?) in

29. Ibid., 115. For explanations similar to Stump's see Hill, "Does the World Makes a Difference to God?" 157; Clarke, "What is Most and Least Relevant in the Metaphysics of St. Thomas Today?" 43; and Clarke, *Explorations in Metaphysics*, 183–210.

order to be meaningfully different in each world. Simply denying that this determination is an accident in God does not make her position any more agreeable to the classical DDS.

In sum, Stump's notion of non-accidental difference as something God could have willed for himself seems to leave no alternative but to conclude that God could have been essentially or substantially different. Assuming that Stump does not allow this conclusion, it is difficult to conceive how God could have been really different from what he is without that difference being either accidental or essential/substantial. Moreover, if the way God actually is in this world is *really* different from how he might have been, then it would seem that there is some *differentia* in God that makes this the case. How is this *differentia* not an accident?[30] Seeking to preserve God's simplicity by concurring with Thomas's denial of divine accidents, while at the same time trying to uphold divine contra-causal free will by affirming that God is really different in this world from the way he would have been in another, appears to be an impossible explanation. Katherin Rogers perceptively expresses the difficulty of Stump's solution:

> If Stump and Kretzmann have Aquinas right, there is some sense in which "there are possible worlds in which God wills not to create . . ." But it is very difficult to see how God in the actual world could be the same being as God in some other possible world, if (1) God in the actual world is identical to His eternal and immutable act in the world, (2) God in a different possible world is identical to His act in that world, and (3) God's act in the actual world is *not* identical to His act in the other possible world. One could suppose that the principle of the transitivity of identity (if A is identical to B and B is identical to C, then A is identical to C) does not hold at the divine level across possible worlds, but I take it this entails the view that we probably can't say anything about what might be possible for God, in which case we have not solved

---

30. A similar argument is tendered by James Ross in "Comments on 'Absolute Simplicity,'" 383–85. In a similar vein Brian Leftow writes, "Thomas never tries to say what a contingent intrinsic difference without a difference in accident can be. And it's not clear that his DDS would let him give an account of this. Anything we could point to that might differ intrinsically in God would be a distinguishable aspect of Him, and His having such aspects is not obviously compatible with DDS. So . . . there would in Thomas' eyes be no metaphysical account at all of what makes God intrinsically different from world to world" ("Aquinas, Divine Simplicity and Divine Freedom," 34).

the difficulty of distinguishing the necessary from the contingent in the divine nature.[31]

FREE WILL WITHOUT COUNTERFACTUAL OPENNESS

Most adherents to the DDS have historically attempted to reconcile God's simplicity and free will by arguing for a conception of freedom that does not require God to stand deliberatively before a range of possibilities. Of course, this understanding tends to militate against general assumptions about human free will in which the nature of freedom is located primarily in the agent's power to do otherwise, the ability to change course and to actualize counterfactuals. To suggest that God might not possess his volitional power in the same way that humans do seems, *prima facie*, to place restrictions on God and to weaken the power of his will. Now, a human's ability to choose among options is regarded as a power precisely because it enables a person to either (1) *begin* on a desirable course of action or (2) to *change* course from one less desirous to one more beneficial. The counterfactual power of volitional freedom in this context is meaningful because it assumes that the one choosing is changeable, or mutable. But, in an agent without any real possibility for beginning or change, it is not clear that freedom needs to be construed as the possibility of doing otherwise. Consequently, choice would not need to be explained as movement from "could choose this or that" to "chooses this or that," that is, as the reduction of volitional potency to act.

Given that adherents to the classical DDS are also firmly committed to God's atemporal eternity and absolute immutability, it is not surprising that they tend to characterize God's volitional freedom in a manner wholly unsuited to temporal and mutable free creatures.[32] The modality of volitional freedom cannot be abstracted from the nature of the volitional agent and, thus, the modality of human freedom cannot be univocally attributed to God's exercise of free will. Herman Bavinck, accordingly, ties the unique modality of God's free will to his absolute simplicity and thereby concludes that God does not possess "choice" as one might ordinarily understand it:

31. Rogers, *Perfect Being Theology*, 34. It is difficult to acknowledge that Stump and Kreztmann "have Aquinas right" inasmuch they fail to meaningfully engage his teaching on God as *ipsum esse subsistens*.

32. For a fine treatment of the relation between divine atemporality and freedom see Helm, *Eternal God*, 171–94.

We can almost never tell why God willed one thing rather than another, and are therefore compelled to believe that he could just as well have willed one thing as another. But *in God there is actually no such thing as choice* inasmuch as it always presupposes uncertainty, doubt, and deliberation. He, however, knows what he wills—eternally, firmly, and immutably. Every hint of arbitrariness, contingency, or uncertainty is alien to his will, which is eternally determinate and unchanging. Contingency characterizes creatures and—let it be said in all reverence—not even God can deprive the creature of this characteristic. In God alone existence and essence are of one piece; by virtue of its very nature a creature is such that it could also not have existed.[33]

That God cannot alter his will is not a weakness in him as it would be in us.[34] As composite and contingent creatures, it is fitting that our volitional freedom consists in the power to will counterfactuals. But our free willing must function in the context of our ontological mutability and contingency. Such a freedom for God would actually signal a weakness in him inasmuch as it would make him dependent upon accidental acts of volition, with which he is not strictly identical, in order to actually possess the will he possesses. In other words, he would not have his will entirely in and through himself. His will would have a beginning and would inhere in him as accident determining him to be this or that way. Human free will, even in its strongest moments, cannot be most absolute inasmuch and it might come and go. God's will, though, is most absolute, without beginning or end, because it is identical with his very act of existence.

Some have gone so far as to deny that God's will is a distinct faculty in him as it is in humans. God's free will is most absolute because it is identical with his essence. Stephen Charnock concludes, via the DDS, that God's will is nothing other than "God willing":

33. Bavinck, *RD*, II: 239–40 (emphasis added). Aquinas offers a similar assessment of divine choice in light of God's immutability: "Mutability . . . is not required—For, if there is no potentiality in the divine will, God does not thus prefer one of the opposites among His effects as if He should be thought as being in potency to both, so that He first wills both in potency and afterward He wills in act; rather, He wills in act whatever He wills, not only in relation to Himself but also in relation to His effects"(*SCG* I.82 [7]). See also, Miller, *A Most Unlikely God*, 103–4.

34. Michael Dodds notes that an unchangeable will for humans may not be a good thing: "It might signify the virtue of steadfastness but could also indicate the vices of stubbornness or indifference" (*Unchanging God of Love*, 171).

> The will of God is the same with his essence. If God had a will
> distinct from his essence, he would not be the most simple Being.
> God hath not a faculty of will distinct from himself; as his under-
> standing is nothing else but *Deus intelligens*, God understanding;
> so his will is nothing else but *Deus volens*, God willing; being,
> therefore, the essence of God; though it is considered, accord-
> ing to our weakness, as a faculty, it is as his understanding and
> wisdom, eternal and immutable; and can no more be changed
> than his essence. The immutability of the divine counsel depends
> upon that of his essence.[35]

Clearly, whatever function free will is to have within this conception of
divine ontology it cannot be taken as God's actual openness to contrary
choice. If God's free will is *Deus volens* it is no more open to being otherwise than is God's very existence and essence.[36]

Charnock argues that the freedom of God's will does not so much
consist in its openness and indifference toward a host of possibilities,
but in its non-dependence upon those creaturely things that he does in
fact will. His freedom of will is the freedom of realizing his necessary
and desired end without dependence upon anything outside himself.
Consider Charnock's remarks:

> The immutability of God's will doth not infringe the liberty of
> it. The liberty of God's will consists with the necessity of con-
> tinuing his purpose. God is necessarily good, immutably good;
> yet he is freely so, and would not be otherwise than what he is.
> God was free in his first purpose; and purposing this or that by
> an infallible and unerring wisdom, it would be a weakness to
> change the purpose. But, indeed, the liberty of God's will doth
> not seem so much to consist in an indifferency to this or that, as
> in an independency on anything without himself: his will was

---

35. Charnock, *Existence and Attributes of God*, I: 325–26. See also, Renard, *The Philosophy of God*, 150.

36. Characterizing God's will as *Deus volens* rather than as a faculty in God seems
to fit well with notion that God is pure act, although it raises insuperable difficulties for
depicting his freedom as the power to do otherwise. Katherin Rogers writes, "[I]f omnipotence, omniscience, and perfect goodness refer only to a power, then God might
be omnipotent, omniscient, and perfectly good, yet not do anything, know anything
or actually exhibit any goodness, and this seems odd to say the least. But if God is His
Act, as the tradition holds, the current difficulty [of counterfactual freedom] remains.
God cannot do other than He does without being other than He is" ("The Traditional
Doctrine of Divine Simplicity," 178–79).

free, because it did not depend upon the objects about which his will was conversant.[37]

God's purpose, whether or not he creates, is the enjoyment of his own goodness. Whatever he wills *must* have his goodness as its end. But it is also a fact that this necessity does not restrict God's freedom in willing insofar as his goodness is what he most desires. Charnock assumes that freedom is the power to possess what one most desires without hindrance from or dependence upon external things. God does not ultimately desire anything other than himself. His freedom with respect to creatures, then, consists in the fact that he is not dependent upon them in order to possess his chief desire. He is free in creating because he does not *need* creatures in order to attain his goodness.[38] This free will, then, is the freedom of independence, not the freedom of either changing his purpose or beginning to will something not previously willed. Such freedom can only characterize temporal creatures that come to possess new desires. But God's desire never changes.

Strictly speaking, Charnock's explanation of God's freedom does not proscribe the possibility that God may also possess deliberative freedom; that denial, rather, is accomplished by emphasizing God's ontological immutability, eternality, and pure actuality. What his explanation does do is show that there is some other way of confessing that God is most free in willing the world without requiring that it be the freedom of *moving*, either temporally or logically, from undecided openness to a specific choice. This alternate way of expressing divine freedom seems necessary insofar as counterfactual indifference is not an option for describing the free will of a simple, immutable, eternal God.

What are we to say, then, about the modal status of "could have" in statements affirming that God "could have" willed differently than he has? Do these affirmations not suggest some intrinsic ontological

---

37. Ibid., I: 328. As with Aquinas's view, this echoes Aristotle's notion that a free agent is the one who is for its own sake. God is most for his own sake since he alone is the final end of all his willing. It follows that he is also most free.

38. In similar fashion, Rudi te Velde writes, "The independence, or absoluteness of God characterizes the way He relates as cause to all other things; it is the independence of the perfect goodness of God, who is not under any obligation or necessity to fulfill himself by creating, but who acts out of his own goodness, establishing all other things in being by letting them share in his own perfection" (*Aquinas on God*, 85). Thomas states, "The reason rather [that God does not will creatures with an absolute necessity] is because the object willed does not have a necessary order to the divine goodness, which is the proper object of the divine will" (*SCG* I.82 [7]).

contingency in God?[39] Many DDS subscribers have concluded that such statements are simply imprecise ways of expressing the non-absolute necessity of the actual world. God's essence would not have been different, they contend, if he had willed some other possible world.[40] Others go further by explicitly stipulating that such modal contingencies are not really applicable to God. Barry Miller, for instance, devises a formula for ensuring that the contingency of "could have" is applied to the non-divine things God wills and not to God himself.[41]

To begin with, Miller insists that internal contingency must be sharply distinguished from external. Internal contingency would indicate that God contingently has cognitive state$_w$ rather than cognitive state$_{w^*}$. External contingency, conversely, would propose that it is contingent that God have cognitive statew rather than cognitive state$_{w^*}$. Miller considers whether either of these forms of contingency imputes potentiality to God. Internal contingency seems to do so since it represents God's knowledge as something actualized in one way and potentially in another. On the other hand, external contingency does not imply such potentiality in God. Miller denies that statements indicating that God "could be" other than he is demand that there be any real potentiality in God. To say it could be that God could have cognitive state$_{w^*}$ does not mean that he is in potency to cognitive state$_{w^*}$. Miller stresses the subtle distinction between the statements "It could be that (God have cognitive state$_{w^*}$)" and "God could have cognitive state$_{w^*}$."[42] The former is acceptable and does not suggest passive potency in God while the latter does seem to locate passive potency in God himself. The contingency in the first formulation lies with "it" and not with "God"; *it* could be, though *God* could not be otherwise than he is.[43] Although this formulation may suffer on account of its abstrusity, it does seem to provide one way of making statements about the contingency of creation without imputing that contingency to the divine nature itself.

39. This is regarded as a serious challenge both by Leftow, "Is God an Abstract Object?" 594–95, and Hughes, *On a Complex Theory*, 108.

40. See Maritain, *Existence and the Existent*, 106.

41. See Miller, *A Most Unlikely God*, 99–105.

42. Ibid., 101.

43. Miller argues that it is wrong to speak of God using an internal modal operator. Ergo, it is wrong to say that God "can" either create or not create the world. The more precise expression is: "It can be that (God create the Universe), or it can be that (God not create the Universe)" (ibid., 102).

Miller is insistent that not every affirmation of contingency is repugnant to the DDS or to divine immutability. As he states, *"[T]he only contingency that is alien to him [God] is one that would impute potentiality to him."*[44] The great issue is to deny that God can change from a state of passive potency to a state of actuality. "[T]he necessity of his omniscience," Miller writes, "conflicts not with the contingency of his *being* in any particular cognitive state, but merely with the possibility of his *changing* from one state to another."[45] In this sense, it is permissible to say, abstractly, that God could have known or willed the world to be different than it is, assuming that such a difference does not conflict with the end and purpose of his own goodness and glory. But this abstract "possibility" should not be regarded as a real passive potency in the divine nature inasmuch as God has never stood in actual passive openness to "the way things might have been but are not." It is when unwilled "possible worlds" are elevated from logical or hypothetical possibility to the status of *actual* possibility in the divine nature that they present problems for the DDS.

Thomas Aquinas makes a distinction between the absolute necessity in God's willing of himself and the suppositional necessity in his willing of other things. Non-divine things are only necessary because God wills them and do not, in themselves, require or coerce God to choose them. Consider Thomas's explanation: "[E]verything eternal is necessary. Now, that God should will some effect to be is eternal, for, like His being, so, too, His willing is measured by eternity, and is therefore necessary. But it is not necessary considered absolutely, because the will of God does not have a necessary relation to this willed object. Therefore, it is necessary by supposition."[46] Again, because God's end of his own goodness and glory does not depend upon the non-divine things he wills, they cannot be considered as absolutely necessary to him in the way that his own nature is. Nevertheless, we cannot say that God's free will could have *actually* been otherwise since it is eternally and immutably *actual* in just the way it is. Thus, Thomas writes: "Furthermore, whatever God could He can, for His power is not decreased, as neither is His essence. But He cannot now not will what He is posited as having willed, because His will cannot be changed. Therefore, at no time could

He not will what He has willed. It is therefore necessary by supposition that He willed whatever He willed, and also that He wills it; neither, however, is absolutely necessary, but, rather, possible in the aforementioned way."[47] Undoubtedly, this sort of "possibility" cannot but fail to inspire those for whom free will is essentially characterized by an agent's *actual* openness to counterfactuals.[48] The precise character of a free will that never moves from "could will" to "does will" seems to be beyond all human analysis. Indeed, the DDS adherent readily owns such inscrutability inasmuch as it is of a single piece with the incomprehensibility of God as *ipsum esse subsistens* or *actus purus*.[49] But this impenetrability is no conclusive argument against the necessity and usefulness of these doctrines for confessing God as "most absolute."

SIMPLICITY AND FREEDOM BEYOND ANALYSIS

There has never been a temporal or logical "moment" in the divine life in which God stood volitionally open to other possible worlds. The actual world is conditionally necessary and every other possible world is conditionally impossible by virtue of the fact that God has *eternally* willed just this particular world.[50] His will for the world is free inasmuch as it

47. Ibid. I.83 [4].

48. Thomas Morris charges that the eternal suppositional necessity of the world destroys the meaningfulness of its contingency. Anything that is not *actually* open to being otherwise cannot be characterized by modal possibility or as a genuine accident. From the DDS it follows that "the actual world is the only possible world, that all our properties are essential, and so on. This is extreme modal uniformity" ("On God and Mann," 311). It may be responded that it is actually Morris who endorses an "extreme modal uniformity" inasmuch as he assumes that those modalities governing human freedom and contingency must also govern divine necessity and freedom in exactly that same way. This is not a uniformity within modality itself, but between the divine and human agents of modality. It follows quite naturally from Morris's ontological univocism.

49. What Gilson says of God's creation without movement is equally suitable for describing the incomprehensibility of his free will: "It is absolutely true that all movement is a changing of the state of being. But when we hear of an act which is not a movement we are at a loss how to think about it. No matter how we try, we always *imagine* that creation [or divine free will] is a kind of change . . . But in actual fact it is something quite different, something we are at a loss to put into words, so unfamiliar is it to the conditions of human experience" (*The Christian Philosophy of St. Thomas Aquinas*, 122). For a fine account of how divine incomprehensibility may function within a philosophical theology see James Anderson, *Paradox in Christian Theology*.

50. On the suppositional impossibility of all other possible worlds see Rogers, *Perfect Being Theology*, 36. Rogers is skeptical of making too much out of possible

is not required in order for God to be God or to fulfill perfectly his end, the enjoyment of his own goodness and glory. Had he willed some other possible world or no world at all, he would not have been in the least bit hindered in his final purpose. Even so, there does seem to be biblical and theological warrant for saying that God could do things other than he does. Insofar as the DDS insists upon the eternal pure actuality of his will it is incumbent upon DDS subscribers to make some sense of God's knowledge of and power for counterfactuals.

Thomas proves God's power to do otherwise from the words of Jesus in Matthew 26:53: "Do you think that I cannot appeal to my Father, and he will at once send me more than twelve legions of angels?" But Christ neither makes this request nor does the Father perform the action. Thomas concludes, "Therefore God can do what He does not."[51] This affirmation is qualified in two ways. First, against those who hold that all of God's actions are performed by a natural necessity, it is argued that the present course of things follows from God's free will and not any necessity in his nature "so that other things could not happen."[52] Second, Thomas responds to those who hold that since God's wisdom and justice cannot be otherwise, and God's will is identical in him with his wisdom and justice, his free will could not be otherwise. This incorrectly presumes that the present creation is adequate to God's wisdom such that "the divine wisdom should be restricted to this present order of things."

---

worlds in our treatment of God's free will. She writes, "It is only the temporal and limited point of view which allows discussion of other possible worlds" ("The Traditional Doctrine of Divine Simplicity," 185). Michael Dodds also highlights the dubious status of possible worlds in seeking to explain how God "might" have been: "Rather than try to find some dimension in the absolute simplicity of God in which to locate a 'real difference' in God resulting from God's not having willed anything other than what God has in fact willed, we would simply point out that the series of arguments leading to the assertion that there is presently some 'real difference' in God is based upon the rather ephemeral foundation of a counter-to-fact supposition about a world that God might have created, but didn't" (Unchanging God of Love, 177). Dodds is specifically targeting proposals by Stump, Kretzmann, and Norris Clarke that claim the way God is is "really different" than the way he might have been. Dodds dislikes ascribing "real difference" to God because it seems to function like the specific difference of some species within a genus that might be denominated as "ways God could possibly be." As there is no such genus, God in his actuality cannot be differentiated from the other possible ways he might have been by some specific or real difference. In fine, his free will should not be characterized as a piece of specifying differentia somehow inhering in him.

51. ST I.25.5.
52. Ibid.

Furthermore, this view assumes that the things created are adequate to the end for which they were created, namely, God. But if God is the end of all things and is infinite in himself, then no finite order of things could possibly be proportionate to its end. Thomas observes, "[T]he divine goodness is an end exceeding beyond all proportion things created." Only an infinite creation could be adequate to the end of God himself and an infinite creation is, by definition, impossible. "Wherefore," Thomas concludes, "we must simply say that God can do other things than those He has done."[53]

The difficulty is in understanding how such power to do otherwise can be reconciled with the denial that God exhibits any sense of passive potency. It would seem that some measure of volitional openness is necessary in order for the "power to do otherwise" to make sense. But in stressing God's power to do otherwise Thomas's concern is not so much in locating a point in the divine life in which God chooses among equally open alternatives, but rather to highlight that the world he has eternally chosen is not *absolutely* necessary according to his nature. The world is dependent upon God and not vice versa. Thus, it is the contingency of the world that is the primary focus when affirming divine contra-causal power. Moreover, it is important to recognize that contra-causal *power* is not to be equated with contra-causal *openness* in God's volition. In fact, Thomas insists that power is not properly attributed to God's will at all, but to his nature: "God does things because He wills so to do; yet the power to do them does not come from His will, but from His nature."[54] In locating God's absolute power in his nature rather than in his will, Thomas removes any need for volitional openness in God. God's power for counterfactuals is not a power of his will as such.

For all this, though, we are still faced with the fact that there seems to be something in God that is less than absolutely necessary, namely, his will to create this particular world. Surely, critics contend, this indicates at least one area in which divine simplicity subverts divine absoluteness, namely, the absoluteness of his freedom. God's ontological absoluteness appears to be endangered if one insists that God is not free in his act of willing the world. If he wills the world with absolute necessity then something non-divine would be necessary to him and he would be

53. Ibid.
54. Ibid. I.25.5, ad 1.

correlative in being and essence. God would depend upon something outside himself for his end and purpose.

Whether his will for the universe is free or necessary, then, it seems that the doctrine of divine absoluteness is doomed. If God's will is free then seemingly he must be composed of act and potency, and thus cannot be existentially absolute (which requires that he be eternally pure act). If his will for the world is absolutely necessary then his nature requires the world and thus God cannot be essentially absolute. For Christians, both of these alternatives are unacceptable. If divine absoluteness is doomed, so is any prospect of offering a sufficient reason for the existence of anything at all.

It must be reiterated at this point that only that which is identical with its own existence is *ultimately* sufficient to account for itself or anything else. For this reason the first cause of being must be subsistent pure act (and all that is entailed in *actus purus* such as being *a se*, indivisibly one, infinite, immutable, and eternal). Moreover, the first cause of being must be *free* in his production of other things since, if he were not, he would stand in existential need of those things in order to be fully actualized in his nature. But then he would not be pure act apart from his production of creatures. God would need the world for his being and the world would need him for its being. Such a pantheistic tautology spells the end of ever offering a sufficient reason for the universe. Needless to say, if one is to uphold the Christian doctrine of creation *ex nihilo* then it is crucial to confess God as *both* simple pure act and free in his act of willing the world.

It should be readily confessed that the exact function of free will in God who is himself pure act is beyond the scope of human knowledge. Just as we cannot comprehend God as *ipsum esse subsistens*, we cannot comprehend the identity between God as eternal, immutable, pure act and his will for the world as free and uncoerced. Though we discover strong reasons for confessing both simplicity and freedom in God, we cannot form an isomorphically adequate notion of *how* this is the case.[55]

---

55. Gregory Doolan has suggested to me that this acknowledgment of ignorance may be analogous to the acknowledgement that we do not know *how* it is that light behaves as both a wave and a particle. The inability of account for *how* a thing might be does not in itself undermine the fact *that* a thing is just that way. There are compelling reasons for confessing *that* God is both simple and free, our inability to explain *how* notwithstanding. It seems that many who dismiss either God's freedom or simplicity do so exclusively on the basis of their inability to answer the *how* question. Again, though,

In fact, this confession of ignorance is precisely what one finds in the Thomist and Reformed traditions.

Richard Muller is representative of the Reformed tradition generally when he writes, "This view of God as possessing a freedom of contrariety with regard to the world renders a whole series of questions concerning the origin and nature of the created order *impossible of purely rational resolution*."[56] Edith Stein doubts that humans possess sufficient modal categories suitable to understanding how God is in himself: "And such an ultimate, impenetrable fact for us is the differentiation between necessity and contingency which we find even in the realm of essential being. It seems to me that it indeed transcends the possibilities of natural reason to demonstrate that the cause of this differentiation lies in the divine essence."[57] Louis De Raeymaeker appears to agree with Stein when he writes, "The absolute necessity and absolute liberty of God transcend the opposition of the relative necessity and limited liberty of man."[58] Michael Dodds does not shirk the mystery in confessing the simplicity of God's will by which he wills himself with absolute necessity and other things freely: "We cannot understand how, in the one act by which God necessarily wills his own goodness, he also freely wills the existence of creatures. We recognize, nonetheless, that this one act, insofar as it is one with the divine essence, is a necessary act that in no way requires the existence of creatures. This same act, insofar as it results in the existence of creatures, is not necessary but free, and would imply no difference with respect to the divine essence by its absence."[59]

We cannot do better than to consider an additional passage from Dodds as a fitting and bracing conclusion to this point:

---

this seems to follow quite naturally from an overarching commitment to ontological univocity.

56. Muller, *PRRD*, III: 448–49 (emphasis added).

57. Stein, *Finite and Eternal Being*, 308. Stein confesses that our discussions of necessity and contingency in God's one act of will and of God's plurality of ideas in his one simple act of knowledge "bears the marks of reason illumined by faith, a reason which—impelled by the words of revealed truth—seeks to grasp mysteries which defy and confound all human concepts" (ibid.).

58. Raeymaeker, *Philosophy of Being*, 286. In a proposal similar to this, Hugh McCann argues that, assuming God's simplicity, "[God's] freedom as creator is such as to transcend all modality" (*Creation and the Sovereignty of God*, chap. 11, sect. 6, not yet paginated).

59. Dodds, *Unchanging God of Love*, 179.

Our remarks regarding the act of the divine will are necessarily halting and inadequate since the operation of God's will infinitely exceeds the capacity of our thought and language. In what we say, we do not seek to explain the mystery of God's will, but only to preserve it from our all-too-human tendency to reduce God to something we can understand. At the same time in answering the hypothetical question that we have posed regarding what God "might do" or how God "might be," we refuse to abandon the actual truth that we have discovered about what God is: that God is pure actuality, *ipsum esse subsistens*, and that as such he is (unlike us) absolutely simple and unchanging. It is of course tempting to deny our ignorance and to pretend instead that God's will is like our own, with a multitude of acts, some of which would be different or changed if God did not will the creation of the world. But if we yield to that temptation, the God of whom we speak will be only a human God, made in our own image. He will be only a "pretend" God who "might be this" or "could be that." He will no longer be the God of transcendent mystery who has made us in his own image and likeness and reveals himself as "He who is" (Ex. 3:14).[60]

CONCLUSION

The difficulty that divine freedom poses for God's simplicity is not such as to render the DDS impossible or necessarily incoherent. Certainly, one must readily acknowledge the incomprehensibility of the divine nature (WCF 2.1) if both are to be maintained. But the inability to say *how* it is that God is both simple and free does not necessarily obviate the fact *that* he is both. Indeed, the absoluteness of the first cause of being demands a firm affirmation of his simplicity and freedom. Moreover, for whatever tension there appears to be in this affirmation, it should also be emphasized that it is God's simplicity that ensures his will is genuinely free from dependence upon creatures.

60. Ibid., 180.

Conclusion

THE DOCTRINE OF DIVINE simplicity has no shortage of detractors in the modern philosophical-theological milieu. Indeed, its austere and sometimes shocking demands grate against the modern proclivity for a God that is more easily understood, more manageable, more like us. It is not at all surprising that most modern opponents of the DDS are firmly committed to a univocal doctrine of being. Many analytic philosophers and Perfect-being theologians are willing to grant that God is above all creatures in his existence and essence; this transcendence, however, is measured by degrees and is not attributed to God's entirely different order of being as *ipsum esse subsistens* or *actus purus*. To be sure, saying that God is *being itself* just sounds like nonsense to minds habituated to conceive only of essences that possess existence as the thinnest or most common of properties.

It has been my contention throughout this study that unless God is identical with all that is in him, and is entirely devoid of all passive potency, one cannot designate him as "most absolute." If he were composed of parts then whatever absoluteness he exhibited would have to be correlative to those parts and thus weakened by relativity, contingency, and dependence. What's more, without an absolutely simple God who is identical with all that is in him one can offer no account for God or for anything else. If God is not the ontological sufficient reason for himself and all other things then he is not God.

My reason for offering a prolonged investigation of the models of composition was to clarify just what it is about God that simplicity denies. Obviously, many who deny absolute simplicity are willing to grant some aspects of the classical doctrine, such as God's incorporeity. I have argued, however, that unless one denies of God *all* of the various act-potency compositional schemes, God himself cannot be wholly *self-sufficient* since he apparently receives further determination to being from some actuating principle with which he is not identical. Something non-divine would then make God to be actual in some sense. That "something" would have to possess a measure of self-sufficiency in itself over against God. But then God is not God. Everything other than God is dependent and cannot existentially account for itself, much less for some actuality in God.

In surveying the way in which simplicity functions in the classical accounts of God's aseity, unity, infinity, immutability, and eternity my aim has been to demonstrate that apart from simplicity it is difficult for any classical account of God's transcendence to stand up or to achieve its design in definitively setting God apart from his creatures. Many of these doctrines make no sense without a strong account of God's simplicity undergirding them.

The consideration of God as *ipsum esse subsistens* and *actus purus* is crucial for any confession of God's absolute existence. In created things, "to be" (*esse*) is always a *principle* of the subject's complete being (*ens*). But as first and absolute being God is, in a sense, existentially unprincipled. He is not the product of a fortuitous combination of excellent parts; neither is he self-made. In truth, God follows from nothing and so nothing is in him as a principle of his being or essence. The only explanation for God's existence is God himself existing.

As for God's attributes, we encounter great difficulties if it is assumed that our many and varied predications about God must correspond to some ontological complexity in him. The DDS rejects the assumption that the mode of human knowledge and speech is adequate to the mode of God's subsistence. His attributes are not in him as their creaturely likenesses are in those things that bear God's image. To this end it has been argued that the divine attributes are not properly considered to be "properties." By way of accommodation and analogy we may certainly speak of "divine properties." Nevertheless, in seeking to account for how God's perfections subsist in him, all property accounts fail. This is because it is the nature of any property to inhere in a substance and thus receive its actuality from that substance. Also, a property adds some further determination of being that does not belong to a substance *qua* substance. But if God is pure act he cannot possess properties in this sense. The "truthmaker" account of predication was proposed to explain how it is that we may ascribe many and diverse perfections to God while maintaining that those perfections do not exist by inherence in him, determining him to be in this way or that. Rather, God himself is the one minimal truthmaker (back of which there is nothing) for all of his attributes and each attribute is ontologically accounted for by the same undifferentiated reality, namely, God himself as pure act.

Specific consideration was given to God's knowledge and will inasmuch as many regard these divine perfections as uniquely challenging to the classical understanding of simplicity. It was argued that, far from being a liability, the DDS actually secures the absoluteness of divine knowledge and volition. God is absolute in his knowledge because he knows all things in knowing himself. He does not discover any truth or fact outside himself. Rather, he knows all things *ad extra* in knowing his essence as imitable and in knowing his will for their existence. Furthermore, God is absolute in his will inasmuch as he himself is the end at which all his willing is directed. The end supplies the reason for the will and thus God himself is the sufficient reason for all his willing. Furthermore, as he is identical with the end or goal of his will, God's *act* of will does not function in him as a mediator between willer and willed. As these are identical in him, his act of will also is identical with him; the divine will is nothing other than God willing.

Finally, we considered the difficulty in explaining how it is that a simple God *freely* wills non-divine things. Would not simplicity cancel out divine freedom, or vice versa? Some recent scholars are content to simply choose one over the other. Yet the fact that we cannot explain ontologically or modally *how* God is simple yet free does not prevent us from affirming *that* he is both. God could not be absolute if he were not pure act inasmuch as only a being that is pure act is sufficient to account for the existence of anything at all. But this one who is simple pure act must also be free in his will to create. If he created from natural necessity then God would, by nature, need the world in order to complete his purpose and enjoyment of himself. If he were compelled to create from some necessity in creation itself, then he would be acted upon from without and would be determined to be "Creator," even if only accidentally. Of course, neither would he be the absolute first cause of being if he were compelled to create by some extrinsic force. All this was to conclude that, inscrutable as the relation between divine simplicity and freedom may be, they are both indispensable to the confession of God as most absolute. Moreover, it seems that God's ontological simplicity makes his will to be free and independent of the creature in an absolute sense, thus securing the absoluteness even of his freedom.

Based on the conclusions of this study, dispensing with the DDS is not advisable. In fact, restoring it to its traditional role as a controlling and vital concern in the orthodox Christian doctrine of God is a non-negotiable for all who would uphold the confession that he is *most absolute*.

Bibliography

Acar, Rahim. *Talking about God and Talking about Creation: Avicenna's and Thomas Aquinas' Positions*. Leiden: Brill, 2005.

Aertsen, Jan A. "*Good* as Transcendental and the Transcendence of the Good." In *Being and Goodness: The Concept of the Good in Metaphysics and Philosophical Theology*, edited by Scott MacDonald, 56–73. Ithaca: Cornell University Press, 1991.

———. *Medieval Philosophy and the Transcendentals: The Case of Thomas Aquinas*. Leiden: Brill, 1996.

———. *Nature and Creature: Thomas Aquinas's Way of Thought*. Translated by Herbert Donald Morton. Leiden: Brill, 1988.

Alston, William P. "Aquinas on Theological Predication: A Look Backward and a Look Forward." In *Reasoned Faith: Essays in Philosophical Theology in Honor of Honor of Norman Kretzmann*, edited by Eleonore Stump, 145–78. Ithaca: Cornell University Press, 1993.

———. "Divine and Human Action." In *Divine and Human Action: Essays in the Metaphysics of Theism*, edited by Thomas V. Morris, 257–80. Ithaca: Cornell University Press, 1988.

Anderson, James. *Paradox in Christian Theology: An Analysis of Its Presence, Character, and Epistemic Status*. Milton Keynes, UK: Paternoster, 2007.

Anderson, James F. *The Bond of Being: An Essay on Analogy and Existence*. St. Louis: Herder, 1949.

———. *The Cause of Being: The Philosophy of Creation in St. Thomas*. St. Louis: Herder, 1952.

———. *Natural Theology: The Metaphysics of God*. Milwaukee: Bruce, 1962.

Anselm [Archbishop of Canterbury]. *Monologium*. In *St. Anselm: Proslogium; Monologium; An Appendix in Behalf of the Fool by Gaunilon; and Cur Deus Homo*. Translated by Sidney Norton Deane. La Salle, IL: Open Court, 1948.

———. *Proslogium*. In *St. Anselm: Proslogium; Monologium; An Appendix in Behalf of the Fool by Gaunilon; and Cur Deus Homo*. Translated by Sidney Norton Deane. La Salle, IL: Open Court, 1948.

Aquinas, Thomas. *Commentary on Aristotle's Metaphysics*. Translated by John P. Rowan. Notre Dame, IN: Dumb Ox, 1995.

———. *Commentary on the Book of Causes*. Translated by Vincent A. Guagliardo, Charles R. Hess, and Richard C. Taylor. Washington, DC: The Catholic University of America Press, 1996.

———. *Compendium theologiae*. Translated by Cyril Vollert as *Compendium of Theology*. St. Louis: Herder, 1947.

———. *De Principiis Naturae*. Translated by Robert P. Goodwin as *The Principles of Nature*. In *Selected Writings of St. Thomas Aquinas*, edited by Robert P. Goodwin, 7–28. New York: Macmillan, 1965.

———. *De Spiritualibus Creaturis.* Translated by Mary C. FitzPatrick and John J. Wellmuth as *On Spiritual Creatures.* Milwaukee, WI: Marquette University Press, 1949.

———. *Quaestiones disputatae De potentia Dei.* Translated by the English Dominican Fathers as *On the Power of God.* 3 vols. London: Burns Oates & Washbourne, 1932.

———. *Questiones Disputatae de Veritate.* Translated by Robert W. Mulligan, James V. McGlynn and Robert W. Schmidt as *Truth.* 3 vols. Chicago: Regnery, 1952–54.

———. *Quodlibetal Questions 1 and 2.* Translated by Sandra Edwards. Toronto: Pontifical Institute of Medieval Studies, 1983.

———. *Scriptum super libros Sententiarum.* Translated by E. M. Macierowski as *Thomas Aquinas's Earliest Treatment of the Divine Essence:* Scriptum super libros Sententiarum, *Book I, Distinction 8.* Binghamton, NY: Binghamton University, 1998.

———. *Sententia super Physicam.* Translated by Richard J. Blackwell, Richard J. Spath, and W. Edmund Thirlkel as *Commentary on Aristotle's* Physics. Notre Dame, IN: Dumb Ox, 1999.

———. *Summa contra gentiles.* Translated by Anton C. Pegis, James F. Anderson, Vernon J. Bourke, and Charles J. O'Neil as *On the Truth of the Catholic Faith.* 5 vols. Garden City, NY: Doubleday, 1955.

———. *Summa theologiae.* Translated by Fathers of the English Dominican Province as *Summa Theologica.* Allen, TX: Christian Classics, 1981.

Archbishop Basil [Krivocheine]. "Simplicity of the Divine Nature and the Distinctions in God, according to St. Gregory of Nyssa." *St. Vladimir's Theological Quarterly* 21 (1977) 76–104.

Aristotle. *The Complete Works of Aristotle: The Revised Oxford Translation.* Edited by Jonathan Barnes. 2 vols. Princeton, NJ: Princeton University Press, 1984.

Arlig, Andrew W. "A Study in Early Medieval Mereology: Boethius, Abelard, and Pseudo-Joscelin." PhD diss., The Ohio State University, 2005.

Augustine. *The City of God.* Translated by Marcus Dods. New York: Random House, 1950.

———. *The Confessions.* Edited by John E. Rotelle. Translated by Maria Boulding. Hyde Park, NY: New City, 1997.

———. *The Trinity.* Edited by John E. Rotelle. Translated by Edmund Hill. Brooklyn, NY: New City, 1991.

Ayres, Lewis. *Augustine and the Trinity.* Cambridge: Cambridge University Press, 2010.

———. *Nicaea and its Legacy: An Approach to Fourth-Century Trinitarian Theology.* Oxford: Oxford University Press, 2004.

Barth, Karl. *Church Dogmatics.* Vol. II/1: *The Doctrine of God.* Translated by T. H. L. Parker et al. Edinburgh: T. & T. Clark, 1957.

Bavinck, Herman. *Reformed Dogmatics.* Edited by John Bolt. Translated by John Vriend. 4 vols. Grand Rapids: Baker Academic, 2004.

Benignus [Brother Benignus Gerrity]. *Nature, Knowledge, and God: An Introduction to Thomistic Philosophy.* Milwaukee, WI: Bruce, 1947.

Bennett, Daniel C. "The Divine Simplicity." In *Logical Analysis and Contemporary Theism,* edited by John Donnelly, 94–105. New York: Fordham University Press, 1972.

Bergmann, Michael, and Jeffrey Brower. "A Theistic Argument against Platonism (and in Support of Truthmakers and Divine Simplicity)." In *Oxford Studies in Metaphysics*, edited by Dean W. Zimmerman, 357–86. Vol. 2. Oxford: Clarendon, 2006.

Berkhof, Louis. *Systematic Theology*. Grand Rapids: Eerdmans, 1996.

Bobik, Joseph. *Aquinas on Being and Essence: A Translation and Interpretation*. Notre Dame, IN: University of Notre Dame Press, 1965.

———. *Aquinas on Matter and Form and the Elements: A Translation and Interpretation of the* de Principiis Naturae *and the* De Mixtione Elementorum *of St. Thomas Aquinas*. Notre Dame, IN: University of Notre Dame Press, 1998.

Boedder, Bernard. *Natural Theology*. New York: Longmans, Green, and Co., 1896.

Boethius. *Philosophiae Consolationis*. In *The Theological Tractates / The Consolation of Philosophy*. Translated by H. F. Stewart, E. K. Rand, and S. J. Tester. Cambridge: Harvard University Press, 1973

———. *De Trinitate*. In *The Theological Tractates / The Consolation of Philosophy*. Translated by H. F. Stewart, E. K. Rand, and S. J. Tester. Cambridge: Harvard University Press, 1973.

Boland, Vivian. *Ideas in God according to Saint Thomas Aquinas: Sources and Synthesis*. Leiden: Brill, 1996.

Bonansea, Bernardino M. *God and Atheism: A Philosophical Approach to the Problem of God*. Washington, DC: The Catholic University of America Press, 1979.

Brakel, Wilhelmus à. *The Christian's Reasonable Service*. Edited by Joel R. Beeke. Translated by Bartel Elshout. 4 vols. Grand Rapids: Reformation Heritage, 1992.

Braine, David. "Aquinas, God and Being." In *Analytical Thomism: Traditions in Dialogue*, edited by Craig Paterson and Matthew S. Pugh, 1–24. Aldershot, UK: Ashgate, 2006.

———. *The Reality of Time and the Existence of God: The Project of Proving God's Existence*. Oxford: Clarendon, 1988.

Branick, Vincent P. "The Unity of the Divine Ideas." *The New Scholasticism* 42 (1968) 171–201.

Brennan, Robert Edward. *Thomistic Psychology: A Philosophic Analysis of the Nature of Man*. New York: MacMillan, 1941.

Brosnan, William J. *God Infinite and Reason*. New York: America, 1928.

Brower, Jeffrey E. "Aquinas's Metaphysics of Modality: A Reply to Leftow." *The Modern Schoolman* 82 (March 2005) 201–12.

———. "Making Sense of Divine Simplicity." *Faith and Philosophy* 25 (2008) 3–30.

———. "Simplicity and Aseity." In *The Oxford Handbook of Philosophical Theology*, edited by Thomas P. Flint and Michael C. Rea, 105–28. Oxford: Oxford University Press, 2009.

Brown, Patterson. "St. Thomas' Doctrine of Necessary Being." *Philosophical Review* 73 (1964) 76–90.

Burns, Peter. "The Status and Function of Divine Simpleness in *Summa theologiae* Ia, qq. 2–13." *The Thomist* 57 (1993) 1–26.

Burns, Robert M. "The Divine Simplicity in St. Thomas." *Religious Studies* 25 (1989) 271–93.

Burrell, David B. "Act of Creation with Its Theological Consequences." In *Aquinas on Doctrine: A Critical Introduction*, Thomas G. Weinandy et al., 27–44. London: T. & T. Clark, 2004.

———. *Aquinas: God and Action.* Notre Dame, IN: University of Notre Dame Press, 1979.

———. "Creation, Will and Knowledge in Aquinas and Duns Scotus." In *Pragmatik I: Handbuch Pragmatischen Denkens,* edited by Herbert Stachowiak, 246–57. Hamburg: Meiner, 1986.

———. "Distinguishing God from the World." In *Language, Meaning, and God: Essays in Honour of Herbert McCabe,* edited by Brian Davies, 75–91. London: Chapman, 1987.

———. "Divine Practical Knowing: How an Eternal God Acts in Time." In *Divine Action: Studies Inspired by the Philosophical Theology of Austin Farrer,* edited by Brian Hebblethwaite and Edward Henderson, 93–102. Edinburgh: T. & T. Clark, 1990.

———. *Freedom and Creation in Three Traditions.* Notre Dame, IN: University of Notre Dame Press, 1993.

———. *Knowing the Unknowable God: Ibn-Sina, Maimonides, Aquinas.* Notre Dame, IN: University of Notre Dame Press, 1986.

———. "Simpleness." In *Philosophy of Religion: A Guide to the Subject,* edited by Brian Davies, 70–75. Washington, DC: Georgetown University Press, 1998.

Cajetan [Thomas de Vio]. *Commentary on Being and Essence.* Translated by Lottie H. Kendzierski and Francis C. Wade, S.J. Milwaukee, WI: Marquette University Press, 1964.

Cantens, Bernardo. "The Interdependency between Aquinas's Doctrine of Creation and his Metaphysical Principle of the Limitation of Act by Potency." *Proceedings of the American Catholic Philosophical Association* 74 (2001) 121–39.

Carlo, William E. "The Role of Essence in Existential Metaphysics: A Reappraisal." *International Philosophical Quarterly* 2 (1962) 557–90.

———. *The Ultimate Reducibility of Essence to Existence in Existential Metaphysics.* The Hague: Nijhoff, 1966.

Carrington, William Thomas, Jr. "Divine Immutability Revisited: The Doctrine of St. Thomas Aquinas in the Face of Some Contemporary Challenges." PhD diss., Fordham University, 1973.

Charnock, Stephen. *The Existence and Attributes of God.* 2 vols. 1853. Reprint. Grand Rapids: Baker, 1979.

Clarke, W. Norris. *Explorations in Metaphysics: Being-God-Person.* Notre Dame, IN: University of Notre Dame Press, 1994.

———. "The Limitation of Act by Potency: Aristotelianism or Neoplatonism?" *The New Scholasticism* 26 (1952) 167–94.

———. "The Meaning of Participation in St. Thomas." *Proceedings of the American Catholic Philosophical Association* 26 (1952) 147–57.

———. *The One and the Many: A Contemporary Thomistic Metaphysics.* Notre Dame, IN: University of Notre Dame Press, 2001.

———. *The Philosophical Approach to God: A New Thomistic Perspective.* 2nd ed. New York: Fordham University Press, 2007.

———. "What Cannot be Said in St. Thomas' Essence-Existence Doctrine." *The New Scholasticism* 48 (1974) 19–39.

———. "What is Most and Least Relevant in the Metaphysics of St. Thomas Today?" *International Philosophical Quarterly* 14 (1974) 411–34.

———. "What is Really Real?" In *Progress in Philosophy: Philosophical Studies in Honor of Rev. Dr. Charles A. Hart*, edited by James A. McWilliams, 61–90. Milwaukee, WI: Bruce, 1955.

Coffey, Peter. *Ontology or the Theory of Being: An Introduction to General Metaphysics.* Gloucester, MA: Smith, 1970.

Cooper, Burton Z. *The Idea of God: A Whiteheadian Critique of St. Thomas Aquinas' Concept of God.* The Hague: Nijhoff, 1974.

Cooper, John W. *Panentheism, the Other God of the Philosophers: From Plato to the Present.* Grand Rapids: Baker Academic, 2006.

Copleston, Frederick. *Augustine to Scotus.* Vol. 2 of *A History of Philosophy.* Westminster, MD: Newman, 1950.

———. *Ockham to Suarez.* Vol. 3 of *A History of Philosophy.* Westminster, MD: Newman, 1953.

Crisp, Oliver D. "Jonathan Edwards on the Divine Nature." *Journal of Reformed Theology* 3 (2009) 175–201.

———. "Jonathan Edwards on Divine Simplicity." *Religious Studies* 39 (March 2003) 23–41.

Cronin, Paul J. "The Various Forms of Pantheism Refuted by the Thomistic Doctrine of the Simplicity of God." Master's thesis, The Catholic University of America, 1946.

Cross, Richard. *Duns Scotus.* Oxford: Oxford University Press, 1999.

———. *Duns Scotus on God.* Aldershot, UK: Ashgate, 2005.

———. "Scotus's Parisian Teaching on Divine Simplicity." In *Duns Scot à Paris: Actes du colloque de Paris, 2–4 septembre 2002*, edited by Oliver Boulnois, 519–62. Turnhout, Belgium: Brepols, 2004.

Cunningham, Francis A. *Essence and Existence in Thomism: A Mental vs. the "Real Distinction"?* Lanham, MD: University Press of America, 1988.

Davies, Brian. "A Modern Defense of Divine Simplicity." In *Philosophy of Religion: A Guide and Anthology*, edited by Brian Davies, 549–64. Oxford: Oxford University Press, 2000.

———. *The Thought of Thomas Aquinas.* Oxford: Clarendon, 1992.

Dever, Vincent Michael. "Divine Simplicity: Aquinas and the Current Debate." PhD diss., Marquette University, 1994.

Dewan, Lawrence. *Form and Being: Studies in Thomistic Metaphysics.* Washington, DC: The Catholic University of America Press, 2006.

———. "Saint Thomas, Alvin Plantinga, and the Divine Simplicity." *The Modern Schoolman* 66 (1989) 141–51.

———. "St. Thomas and the Possibles." *The New Scholasticism* 53 (1979) 76–85.

———. "St. Thomas, James Ross, and Exemplarism: A Reply." *American Catholic Philosophical Quarterly* 65 (1991) 221–34.

———. "St. Thomas, Joseph Owens, and the Real Distinction between Being and Essence." *The Modern Schoolman* 61 (1984) 145–56.

DeWeese, Garrett. "Atemporal, Sempiternal, or Omnitemporal: God's Temporal Mode of Being." In *God and Time: Essays on the Divine Nature*, edited by Gregory E. Ganssle and David M Woodruff, 49–61. Oxford: Oxford University Press, 2002.

Dodds, Michael J. "Ultimacy and Intimacy: Aquinas and the Relation between God and the World." In *Ordo Sapientiae et Amoris: Image et message de Saint Thomas d'Aquin à travers les récentes études historiques, herméneutiques et doctrinales: Hommage au Professeur Jean-Pierre Torrell, OP*, 211–27. Fribourg: Editiones Universitaires, 1993.

———. *The Unchanging God of Love: Thomas Aquinas and Contemporary Theology on Divine Immutability*. 2nd ed. Washington, DC: The Catholic University of America Press, 2008.

———. "Unlocking Divine Causality: Aquinas, Contemporary Science, and Divine Action." *Angelicum* 86 (2009) 67–86.

Donnelly, John Patrick. "Calvinist Thomism." *Viator* 7 (1976) 441–55.

Doolan, Gregory T. *Aquinas on the Divine Ideas as Exemplar Causes*. Washington, DC: The Catholic University of America Press, 2008.

———. "Is Thomas's Doctrine of Divine Ideas Thomistic?" In *Wisdom's Apprentice: Thomistic Essays in Honor of Lawrence Dewan, O.P.*, edited by Peter A. Kwasniewski, 153–69. Washington, DC: The Catholic University of America Press, 2007.

———. "Substance as a Metaphysical Genus." In *The Science of Being as Being: Metaphysical Investigations*, edited by Gregory T. Doolan. Washington, DC: The Catholic University of America Press, forthcoming.

Driscoll, John T. *Christian Philosophy: God; Being a Contribution to a Philosophy of Theism*. New York: Benziger, 1904.

Dulles, Avery, et al. *Introductory Metaphysics: A Course Combining Matter Treated in Ontology, Cosmology and Natural Theology*. New York: Sheed and Ward, 1955.

Dumont, Stephen D. "Scotus's Doctrine of Univocity and the Medieval Tradition of Metaphysics." In *Was ist Philosophie im Mittelalter?* edited by Jan A. Aertsen and Andreas Speer, 193–212. Berlin: de Gruyter, 1998.

Elders, Leo J. *The Metaphysics of Being of St. Thomas Aquinas in a Historical Perspective*. Leiden: Brill, 1993.

———. *The Philosophical Theology of St. Thomas Aquinas*. Leiden: Brill, 1990.

Emery, Gilles. *The Trinitarian Theology of Saint Thomas Aquinas*. Translated by Francesca Aran Murphy. Oxford: Oxford University Press, 2007.

Erickson, Millard J. *God the Father Almighty: A Contemporary Exploration of the Divine Attributes*. Grand Rapids: Baker, 1998.

Fabro, Cornelio. "The Intensive Hermeneutics of Thomistic Philosophy: The Notion of Participation." Translated by B. M. Bonansea. *The Review of Metaphysics* 27 (1973–74) 449–91.

———. "Platonism, Neo-Platonism, and Thomism: Convergences and Divergences." *The New Scholasticism* 44 (1970) 69–100.

Farthing, John L. "The Problem of Divine Exemplarity." *The Thomist* 49 (1985) 183–222.

Feinberg, John S. *No One Like Him: The Doctrine of God*. Wheaton, IL: Crossway, 2001.

Feser, Edward. *Aquinas: A Beginner's Guide*. Oxford: Oneworld, 2009.

Fütscher, Lorenz. *Act and Potency*. Translated by Arnold J. Benedetto and S. Y. Watson. N.p., 1950.

Fox, John. "Truthmaker." *Australasian Journal of Philosophy* 65 (1987) 188–207.

Frame, John M. *The Doctrine of God*. Phillipsburg, NJ: P & R, 2002.

Franks, Christopher A. "The Simplicity of the Living God: Aquinas, Barth, and Some Philosophers." *Modern Theology* 21 (2005) 275–300.

Gale, Richard M. *On the Nature and Existence of God*. Cambridge: Cambridge University Press, 1991.

Garrigou-Lagrange, Réginald. *God: His Existence and His Nature*. 2 vols. St. Louis: Herder, 1934.

———. *The One God: A Commentary on the First Part of St. Thomas' Theological Summa*. St. Louis: Herder, 1943.

Geach, Peter T. "Form and Existence." In *Aquinas: A Collection of Critical Essays*, edited by Anthony Kenny, 29–53. Notre Dame, IN: University of Notre Dame Press, 1976.

———. *God and the Soul*. New York: Schocken, 1969.

Geddes, L. W. "God, the Fullness of Being, Spirit and Personal." In *God*, edited by C. Lattey, 117–35. London: Sheed and Ward, 1931.

Giles of Rome. *Theorems on Existence and Essence*. Translated by Michael V. Murray. Milwaukee, WI: Marquette University Press, 1949.

Gill, John. *A Body of Divinity*. Grand Rapids: Sovereign Grace, 1971.

Gilson, Etienne. *Being and Some Philosophers*. 2nd ed. Toronto: Pontifical Institute of Mediaeval Studies, 1952.

———. *Christian Philosophy: An Introduction*. Translated by Armand Maurer. Toronto: Pontifical Institute of Medieval Studies, 1993.

———. *The Christian Philosophy of St. Thomas Aquinas*. Translated by L. K. Shook. New York: Random House, 1956.

———. *Elements of Christian Philosophy*. Garden City, NY: Doubleday, 1960.

———. *God and Philosophy*. New Haven: Yale University Press, 1941.

———. *History of Christian Philosophy in the Middle Ages*. New York: Random House, 1955.

———. *The Spirit of Medieval Philosophy*. Translated by A. H. C. Downes. New York: Scribner, 1936.

Glenn, Paul J. *Ontology: A Class Manual in Fundamental Metaphysics*. St. Louis: Herder, 1946.

Goad, Keith. "Simplicity and Trinity in Harmony." *Eusebeia* 8 (Fall 2007) 97–118.

Goheen, John. *The Problem of Matter and Form in the* De Ente et Essentia *of Thomas Aquinas*. Cambridge, MA: Harvard University Press, 1940.

Goris, Harm. *Free Creatures of an Eternal God: Thomas Aquinas on God's Foreknowledge and Irresistible Will*. Leuven: Peeters, 1996.

———. "Thomism in Zanchi's Doctrine of God." In *Reformation and Scholasticism: An Ecumenical Enterprise*, edited by Willem J. van Asselt and Eef Dekker, 121–39. Grand Rapids: Baker Academic, 2001.

Gorman, Michael. "The Essential and the Accidental." *Ratio* 18 (2005) 276–89.

Greenstock, David L. "Exemplar Causality and the Supernatural Order." *The Thomist* 16 (1953) 18–31.

Gregory of Nyssa. *Against Eunomius*. In vol. 5 of *A Select Library of Nicene and Post-Nicene Fathers of the Christian Church: Second Series*. Edited by Philip Schaff and Henry Mace. Translated by William Moore and Henry Austin Wilson. Grand Rapids: Eerdmans, 1979.

———. *On the Holy Spirit*. In vol. 5 of *A Select Library of Nicene and Post-Nicene Fathers of the Christian Church: Second Series*. Edited by Philip Schaff and Henry Mace. Translated by William Moore and Henry Austin Wilson. Grand Rapids: Eerdmans, 1979.

Grudem, Wayne. *Systematic Theology: An Introduction to Biblical Doctrine*. Grand Rapids: Zondervan, 1994.

Hall, Alexander W. *Thomas Aquinas and John Duns Scotus: Natural Theology in the High Middle Ages*. New York: Continuum, 2007.

Hankey, W. J. *God in Himself: Aquinas' Doctrine of God as Expounded in the* Summa Theologiae. Oxford: Oxford University Press, 1987.

Hart, Charles A. *Thomistic Metaphysics: An Inquiry into the Act of Existing.* Englewood Cliffs, NJ: Prentice-Hall, 1959.

Hasker, William. "Simplicity and Freedom: A Response to Stump and Kretzmann." *Faith and Philosophy* 3 (1986) 192–201.

Hawkins, D. J. B. *Being and Becoming: An Essay Towards a Critical Metaphysic.* New York: Sheed and Ward, 1954.

Helm, Paul. "Eternal Creation." *Tyndale Bulletin* 45 (1994) 321–38.

———. *Eternal God: A Study of God without Time.* Oxford: Oxford University Press, 1989.

Henninger, Mark G. *Relations: Medieval Theories 1250–1325.* Oxford: Clarendon, 1989.

Henry, Desmond Paul. *Medieval Mereology.* Amsterdam: Grüner, 1991.

Henry of Ghent. *Henry of Ghent's Summa: The Questions on God's Unity and Simplicity (Articles 25–30).* Translated and edited by Roland J. Teske. Paris: Peeters, 2006.

Hill, William. "Does the World Make a Difference to God?" *The Thomist* 38 (1974) 146–64.

Hillman, T. Allan. "Substantial Simplicity in Leibniz: Form, Predication, and Truth-makers." *The Review of Metaphysics* 63 (September 2009) 91–138.

Hodge, Charles. *Systematic Theology.* 3 vols. Grand Rapids: Eerdmans, 1952.

Hoffman, Joshua, and Gary R. Rosenkrantz. *The Divine Attributes.* Oxford: Blackwell, 2002.

Holloway, Maurice R. *An Introduction to Natural Theology.* New York: Appelton-Century-Crofts, 1959.

Holmes, Stephen R. "Something Much Too Plain to Say: Towards a Defense of the Doctrine of Divine Simplicity." *Neue Zeitschrift für Systematische Theologie und Religionsphilosophie* 43 (2001) 137–54.

Hovda, Paul. "What is Classical Mereology?" *Journal of Philosophical Logic* 38 (2009) 55–82.

Hughes, Christopher. *On a Complex Theory of a Simple God: An Investigation into Aquinas' Philosophical Theology.* Ithaca, NY: Cornell University Press, 1989.

Hughes, Gerard J. *The Nature of God.* London: Routledge, 1995.

Immink, Frederik Gerrit. *Divine Simplicity.* Kampen: Kok, 1987.

Irenaeus. *Against Heresies.* In *The Apostolic Fathers—Justine Martyr—Irenaeus.* Vol. 1 of *The Ante-Nicene Fathers.* Edited by Alexander Roberts and James Donaldson. Translated by Ernest Cushing Richardson and Bernhard Pick. New York: Scribner, 1903.

John Duns Scotus. *God and Creatures: The Quodlibetal Questions.* Translated and edited by Felix Alluntis and Allan B. Wolter. Princeton: Princeton University Press, 1975.

———. *Philosophical Writings: A Selection.* Translated and edited by Allan B. Wolter. Edinburgh: Nelson, 1962.

———. *A Treatise on God as First Principle.* Translated and edited by Allan B. Wolter. Chicago: Franciscan Herald, 1966.

Jordan, Mark D. "The Intelligibility of the World and the Divine Ideas in Aquinas." *The Review of Metaphysics* 38 (September 1984) 17–32.

———. "The Names of God and the Being of Names." In *The Existence and Nature of God,* edited by Alfred J. Freddoso, 161–90. Notre Dame and London: University of Notre Dame Press, 1983.

Joyce, George Hayward. *Principles of Natural Theology.* 3rd ed. London: Longmans, Green and Co., 1951.

Kane, William J. *The Philosophy of Relation in the Metaphysics of St. Thomas.* Washington, DC: The Catholic University of America Press, 1958.

Kaufman, Dan. "Divine Simplicity and the Eternal Truths in Descartes." *British Journal for the History of Philosophy* 11 (2003) 553–80.

Kelly, J. N. D. *Early Christian Doctrines.* 5th ed. London: Black, 1977.

Kenny, Anthony. *Aquinas.* Oxford: Oxford University Press, 1980.

———. *Aquinas on Being.* Oxford: Clarendon, 2002.

———. *Aquinas on Mind.* London and New York: Routledge, 1993.

———. *The Five Ways: St. Thomas Aquinas' Proofs of God's Existence.* New York: Schocken, 1969.

Klima, Gyula. "Existence and Reference in Medieval Logic." In *New Essays in Free Logic,* edited by Alexander Hieke and Edgar Morscher, 197–226. Dordrecht: Kluwer Academic, 2001.

———. "On Kenny on Aquinas on Being: A Critical Review of *Aquinas on Being* by Anthony Kenny." *International Philosophical Quarterly* 44 (2004) 567–80.

———. "The Semantic Principles Underlying Saint Thomas Aquinas's Metaphysics of Being." *Medieval Philosophy and Theology* 5 (1996) 87–141.

Klubertanz, George P. *Introduction to the Philosophy of Being.* 2nd ed. New York: Appelton-Century-Crofts, 1963.

———. *St Thomas Aquinas on Analogy: A Textual Analysis and Systematic Synthesis.* Chicago: Loyola University Press, 1960.

Knasas, John F. X. *Being and Some Twentieth-Century Thomists.* New York: Fordham University Press, 2003.

———. "*Contra* Spinoza: Aquinas on God's Free Will." *American Catholic Philosophical Quarterly* 76 (2002) 417–29.

———. "Haldane's Analytic Thomism and Aquinas's *Actus Essendi.*" In *Analytical Thomism: Traditions in Dialogue,* edited by Craig Paterson and Matthew S. Pugh, 233–51. Aldershot, UK: Ashgate, 2006.

Knuuttila, Simo. "Being qua Being in Thomas Aquinas and John Duns Scotus." In *The Logic of Being: Historical Studies,* edited by Simo Knuuttila and Jaakko Hintikka, 201–22. Dordrecht: Kluwer Academic, 1986.

Kopaczynski, Germain. *Linguistic Ramifications of the Essence-Existence Debate.* Washington, DC: University Press of America, 1979.

Kossel, Clifford G. "The Problem of Relation in Some Non-Scholastic Philosophies." *Journal of Symbolic Logic* 11 (1946) 61–81.

———. "Principles of St. Thomas's Distinction between the *Esse* and *Ratio* of Relation." *The Modern Schoolman* 24 (1947) 19–36.

———. "St. Thomas's Theory of the Causes of Relation." *The Modern Schoolman* 25 (1948) 151–172.

Kretzmann, Norman. "A General Problem of Creation: Why Would God Create Anything at All?" In *Being and Goodness: The Concept of the Good in Metaphysics and Philosophical Theology,* edited by Scott MacDonald, 208–28. Ithaca: Cornell University Press, 1991.

———. "A Particular Problem of Creation: Why Would God Create This World?" In *Being and Goodness: The Concept of the Good in Metaphysics and Philosophical Theology,* edited by Scott MacDonald, 229–49. Ithaca: Cornell University Press, 1991.

―――. *The Metaphysics of Creation: Aquinas's Natural Theology in* Summa contra gentiles *II*. Oxford: Clarendon, 1999.

―――. *The Metaphysics of Theism: Aquinas's Natural Theology in* Summa contra gentiles *I*. Oxford: Clarendon, 1997.

La Croix, Richard. "Augustine on the Simplicity of God." *New Scholasticism* 51 (1977) 453–69.

Lamont, John. "Aquinas on Divine Simplicity." *The Monist* 80 (1997) 521–38.

Leftow, Brian. "Aquinas, Divine Simplicity and Divine Freedom." In *Metaphysics and God: Essays in Honor of Eleonore Stump*, edited by Kevin Timpe, 21–38. London: Routledge, 2009.

―――. "Aquinas on Attributes." *Medieval Philosophy and Theology* 11 (2003) 1–41.

―――. "Aquinas on God and Modal Truth." *The Modern Schoolman* 82 (March 2005) 171–200.

―――. "Divine Simplicity." *Faith and Philosophy* 23 (2006) 365–80.

―――. "God and the Problem of Universals." In *Oxford Studies in Metaphysics*, Vol. 2, edited by Dean W. Zimmerman, 325–56. Oxford: Clarendon, 2006.

―――. "Is God an Abstract Object?" *Nous* 24 (1990) 581–98.

―――. "On a Principle of Sufficient Reason." *Religious Studies* 39 (2003) 269–86.

―――. "Parts, Wholes and Eternity." *Philosophical Studies Series* 87 (2001) 199–206.

―――. "Rowe, Aquinas and God's Freedom." *Philosophical Books* 48 (July 2007) 195–206.

―――. "Simplicity and Eternity." PhD diss., Yale University, 1984.

―――. *Time and Eternity*. Ithaca: Cornell University Press, 1991.

Leigh, Edward. *A Systeme or Body of Divinity*. London: Lee, 1662.

Levering, Matthew. *Scripture and Metaphysics: Aquinas and the Renewal of Trinitarian Theology*. Oxford: Blackwell, 2004.

Long, Steven A. "Divine and 'Creaturely': The Search for a Middle Term." *Communio* 21 (1994) 151–61.

―――. "On the Natural Knowledge of the Real Distinction of Essence and Existence." *Nova et Vetera* 1 (Spring 2003) 75–108.

Lyttkens, Hampus. *The Analogy between God and the World: An Investigation of its Background and Interpretation of its Use by Thomas of Aquino*. Uppsala: Almquist & Wiksells, 1952.

MacDonald, Scott. "The *Esse/Essentia* Argument in Aquinas's *De ente et essentia*." In *Thomas Aquinas: Contemporary Philosophical Perspectives*, edited by Brian Davies, 141–57. Oxford: Oxford University Press, 2002.

―――. "The Metaphysics of Goodness and the Doctrine of the Transcendentals." In *Being and Goodness: The Concept of the Good in Metaphysics and Philosophical Theology*, edited by Scott MacDonald, 31–55. Ithaca: Cornell University Press, 1991.

Mahoney, Edward P. "Metaphysical Foundations of the Hierarchy of Being according to Some Late-Medieval and Renaissance Philosophers." In *Philosophies of Existence: Ancient and Medieval*, edited by Parviz Morewedge, 165–257. New York: Fordham University Press, 1982.

Maimonides, Moses. *The Guide for the Perplexed*. Translated by M. Friedländer. 2nd ed. New York: Dover, 1956.

Maloney, Christopher. "*Esse* in the Metaphysics of Thomas Aquinas." *The New Scholasticism* 55 (1981) 159–77.

Mann, William E. "The Divine Attributes." *American Philosophical Quarterly* 12 (April 1975) 151–59.

———. "Divine Simplicity." *Religious Studies* 18 (1982) 451–71.

———. "Simplicity and Immutability in God." *International Philosophical Quarterly* 23 (1983) 267–76.

———. "Simplicity and Properties: A Reply to Morris." *Religious Studies* 22 (1986) 343–53.

Maritain, Jacques. *The Degrees of Knowledge.* Translated by Gerald B. Phelan. New York: Scribner, 1959.

———. *Existence and the Existent: The Christian Answer.* Translated by Lewis Galantière and Gerald B. Phelan. New York: Pantheon, 1948.

———. *A Preface to Metaphysics: Seven Lectures on Being.* New York: Sheed and Ward, 1948.

Martin, Aaron. "Reckoning with Ross: Possible, Divine Ideas, and Virtual Practical Knowledge." *Proceedings of the American Catholic Philosophical Association* 78 (2005) 193–208.

Martin, C. B. "God, the Null Set, and Divine Simplicity." In *The Challenge of Religion Today: Essays on the Philosophy of Religion,* edited by John King-Farlow, 138–43. New York: Science History, 1976.

Mascall, E. L. *Existence and Analogy.* London: Longmans, Green and Co., 1949.

———. *He Who Is: A Study in Traditional Theism.* London: Longmans, Green and Co., 1943.

Maurer, Armand A. "Form and Essence in the Philosophy of St. Thomas." In *Being and Knowing: Studies in Thomas Aquinas and Later Medieval Philosophers,* 3–18. Toronto: Pontifical Institute of Medieval Studies, 1990.

———. *Medieval Philosophy.* 2nd ed. Toronto: Pontifical Institute of Mediaeval Studies, 1982.

———. "St. Thomas and the Analogy of Genus." In *Being and Knowing: Studies in Thomas Aquinas and Later Medieval Philosophers,* 19–31. Toronto: Pontifical Institute of Medieval Studies, 1990.

———. "Scotism and Ockhamism." In *A History of Philosophical Systems,* edited by Vergilius Ferm, 212–24. New York: Philosophical Library, 1950.

McCann, Hugh J. *Creation and the Sovereignty of God.* Bloomington, IN: Indiana University Press, forthcoming.

McCormack, Bruce L. "The Actuality of God: Karl Barth in Conversation with Open Theism." In *Engaging the Doctrine of God: Contemporary Protestant Perspectives,* edited by Bruce L. McCormack, 185–242. Grand Rapids: Baker Academic, 2008.

McDaniel, Kris. "Structure-Making." *Australasian Journal of Philosophy* 87 (2009) 251–74.

McInerny, Ralph M. *Aquinas and Analogy.* Washington, DC: The Catholic University of America Press, 1996.

———. *Being and Predication: Thomistic Interpretations.* Washington, DC: The Catholic University of America Press, 1986.

———. Can God be Named by Us? Prolegomena to Thomistic Philosophy of Religion." *Review of Metaphysics* 32 (Sept. 1978) 53–73.

McKian, John D. "The *raison d'être* of the Human Composite, according to St. Thomas Aquinas." In *Essays in Modern Scholasticism,* edited by Anton C. Pegis, 134–67. Westminster, MD: The Newman Bookshop, 1944.

Meng, Jude Chua Soo. "Reginald Garrigou-Lagrange OP on Aristotle, Thomas Aquinas and the Doctrine of Limitation of Act by Potency." *The Modern Schoolman* 78 (2000) 71–88.

Merricks, Trenton. "Composition as Identity, Mereological Essentialism, and Counterpart Theory." *Australasian Journal of Philosophy* 77 (1999) 192–95.

Miller, Barry. *From Existence to God: A Contemporary Philosophical Argument*. London: Routledge, 1992.

———. *The Fullness of Being: A New Paradigm for Existence*. Notre Dame, IN: University of Notre Dame Press, 2002.

———. *A Most Unlikely God: A Philosophical Inquiry into the Nature of God*. Notre Dame, IN: University of Notre Dame Press, 1996.

———. "On 'Divine Simplicity: A New Defense.'" *Faith and Philosophy* 11 (1994) 474–77.

Montagnes, Bernard. *The Doctrine of the Analogy of Being according to Thomas Aquinas*. Translated by E. M. Macierowski. Milwaukee, WI: Marquette University Press, 2004.

Moreland, J. P., and William Lane Craig. *Philosophical Foundations for a Christian Worldview*. Downers Grove, IL: InterVarsity, 2003.

Morewedge, Parviz, ed. *Philosophies of Existence: Ancient and Medieval*. New York: Fordham University Press, 1982.

Morreall, John S. *Analogy and Talking About God: A Critique of the Thomistic Approach*. Washington, DC: University of America Press, 1979.

———. "The Aseity of God in St. Anselm." *Sophia* 23 (October 1984) 35–44.

Morris, Thomas V. *Anselmian Explorations: Essays in Philosophical Theology*. Notre Dame: University of Notre Dame Press, 1987.

———. "Dependence and Divine Simplicity." *International Journal for Philosophy of Religion* 23 (May 1988) 161–74.

———. "Metaphysical Dependence, Independence, and Perfection." In *Being and Goodness: The Concept of the Good in Metaphysics and Philosophical Theology*, edited by Scott MacDonald, 278–97. Ithaca: Cornell University Press, 1991.

———. "On God and Mann: A View of Divine Simplicity." *Religious Studies* 21 (1985) 299–318.

———. *Our Idea of God: An Introduction to Philosophical Theology*. Notre Dame: University of Notre Dame Press, 1991.

———. "A Theistic Proof of Perfection." *Sophia* 26 (1987) 31–35.

Morris, Thomas V., ed. *The Concept of God*. Oxford: Oxford University Press, 1987.

———. *Divine and Human Action: Essays in the Metaphysics of Theism*. Ithaca: Cornell University Press. 1988.

Morris, Thomas, and Christopher Menzel. "Absolute Creation." *American Philosophical Quarterly* 23 (1986) 353–62.

Muller, Richard A. *Dictionary of Latin and Greek Theological Terms: Drawn Principally from Protestant Scholastic Theology*. Grand Rapids: Baker, 1985.

———. "The Dogmatic Function of St. Thomas' 'Proofs': A Protestant Appreciation." *Fides et Historia* 24 (Summer 1992) 15–29.

———. "Incarnation, Immutability, and the Case for Classical Theism." *Westminster Theological Journal* 45 (Spring 1983) 22–40.

———. *Post-Reformation Reformed Dogmatics: The Rise and Development of Reformed Orthodoxy, ca. 1520–1725*. 4 vols. Grand Rapids: Baker Academic, 2003.

Mulligan, Kevin, et al. "Truth-Makers." *Philosophy and Phenomenological Research* 44 (1984) 287–320.

Nash, Ronald H. *The Concept of God: An Exploration of Contemporary Difficulties with the Attributes of God.* Grand Rapids: Zondervan, 1983.

Nash-Marshall, Siobhan. "God, Simplicity, and the *Consolatio Philosophiae.*" *American Catholic Philosophical Quarterly* 78 (2005) 225–46.

———. "Properties, Conflation, and Attribution: the *Monologion* and Divine Simplicity." *St. Anselm Journal* 4 (Spring 2007) 1–18.

Neele, Adriaan Cornelis. "A Study of Divine Spirituality, Simplicity, and Immutability in Petrus Van Mastricht's Doctrine of God." Master's thesis, Calvin Theological Seminary, 2002.

Noonan, John P. *General Metaphysics.* Chicago: Loyola University Press, 1957.

O'Brien, Andrew Joseph. "Duns Scotus' Teaching on the Distinction between Essence and Existence." *The New Scholasticism* 38 (1964) 61–77.

O'Connor, Timothy. "Simplicity and Creation." *Faith and Philosophy* 16 (1999) 405–12.

Oderberg, David S. *Real Essentialism.* London: Routledge, 2007.

O'Leary, Joseph S. "Divine Simplicity and the Plurality of Attributes (CE II 359–386; 445–560)." In *Gregory of Nyssa: Contra Eunomium II*, edited by Lenka Karfíková et al., 307–37. Vol. 82 of *Supplements to Vigiliae Christianae.* Leiden: Brill, 2007.

Oliphint, K. Scott. *Reasons for Faith: Philosophy in the Service of Theology.* Phillipsburg, NJ: P & R, 2006.

Oppy, Graham Robert. *Arguing about Gods.* Cambridge: Cambridge University Press, 2006.

———. "The Devilish Complexities of Divine Simplicity." *Philo* 6 (Spring-Summer 2003) 10–22.

———. "Pantheism, Quantification and Mereology." *Monist* 80 (1997) 320–36.

O'Rourke, Fran. *Pseudo-Dionysius and the Metaphysics of Aquinas.* Notre Dame, IN: University of Notre Dame Press, 2005.

Owen, John. *Vindicae Evangelicae.* In *The Works of John Owen*, vol. 12, edited by William Goold. 1850–53. Reprint. Edinburgh: Banner of Truth Trust, 1999.

Owens, Joseph. "Being and Natures in Aquinas." *The Modern Schoolman* 41 (1984) 157–68.

———. *The Doctrine of Being in the Aristotelian* Metaphysics. 3rd ed. Toronto: Pontifical Institute of Mediaeval Studies, 1978.

———. *An Elementary Christian Metaphysics.* Milwaukee, WI: Bruce, 1963.

———. *An Interpretation of Existence.* Milwaukee, WI: Bruce, 1968.

——— *St. Thomas Aquinas on the Existence of God: Collected Papers of Joseph Owens.* Edited by John R. Catan. Albany, NY: State University of New York Press, 1980.

Pannenberg, Wolfhart. *Basic Questions in Theology: Collected Essays.* Translated by George H. Kehm. 2 vols. Philadelphia: Fortress, 1971.

———. *Systematic Theology.* Translated by Geoffrey W. Bromiley. Vol. 1. Grand Rapids: Eerdmans, 1991.

Pasnau, Robert. "Form and Matter." In *The Cambridge History of Medieval Philosophy*, edited by Robert Pasnau and Christina Van Dyke, 635–46. Cambridge: Cambridge University Press, 2010.

———. *Thomas Aquinas on Human Nature: A Philosophical Study of* Summa Theologiae *1a 75–89.* Cambridge: Cambridge University Press, 2001.

Pasnau, Robert, and Christopher Shields. *The Philosophy of Aquinas*. Boulder, CO: Westview, 2004.

Patt, Walter. "Aquinas's Real Distinction and Some Interpretations." *The New Scholasticism* 62 (1988) 1–29.

Patterson, Robert Leet. *The Conception of God in the Philosophy of Aquinas*. Merrick, NY: Richwood, 1976.

Pawl, Timothy. "The Possibility Principle and the Truthmaker for Modal Truths." *Australasian Journal of Philosophy* 88 (September 2010) 417–28.

Pegis, Anton C. *Saint Thomas and Philosophy*. Milwaukee, WI: Marquette University Press, 1964.

———. *Saint Thomas and the Greeks*. Milwaukee, WI: Marquette University Press, 1939.

Pelikan, Jaroslav. *Christianity and Classical Culture: The Metamorphosis of Natural Theology in the Christian Encounter with Hellenism*. New Haven: Yale University Press, 1993.

———. *The Emergence of the Catholic Tradition (100–600)*. Vol. 1 of *The Christian Tradition: A History of the Development of Doctrine*. Chicago: University of Chicago Press, 1971.

Perkins, William. *A Golden Chaine: or, The Description of Theology*. In *The Workes of That Famous and Worthy Minister of Christ in the Universitie of Cambridge, Mr. William Perkins*. 3 vols. London: Legatt, 1626.

Peters, John A. *Metaphysics: A Systematic Survey*. Pittsburg, PA: Duquesne University Press, 1963.

Phelan, Gerald B. *G. B. Phelan: Selected Papers*. Edited by Arthur G. Kirn. Toronto: Pontifical Institute of Mediaeval Studies, 1967.

Pieper, Josef. *The Silence of St. Thomas: Three Essays*. South Bend, IN: St. Augustine's, 1999.

Plantinga, Alvin. *Does God Have a Nature?* Milwaukee, WI: Marquette University Press, 1980.

Preller, Victor. *Divine Science and the Science of God: A Reformulation of Thomas Aquinas*. Princeton, NJ: Princeton University Press, 1967.

Pruss, Alexander R. "On Two Problems of Divine Simplicity." In *Oxford Studies in Philosophy of Religion*, Vol. 1, edited by Jonathan L. Kvanvig, 150–67. Oxford: Oxford University Press, 2008.

Pugh, Matthew S. "Kenny on Being in Aquinas." In *Analytical Thomism: Traditions in Dialogue*, edited by Craig Paterson and Matthew S. Pugh, 263–81. Aldershot, UK: Ashgate, 2006.

Radde-Gallwitz, Andrew. *Basil of Caesarea, Gregory of Nyssa, and the Transformation of Divine Simplicity*. Oxford: Oxford University Press, 2009.

Redlon, Reginald A. "St. Thomas and the Freedom of Creative Act." *Franciscan Studies* 20 (1960) 1–18.

Raeymaeker, Louis De. *The Philosophy of Being*. Translated by Edmund H. Ziegelmeyer. St. Louis: Herder, 1954.

Rehnman, Sebastian. "Theistic Metaphysics and Biblical Exegesis: Francis Turretin on the Concept of God." *Religious Studies* 38 (2002) 167–86.

Renard, Henri. *The Philosophy of Being*. 2nd ed. Milwaukee, WI: Bruce, 1946.

———. *The Philosophy of God*. Milwaukee, WI: Bruce, 1951.

Richards, Jay Wesley. *The Untamed God: A Philosophical Exploration of Divine Perfection, Simplicity and Immutability*. Downers Grove, IL: InterVarsity, 2003.

Ridgeley, Thomas. *Commentary on the Larger Catechism*, Vol. 1. Edited by John M. Wilson. 1855. Reprint. Edmonton, AB: Still Waters Revival, 1993.

Robinson, Howard. "Can We Make Sense of the Idea that God's Existence is Identical to His Essence?" In *Reason, Faith and History: Philosophical Essays for Paul Helm*, edited by Martin W. F. Stone, 127–43. Aldershot, UK: Ashgate, 2008.

Rocca, Gregory P. "'Creatio ex Nihilo' and the Being of Creatures: God's Creative Act and the Transcendence-Immanence Distinction in Aquinas." In *Divine Transcendence and Immanence in the Work of Thomas Aquinas*, edited by Harm Goris et al., 1–17. Leuven: Peeters, 2009.

———. *Speaking the Incomprehensible God: Thomas Aquinas on the Interplay of Positive and Negative Theology*. Washington, DC: The Catholic University of America Press, 2004.

Roderiguez-Pereyra, Gonzalo. *Resemblance Nominalism: A Solution to the Problem of Universals*. Oxford: Clarendon, 2002.

Rogers, Katherin A. *Perfect Being Theology*. Edinburgh: Edinburgh University Press, 2000.

———. "The Traditional Doctrine of Divine Simplicity." *Religious Studies* 32 (1996) 165–86.

Ross, James. "Aquinas's Exemplarism; Aquinas's Voluntarism." *American Catholic Philosophical Quarterly* 64 (1990) 171–98.

———. "Comments on 'Absolute Simplicity.'" *Faith and Philosophy* 2 (1985) 383–91.

———. "God, Creator of Kinds and Possibilities: *Requiescant Universalia Ante Res*." In *Rationality, Religious Belief, and Moral Commitment*, edited by Robert Audi and William J. Wainright, 315–34. Ithaca: Cornell University Press, 1986.

Rowe, William L. *Can God Be Free?* Oxford: Clarendon, 2004.

———. "The Problem of Divine Perfection and Freedom." In *Reasoned Faith: Essays in Philosophical Theology in Honor of Honor of Norman Kretzmann*, edited by Eleonore Stump, 223–33. Ithaca: Cornell University Press, 1993.

Saeedimehr, Mohammad. "Divine Simplicity." *Topoi* 26 (2007) 191–99.

Sarot, Marcel. *God, Passibility and Corporeality*. Kampen: Kok Pharos, 1992.

Shanley, Brian J. "On Analytical Thomism." In *Analytical Thomism: Traditions in Dialogue*, edited by Craig Paterson and Matthew S. Pugh, 215–24. Aldershot, UK: Ashgate, 2006.

Simons, Peter. *Parts: A Study in Ontology*. Oxford: Clarendon, 1987.

Smith, George D. "God One and Indivisible: The Divine Attributes." In *God*, edited by C. Lattey, 53–73. London: Sheed and Ward, 1931.

Smith, Gerard. "Avicenna and the Possibles." In *Essays in Modern Scholasticism*, edited by Anton C. Pegis, 116–33. Westminster, MD: The Newman Bookshop, 1944.

———. *Natural Theology: Metaphysics II*. New York: Macmillan, 1951.

Sokolowski, Robert. *The God of Faith and Reason: Foundations of Christian Theology*. Notre Dame, IN: University of Notre Dame Press, 1982.

Stead, Christopher. "Divine Simplicity as a Problem for Orthodoxy." In *The Making of Orthodoxy: Essays in Honour of Henry Chadwick*, edited by Rowan Williams, 255–69. Cambridge: University of Cambridge, 1989.

———. *Divine Substance*. Oxford: Clarendon, 1977.

Stein, Edith. *Finite and Eternal Being*. Edited by L. Gelber and Romaeus Leuven. Translated by Kurt F. Reinhardt. Washington, DC: ICS, 2002.

———. *Potency and Act: Studies Toward a Philosophy of Being.* Edited by L. Gelber and Romaeus Leuven. Translated by Walter Redmond. Washington, DC: ICS, 2009.

Stump, Eleonore. *Aquinas.* London: Routledge, 2003.

———. Review of *Does God Have a Nature? (The Aquinas Lecture: 1980)*, by Alvin Plantinga. *The Thomist* 47 (1983) 616–22.

———. "Simplicity." In *A Companion to Philosophy of Religion*, edited by Philip L. Quinn and Charles Taliaferro, 250–56. Oxford: Blackwell, 1997.

Stump, Eleonore, and Norman Kretzmann. "Absolute Simplicity." *Faith and Philosophy* 2 (1985) 353–82.

———. "Eternity." In *The Concept of God*, edited by Thomas V. Morris, 219–52. Oxford: Oxford University Press, 1987.

———. "Eternity, Awareness, and Action." *Faith and Philosophy* 9 (1992) 463–82.

———. "Simplicity Made Plainer: A Reply to Ross." *Faith and Philosophy* 4 (1987) 198–201.

Sweeney, Leo. *Christian Philosophy: Greek, Medieval, Contemporary Reflections.* New York: Lang, 1997.

———. *Divine Infinity in Greek and Medieval Thought.* New York: Lang, 1992.

———. *A Metaphysics of Authentic Existentialism.* Englewood Cliffs, NJ: Prentice-Hall, 1965.

Swinburne, Richard. *The Christian God.* Oxford: Oxford University Press, 1994.

TeSelle, Eugene. "Divine Action: The Doctrinal Tradition." In *Divine Action: Studies Inspired by the Philosophical Theology of Austin Farrer*, edited by Brian Hebblethwaite and Edward Henderson, 71–91. Edinburgh: T. & T. Clark, 1990.

Teske, Roland. "Properties of God and the Predicaments in *De Trinitate V.*" *The Modern Schoolman* 59 (1981) 1–19.

Thibault, Herve J. *Creation and Metaphysics: A Genetic Approach to Existential Act.* The Hague: Nijhoff, 1970.

Thomas, J. L. H. "The Identity of Being and Essence in God." *Heythrop Journal* 27 (1986) 394–408.

Thornwell, James Henley. *The Collected Writings of James Henley Thornwell.* Vol. 1. Edinburgh: The Banner of Truth Trust, 1986.

Tracy, Thomas F. *God, Action, and Embodiment.* Grand Rapids: Eerdmans, 1984.

Turretin, Francis. *Institutes of Elenctic Theology.* Edited by James T. Dennison, Jr. Translated by George Musgrave Giger. 3 vols. Phillipsburg, NJ: P & R, 1992–1997.

Twetten, David B. "Really Distinguishing Essence from *Esse.*" In *Wisdom's Apprentice: Thomistic Essays in Honor of Lawrence Dewan, O.P.*, edited by Peter A. Kwasniewski, 40–84. Washington, DC: The Catholic University of America Press, 2007.

Vallicella, William F. "Divine Simplicity: A New Defense." *Faith and Philosophy* 9 (1992) 508–25.

Van Inwagen, Peter. "God and Other Uncreated Things." In *Metaphysics and God: Essays in Honor of Eleonore Stump*, edited by Kevin Timpe, 3–20. London: Routledge, 2009.

Van Roo, William. "Act and Potency." *The Modern Schoolman* 18 (1940) 1–5.

Van Steenberghen, Fernand. *Ontology.* Translated by Lawrence Moonan. New York: Wagner, 1970.

Van Til, Cornelius. *An Introduction to Systematic Theology: Prolegomena and the Doctrines of Revelation, Scripture, and God.* Edited by William Edgar. 2nd ed. Phillipsburg, NJ: P & R, 2007.

Veatch, Henry Babcock. *Realism and Nominalism Revisited.* Milwaukee, WI: Marquette University Press, 1954.

Velde, Rudi A. te. *Aquinas on God: The 'divine Science' of the Summa Theologiae.* Aldershot, UK: Ashgate, 2006.

———. "God and the Language of Participation." In *Divine Transcendence and Immanence in the Work of Thomas Aquinas,* edited by Harm Goris et al., 19–36. Leuven: Peeters, 2009.

———. *Participation and Substantiality in Thomas Aquinas.* Leiden: Brill, 1995.

Wainwright, William. "Augustine on God's Simplicity: A Reply." *The New Scholasticism* 53 (1979) 124–27.

Webster, John. "Life in and of Himself: Reflections on God's Aseity." In *Engaging the Doctrine of God: Contemporary Protestant Perspectives,* edited by Bruce L. McCormack, 107–24. Grand Rapids: Baker Academic, 2008.

Weed, Jennifer Hart. "Creation as a Foundation of Analogy in Aquinas." In *Divine Transcendence and Immanence in the Work of Thomas Aquinas,* edited by Harm Goris et al., 129–48. Leuven: Peeters, 2009.

Weigel, Peter. "Aquinas on Divine Simplicity—No Simple Matter." PhD diss., Yale University, 1999.

———. *Aquinas on Simplicity: An Investigation into the Foundations of His Philosophical Theology.* Oxford: Lang, 2008.

Weinandy, Thomas G. *Does God Change?* Still River, MA: St. Bede's, 1985.

———. *Does God Suffer?* Notre Dame, IN: University of Notre Dame Press, 2000.

West, J. L. A. "The Real Distinction between Supposit and Nature." In *Wisdom's Apprentice: Thomistic Essays in Honor of Lawrence Dewan, O.P.,* edited by Peter A. Kwasniewski, 85–106. Washington, DC: The Catholic University of America Press, 2007.

William of Ockham. *Philosophical Writings: A Selection.* Translated and edited by Philotheus Boehner. Indianapolis: Hackett, 1990.

Williams, Dom Raphael. "God Distinct from the Universe." In *God,* edited by C. Lattey, 74–90. London: Sheed and Ward, 1931.

Wippel, John F. "Essence and Existence." In *The Cambridge History of Medieval Philosophy,* edited by Robert Pasnau and Christina Van Dyke, 622–34. Cambridge: Cambridge University Press, 2010.

———. *Metaphysical Themes in Thomas Aquinas.* Washington, DC: The Catholic University of America Press, 1984.

———. *Metaphysical Themes in Thomas Aquinas II.* Washington, DC: The Catholic University of America Press, 2007.

———. *The Metaphysical Thought of Thomas Aquinas: From Finite Being to Uncreated Being.* Washington, DC: The Catholic University of America Press, 2000.

———. "Metaphysics." In *The Cambridge Companion to Aquinas,* edited by Norman Kretzmann and Eleonore Stump, 85–127. Cambridge: Cambridge University Press, 1993.

———. "Norman Kretzmann on Aquinas's Attribution of Will and Freedom to Create to God." *Religious Studies* 39 (2003) 287–98.

———. "The Relationship between Essence and Existence in Late-Thirteenth-Century Thought: Giles of Rome, Henry of Ghent, Godfrey of Fontaines, and James of Viterbo." In *Philosophies of Existence: Ancient and Medieval,* edited by Parviz Morewedge, 131–64. New York: Fordham University Press, 1982.

————. *Thomas Aquinas on the Divine Ideas*. Toronto: Pontifical Institute of Mediaeval Studies, 1993.

Wolter, Allan B. "A Scotist Approach to the Ultimate Why-Question." In *Philosophies of Existence: Ancient and Medieval*, edited by Parviz Morewedge, 109–30. New York: Fordham University Press, 1982.

Wolterstorff, Nicholas. "Divine Simplicity." In *Philosophical Perspectives 5, Philosophy of Religion*, edited by James E. Tomberlin, 531–52. Atascadero, CA: Ridgeview, 1991.

————. "God Everlasting." In *God and the Good*, edited by Clifton Orlebeke and Lewis Smedes, 181–203. Grand Rapids: Eerdmans, 1975.

————. *On Universals*. Chicago: The University of Chicago Press, 1970.

Index

Printed in Great Britain
by Amazon

50122922R00149